REWARD AND PUNISHMENT
IN HUMAN LEARNING

REWARD AND PUNISHMENT

ELEMENTS OF

ACADEMIC PRESS

IN HUMAN LEARNING
A BEHAVIOR THEORY

JOSEPH NUTTIN
DEPARTMENT OF PSYCHOLOGY
UNIVERSITY OF LOUVAIN
LOUVAIN, BELGIUM

in collaboration with ANTHONY G. GREENWALD
DEPARTMENT OF PSYCHOLOGY
OHIO STATE UNIVERSITY
COLUMBUS, OHIO

NEW YORK AND LONDON   1968

ACADEMIC PRESS INC.
111 Fifth Avenue, New York, New York 10003

United Kingdom Edition published by
ACADEMIC PRESS INC. (LONDON) LTD.
Berkeley Square House, London W.1

Chapters 2, 3, 4, 5, 6, and 7 were originally published in French
under the title "Tâche, Réussite et Échec," by Joseph Nuttin,
Louvain: Publications Universitaires de Louvain in 1953.

LIBRARY OF CONGRESS CATALOG CARD NUMBER: 68-23475

PRINTED IN THE UNITED STATES OF AMERICA

PREFACE

The roles of reward and punishment in shaping human and animal behavior have long been subjects of study by psychologists as well as topics of interest to persons who are obliged to control or to modify the behavior of others—that is, persons such as teachers, executives, prison officials, psychotherapists, and, most importantly, parents. In academic psychology, the study of reward and punishment has most often been conducted by asking the questions: "What is the effect of rewarding a response on its subsequent probability of occurrence?" and "Does punishment reduce the probability that a response will be repeated?" The approach taken in this volume is indicated by a different question, once regarded as of fundamental importance in psychology but now rarely heard: "What is learned when a response is rewarded and how does this differ from what is learned when a response is punished?"

The manner of stating the question about reward and punishment effects has significance for the kinds of research designs one uses to obtain answers. It follows that the research reported in this volume has employed some procedures that have been used rarely if at all in studies conducted outside the authors' laboratories. It should not be surprising, then, that the results of this work demand conclusions differing from those usually obtained in research directed by differently stated questions. Further, the present results call into doubt some widely held views concerning reward and punishment effects.

The experimental studies reported in Chapters 2 through 7 of this volume were originally reported in Chapters 2, 3, 4, 6, 7, and 8 of *Tâche, Réussite, et Échec* (Nuttin, 1953). Although small segments of this research have appeared in articles published in English-language journals by the first author (Nuttin, 1947; 1949; 1964), this

v

is the first English presentation for most of this material, and includes all of the experimental research reported in *Tâche, Réussite, et Échec*. The reporting of these experimental studies has been brought up to date by acknowledging significant relevant publications through approximately the middle of 1967.

A separate program of research, of more modest proportions, conducted by the second author, is presented as an Appendix. The conclusions drawn from these two programs are in strong sympathy with one another, and this was the primary source of motivation for the collaboration in which the second author has been translator as well as author of the Appendix.

March, 1968   J. NUTTIN
                                                   A. G. GREENWALD

TRANSLATOR'S PREFACE

I first read Professor Nuttin's work in the course of reviewing literature pertinent to my own research into reward and punishment effects. It was apparent immediately that his work provided a theoretical contrast with the views of American theorists, particularly Thorndike, and was unfortunately not readily available to English-speaking psychologists. Especially since my own theoretical views were in sympathy with Nuttin's, I felt strongly enough about his work to attempt on my own (Greenwald, 1966) to increase its availability to English-speaking psychologists. Later, Professor Nuttin and I agreed to collaborate on this volume, presenting his research program in entirety together with my own related research.

Professor Nuttin has allowed me considerable discretion in translating his work. In order to focus on the results of his experimental research program, I have omitted substantial sections of discussion concerning implications of the research for the understanding of human personality and have condensed much of the description of research procedures where I felt details were not essential to interpreting findings. The introductory and concluding chapters of this volume present Professor Nuttin's theoretical views and have been translated without condensation from drafts written by him during 1967. In translating this theoretical material, I have been allowed considerable freedom by Professor Nuttin to express his ideas in my own words. I have tried to use this freedom to achieve a greater degree of readability than I could have obtained by being more literal. As a corrective against the possibility that I may thereby have altered some ideas, the manuscript has been rather thoroughly examined by Professor Nuttin in early draft stages.

The research reported in the Appendix was conducted with the assistance of Stuart M. Albert, Fred Fanning, Robert E. Love, and my wife, Jean. The manuscript for the Appendix has benefited from comments by Professor Nuttin on an early draft, as well as from discussion with Professors Neal F. Johnson and Delos D. Wickens. In addition, I wish to acknowledge the stimulating value of recent publications by Professors Leo Postman (1966) and Melvin H. Marx (1967) which appeared in *Psychological Bulletin*. These articles have been directly addressed to the topic of Professor Nuttin's work and the theoretical issues raised in it; portions of this volume have been formulated as replies to and further discussions of points raised in Postman's and Marx's papers. Finally, I am grateful to Professor Howard Pollio, who read and commented on the entire manuscript.

March, 1968

A. G. GREENWALD

CONTENTS

Chapter 5. **Does Reward Strengthen Connections?**

Chapter 6. **Task Tension and Learning**

Chapter 7. **Structural Isolation and Learning**

Chapter 8. **Elements of a Behavior Theory**

Appendix. **Further Experimental Analysis of Reward and Punishment**

CHAPTER 1

•

INTRODUCTION:
LEARNING, BEHAVIOR, AND PERSONALITY

This book is principally devoted to the presentation of several series of experiments investigating the roles of reward and punishment in human learning. It will be useful to introduce this empirical program by considering the theoretical context in which it was conceived. The manner of selecting and stating research problems and of interpreting experimental data depends greatly on the theoretical viewpoint one adopts toward the study of behavior.

Extensive simplification and schematization are necessary to subject any behavioral process to experimental study. The investigator is nonetheless obliged not to lose sight of the essential characteristics of behavior as it occurs in its more complex natural state. In this introductory chapter we shall attempt to specify the essential characteristics of human behavior even though we may not have the means at hand to study them experimentally. We do not wish to allow our theoretical analysis to eliminate from consideration those more complex characteristics of behavior that are not currently within the scope of our laboratory technology.[1] The goal of accounting for complex phenomena is frequently sacrificed to the goal of parsimony in the construction of theories of behavior; it is particularly likely to be neglected when one attempts to apply theoretical principles of animal behavior directly to human behavior. In the following exposition, our selection of research problems and operational definitions of variables will be guided by the principle of preserving, in our analysis, the essential characteristics of human behavior.

---

[1]Watson was among those who specified that psychology must explain the natural complexities of behavior and not only the simpler processes that can be observed in the laboratory. He remarked: "... the behaviorist is primarily interested in the behavior of the whole man. From morning to night he watches him perform his daily round of duties. ... In other words, the response the behaviorist is interested in is the common-sense answer to the questions 'What is he [man] doing and why is he doing it?'" (Watson, 1930, p. 15).

1

SUCCESS AND REWARD

In using the terms "reward" and "punishment" in the title of this volume and in its text, we conform to the current usage of these terms in the psychology of learning; they designate, respectively, a positively or negatively valued event contingent on the performance of an action or series of actions.

THE MULTIPLE FUNCTIONS OF BEHAVIORAL OUTCOMES

In commonsense psychology, as well as in philosophical speculation on human behavior, the outcome of an action is regarded as playing a fundamental role in behavioral processes. Specifically, a future outcome can be said to determine behavior in the sense that the outcome is "intended" prior to performance of the action and the anticipation of the outcome subjectively appears to have the power of eliciting the action. In this sense, the outcome may be referred to as the goal of behavior and may be said to have motivational significance — that is, relevance to the satisfaction or frustration of needs. Additionally, a past outcome (received for some act) can be accorded an essential role in determining the conditions under which that act will subsequently be performed. It is in this sense that behavioral outcomes have typically played a basic role in the study of learning; many experiments have been directed at elucidation of the exact processes by which obtained outcomes influence future motivation and performance.

When one observes people in their everyday settings, a primary component of what one notices — perhaps as important as their physical appearance — is their behavior and its success or failure, i.e., its outcomes. Interpersonal perception is, to a large extent, judgment of what others are doing and how successfully they are doing it. It may be argued that this generalization applies equally to the perceiver judging himself. He observes his own activity and forms impressions of himself based in some part on the successful or unsuccessful outcomes he obtains. Thus, outcomes of behavior form an important class of the perceptual objects of daily experience. They provide the perceiver with much information not only about others but also about himself; the successful or unsuccessful nature of one's own outcomes may strongly determine the overall character of one's self-conception.

Both clinical and experimental psychologists have studied the roles of pleasant and unpleasant outcomes in the determination of behavior.

Psychoanalysts, as well as learning theorists, have proposed to explain present behavior as a function of past outcomes. Freud, in his study of pathologies of behavior, focused on the effects of unpleasant outcomes (frustrations) which, in psychoanalytic theory, lead to repetition of responses through the mechanisms of fixation and regression; such repetition of behavior characterizes, for Freud, a state of maladjustment to present circumstances. On the other hand, Thorndike has concentrated on effects of pleasant outcomes ("satisfiers") which play a role in repetition of previous responses through the mechanisms of learning. Learning leads to superior adjustment to present circumstances by selection of adaptive responses in preference to nonadaptive ones.

Freud, as well as Thorndike and Pavlov, employed the reflex, or afferent-efferent neural connection, as the basic theoretical model for behavior. In Freud's conception, the afferent stimulus was the bearer of energy that was discharged, by the organism, through an efferent pathway; Freud's focus of analysis was on the process of discharge of tension through behavior. Thorndike and Pavlov, on the other hand, were concerned with explaining the process of connection between afferent and efferent centers and, for them, the focus of analysis may be said to have been on the process of learning. These two sets of views gave rise, early in the twentieth century, to two major categories of behavior theory that have since been dominant: the tension-reduction model of motivation and the conditioning model for the modification of stimulus-response connections. In both models, the role of cognitive processes in behavior has been minimized, although psychoanalysts as well as clinical psychologists have stressed the cognitive-process distinction between awareness and nonawareness of objects of experience. In the framework of the recent information-processing models of behavior (see, for example, Feigenbaum & Feldman, 1963), it appears that a more favorable climate has been generated for considering the role of cognitive processes in behavior.

THE DISTINCTION BETWEEN SUCCESS AND REWARD

In this volume the roles of positive and negative outcomes will be studied in the context of the learning process. Before proceeding with a theoretical analysis of learning, it will be useful to establish clear definitions for four terms used in describing outcomes—success, failure, reward, and punishment.

When a teacher assigns an arithmetic problem and calls the student's answer *right,* we may say that the student's performance has led to a success.[2] The teacher might, under some circumstances, add a small gift such as a piece of candy or a reprieve from some homework assignment to the outcome. This, however, would be something quite separate from what we are calling the success aspect of the outcome; we shall refer to this additional consequence as a reward. The chief difference between success and reward as presently used is that success is an intrinsic consequence of an action while reward is an extrinsic consequence. It follows that the reward may satisfy some motive that is quite tangential to successful performance; for example, a reward of candy satisfies a hunger motive rather than a motive for achievement at arithmetic problems.

Any response can be discussed in terms of some criterion of success or failure. In general, only a restricted subset of the responses that might be performed in some situation will meet the criterion of success. In the case of the arithmetic problem, success will be achieved by and large only when responses consistent with the rules of arithmetic have been performed. Similarly, in the puzzle boxes typical of Thorndike's earliest learning experiments, the criterion of success will be achieved only when the animal's response falls within the subset of those responses that serve to operate the door-release mechanism. In other words, success or failure is inherent in the response and is determined solely by whether the response performed is within or outside of the subset of responses that meet the performance criterion.

When the teacher responds to the student's answer, the comment *right* is primarily a signal of success rather than a reward. In order to understand the significance of the information provided by *right,* we must note that there are situations in which the performer is incapable of determining for himself whether or not his response meets the criterion of success. When the task consists of opening the latch mechanism of a door, the subject will have no difficulty in determining whether or not his response has been successful. But for the arithmetic problem—and in many other everyday situations—success is not so obvious; it is necessary to have an expert observer (such as a teacher or an experimenter) assess the success of performance. The information provided by *right* adds nothing to the actual success of the subject's performance—no more than if an observer remarked

---

[2]In his early publications, Thorndike (1898) employed the term "success" to designate positive outcomes. For example, he wrote that ". . . the method of trial and error with accidental success is the method of acquiring associations among the animals" (p. 105). James (1890) also used the term *success* in this fashion.

right at the moment when a subject successfully operated a door latch. In the case of the puzzle box, of course, the observer is superfluous, while in many other cases the performer would remain ignorant of his success or failure without the observer's remark of *right* or *wrong*. The observer can, it may be noted, enhance his comment to the performer by saying, for example, "Very well done!" etc. This type of comment would constitute praise or approval and should be considered as adding the extrinsic satisfying property of reward to the information indicating success.

Our analysis to this point should clearly suggest the appropriateness of distinguishing between success and failure, on the one hand, and reward and punishment, on the other. Even more important than making this distinction at the verbal level, however, is conceiving it at the level of operational definition for application to experimental situations, since it is quite possible that this conceptual distinction may have behavioral significance. Let us discuss a number of illustrative situations so as to work toward meaningful operational definitions of the distinction between success-failure and reward-punishment.

For a variety of tasks, the subject is motivated to achieve the criterion of success primarily as a means to a desired extrinsic reward. This is the case when a child's successful operation of a latch mechanism serves to make available some food inside a cupboard; it is also the case when a successful examination performance is the means of obtaining a diploma and a career qualification; the situation is similar also for a cat in a puzzle box who receives a piece of fish outside the box. Nonetheless, it may be useful to distinguish among these three examples in terms of the degree of the subject's interest in the performance itself. For the student, the successful examination performance presumably is of some value in and of itself, while for the cat, success at opening the puzzle box may have no value independent of the food to be found outside or the freedom of being outside (i.e., presumably the cat would not be motivated to open the latch to get into an empty box). The case of the child opening a cupboard door may be an intermediate one, in that the child might enjoy the simple act of opening an empty cupboard, but he is even more interested when the cupboard contains food or playthings.

In selecting examples, we find it relatively easy to illustrate tasks with intrinsic value by reference to human, as opposed to infrahuman, behavior. It is appropriate to ask whether the distinction between success and reward is one that should be extended also to the analysis of infrahuman behavior. The answer to this question takes us into the comparative psychology of motivation. It is typically true that humans are ego-involved in the tasks at which they perform; that is, success or failure at the task is of substantial personal meaning, irrespective of whatever extrinsic rewards or punishments may be contingent on performance. Thus, the child who receives some candy as consolation for failing to solve a problem might prefer strongly to be in the position of the child who succeeded at solving the problem while receiving no additional reward.

In summary, our conceptions of success and reward may be distinguished in two respects: (1) Success is intrinsically linked to performance while reward is extrinsically linked; and (2) in the case of human behavior, substantial ego satisfaction may be attached to success independently of the availability of extrinsic reward.[3] The distinction between failure and punishment can be stated in precisely parallel fashion.

The tradition of research on learning has been typified by emphasis on rather arbitrary, extrinsic relations between actions and rewards — for example, as seen in the study of effects of varying the temporal relation between response and reward. The intrinsic relation between action and success and the role of this relation in learning has either been ignored or, at best, confounded rather extensively with the extrinsic relation involving reward.[4] Nonetheless, it is quite possible that in the context of human behavior, a contingency between a response and a reward has an effect different from that of the more fundamental intrinsic contingency between the response and its success. A reward that occurs in a close temporal contingency with a response but is perceived as irrelevant to the response may, for example, have less effect on subsequent behavior than a delayed indication of the response's success. Thus, when a job applicant, weeks after diligent preparation for a qualifying examination, stubs his toe on the doorsill on his way to the mailbox in which he finds notification of

---

[3]Certain experiments, such as those on manipulation of objects by monkeys (e.g., Harlow, 1950) raise the question of the role of success and failure (as opposed to reward and punishment) in animal behavior. Opening a door latch, for example, could be a source of intrinsic satisfaction to a monkey, as is apparently indicated by continued performance by monkeys at this task in the absence of extrinsic rewards. In regard to the second aspect of success, there would appear to be little basis for imagining that ego-involvement with success is a variable of any significance in infrahuman learning.

[4]It must be noted that Thorndike's conception of the role of "belonging" (Thorndike, 1932) somewhat approximates the notion of intrinsic relation as offered here. Nonetheless, the principle of belonging did not play an important theoretical role for Thorndike; for example, his treatment of "spread of effect" assumed that a belonging relation between response and reward was unnecessary for learning.

winning the job competition, this success experience is more likely to lead to maintenance of his study habits rather than of those that led to stubbing his toe. A related illustration is that of a person trying to start his car; after listening to the starter motor turn over for a few minutes with no success, he stamps on the floor in anger—at which point the motor starts. In this case, the stamping may well be repeated the next time the car won't start, but this repetition is due chiefly to a curiosity to find out if the stamping bears a causal relation to the car's starting; it is a type of exploratory behavior that will persist only so long as it appears that the causal relation between action and success is genuine. Note, of course, that the ability to employ a highly delayed indication of success or the ability to structure temporal contingencies in terms of causality is likely to be dependent on the existence of a level of cognitive development that occurs only among humans. Thus, the distinction between success and reward may be a relatively unimportant one insofar as infrahuman behavior is concerned; subhuman cognitive development may be insufficient for there to be any effective difference between an arbitrary (or extrinsic) contingency and the intrinsic success contingency.

In interpreting data from human learning experiments, it will also be necessary to distinguish between two distinct functions of the experimenter's comment of *right* following a response by the subject. The experimenter's comment acts not only as an indicator of success for the subject's response, but also serves as an informative cue designating that the just-performed response will be of use in successful performance on subsequent repetitions of the experimental task (see Experiments Ti_{1-5}, Chapter 6). The fact that these two functions of *right* have been confounded in the single term "symbolic reward" has led to maintenance of our ignorance about the potentially separable effects of success per se and of information provided by success. (This distinction will be developed further in Chapter 5.)

Moreover, it may be interesting to distinguish between the effects of outcomes that are received purely by chance (e.g., trial and error successes) as opposed to those that are received due to the subject's exercise of some performance skill. If ego-involvement does play some role in the effects of success, it would be reasonable to expect that this role would not come into play when success occurs by chance rather than by skill.[5] In the experiments reported in this volume, we

[5]Observation of the behavior of children in some of the present experiments suggests, however, that this distinction between skill and chance situations may be of significance only for adult performance and learning. Children seem to react identically to success in trial and error and skill situations.

have most often sought to present subjects with tasks in which the experimenter's remarks of *right* and *wrong* indicate successes and failures which the subject is led to interpret as due to his own performance skill. Nevertheless, the terms "reward" and "punishment" will be employed very generally in describing results and procedures to conform to current usage in learning experiments.

LEARNING IN HUMAN BEHAVIOR

There are two more points we wish to discuss as a preliminary to formulating a theory of learning applicable to human behavior. These are (1) the role of learning in a general analysis of human behavior; and (2) the role of the concept of stimulus-response (S-R) connection in the study of human behavior. These two topics are interrelated, since learning has often been conceived in terms of the formation of S-R connections.

It is important that the participants in a developing science recognize clearly the provisional and possibly development-restricting nature of the theories and models that they attempt to generalize from simple to more complex phenomena, as is the case for psychologists when extending principles developed in the study of animal behavior to the greater complexities of human behavior. It seems unlikely that a scientific psychology, concerned only with the study of human behavior, would have taken, as modern psychology has, the learning process as its fundamental focus. That is, human behavior seems inappropriately tied to the paradigm of an animal placed repetitively in a relatively constant stimulus situation such as an unchanging puzzle box or a maze in which the same goal is constantly sought. Man is characteristically an organism who does not return to the same problem situation once he has achieved its solution or obtained its goal; he moves on to other problems and new goals. Change, rather than constancy, is characteristic of the human problem-solving environment; therefore, the study of human behavior should focus on the basis for change in response to novel situations rather than on constancy of response to familiar ones. The psychologist who starts with human behavior as the basis for formulating his research problems would not be expected to be primarily interested in the learning process. The study of learning or habit formation, i.e., the acquisition of highly repetitive performances such as driving a car or typewriting would be secondary to the study of the nonrepetitive aspects of human behavior. This is not to say that understanding of the learning process is not of great importance to the study of human behavior; however, the role of learning in human behavior should be properly conceived. The most striking aspect of human behavior is its constructive character—its modifiability in response to new situations and through formulation of new goals. It seems quite inappropriate to seek to understand this constructive property of behavior by studying the habit formation process.

BEHAVIOR AND THE S-R MODEL

As we noted earlier in this chapter, Freud employed the reflex model of behavior, focusing on the process of discharge of stimulus energy (particularly from internal stimulation) through efferent (or behavioral) pathways. Freud's approach may be seen as an outgrowth of the conceptions of the Helmholtz school of medicine (cf. Jones, 1953). Pavlov and Thorndike, also working within the framework of the reflex model, focused on the problem of association formation, taking their intellectual orientations from the philosophical tradition of associationism and the physiological study of the reflex, respectively.

We may ask how it is that one would arrive at the explanation of human behavior in terms of the S-R reflex unit. In actuality, human behavior involves the interactions between a person and his environment. This behavior, by virtue of the integrity of the person over time, will manifest characteristics of unity and continuity; in other words, the separate actions of the individual will be as links in a larger structure, and the response to a specific situation will depend on this overall structure—the individual's personality. Thus, the study of human behavior might seem to have the human personality in its behavioral interaction with the environment as its primary object of analysis. Each action could be viewed as a phase in the interaction between personality and environment; through this interaction, the personality alters the environment and simultaneously may itself be modified. In making these observations, we do not wish to oppose the legitimate scientific pursuit of dissecting a whole into its smaller parts and processes for purposes of study; rather, we wish to note the incompleteness of any study that loses sight of the relation between part and whole, and the dependence of the part on the whole, in the process of dissecting the parts. For these reasons, the present analysis will keep in mind the human personality as the context in which the response to a specific situation occurs.

Let us now consider why the predominant tendency in contemporary psychology is to formulate explanations of human behavior in S-R terms. In examining the eighteenth- and nineteenth-century antecedents of modern psychology, we find a gradually increasing independence of psychological theorizing from what we believe to be the two fundamental realities of human behavior—the personality and the environment. While we shall not go into extensive historical detail, we may note a few of the highlights of this intellectual evolution. The British philosopher Hobbes (1588—1679) first enunciated the view that the sensory qualities of the objects of perception are not situated in the objects themselves. Berkeley (1685—1753) completely separated the content of perceptual experience from an external environment of real objects; thus mental life became conceptually independent of the outside world. Also during the eighteenth century, Hume (1711—1776) declared that an analysis of mental content showed no "self" or permanent substrate of mental activity; he concluded that mental life could be reduced to sequences of sensations, feelings, and ideas.

In the framework of these philosophical developments, the chief problem for psychology was to formulate the laws describing the process by which idea A is followed by idea B. This, of course, was the problem of association formation; much philosophical and psychological effort was expended in the formulation of laws of association which then were taken as the basis for explaining all aspects of mental life, not just phenomena of memory.

At the end of the nineteenth century, psychology began to acquire its present focus on observable behavior. Despite the new focus, the associationistic model was maintained and psychologists sought to explain the modification of the basic unit of behavior—the reflex—in terms of the already developed principles provided by the associationists. The notion of association of ideas was thus transformed into that of conditioned reflex, or acquired stimulus-response connection.

In the purest forms of the S-R approach (e.g., the behaviorists Thorndike, Watson, Guthrie, and Skinner), the organism is conceived as being under the control of impinging stimuli, these stimuli eliciting responses to which they are connected either innately or by virtue of past experience in accordance with the laws of association. In such a system, human behavior is reduced to the performance of learned associations; the conception of an organism or personality intervening between stimulus and response is assumed to be quite unnecessary. In some of the more complex S-R systems (e.g., the neobehaviorists Hull, Spence, and Osgood), the organism does play some intervening role (e.g., Hull's conception of drive) so that performance can vary as a function of organism factors given a fixed associative history. Such conceptions are, nonetheless, greatly removed from a conception of human behavior in terms of a personality constructively interacting with its environment.

In recent years, the problem of stimulus-response connection formation has most often been studied in experimental situations involving verbal stimuli (usually printed words) and spoken verbal responses. Studies of this sort are intended by contemporary investigators to elaborate not just laws pertaining to the memorization of verbal material, but the general mechanisms by which a behavioral response is elicited by a stimulus.

BEHAVIOR AS A CONSTRUCTIVE PROCESS

When the complexity of human motivation is considered, the inadequacy of reducing human behavior to a collection of segmental S-R connections becomes most noticeable. While man's behavior may be in part reactive and adaptive, the S-R model overlooks its constructive aspect. Man, in other words, does not simply react to changes in the environment, with adaptive reactions being preserved and maladaptive ones eliminated in accordance with the association principles; rather, man acts on his social and physical environment, attempting to make them conform to his personal projects and plans. The performance of adaptive habits or conditioned reflexes is properly conceived as a skill that frees man from environmental rigors sufficiently to allow him to become engaged in his projects. One could say that man is only truly adapted to his environment when he succeeds in modifying the environment to suit himself, i.e., in accordance with his projects and plans. Thus, we suggest that the concept of man as behaving in adaptive fashion, performing S-R connections in accordance with association principles, be replaced or at least supplemented by a conception of the constructiveness of behavior (see also Nuttin, 1967).

Man spends the majority of his waking time engaged in attempts to realize short- or long-term projects. These projects are themselves the cognitively elaborated forms in which needs manifest themselves.[6] A man's endeavors, for example, to earn his living and to enhance his social status by preparing himself for a professional career, constitute a long-term project that organizes and directs a large number of subordinated and coordinated activities. The child trying, in many interrelated ways, to change the behavioral interactions among his father,

---

[6]In regard to the dynamic properties of plans and projects, see Nuttin (1964). The present conception of motivation and of the interaction between cognitive and motivational processes in behavior is further elaborated in Chapter 8, below.

his mother, and himself—i.e., his Oedipus complex—is similarly working at a cognitively elaborated need-relevant project.[7] Both are trying to do, to make, or to realize something, and each action they take is determined to a large extent by its role in the overall project. More passive types of behavior also can fit into such projects and plans. For example, it may be part of a broader project just to wait and see what happens, to be receptive to opportunities.

When man's behavior is conceived in terms of coordinated means-end structures that are implemented in behavior, the learning process is consequently accorded a less important role than it is presumed to play in the case of a rat repeatedly obtaining food in a maze. The behavior of the maze-running rat becomes a repetition of a restricted set of responses directed at an unchanging goal object. Man, on the other hand, continuously constructs and directs himself at new goals, or subgoals heading toward an eventual major goal. Man's habits or S-R connections are behavioral units to be employed in ever-changing combinations in his constructive attempts to obtain subgoals and major goals. These behavioral units may be likened to the bricks used in making a house designed by an architect; much as it is inappropriate to equate the design and construction of a new house with the making of its bricks, so would it be improper to equate the design and construction of human behavior with the formation of habits. It is the prospective and constructive features of human behavior that cannot fully be explained in terms of learning processes. Quite to the contrary, as we shall show later in Chapter 5, the learning process may itself be seen as being directed by man's projects; man preserves, through learning, the information and habits that he expects to be useful in completion of his minor or major projects. This is not to deny the involvement of the learning process in the acquisition of new goals and means-end structures. Nonetheless, the process by which new goals are set and new projects are constructed is not to be equated with the process by which they, in interaction with learned habits, determine behavior. The behavioral process is characterized by progression beyond goals already obtained, toward the completion of new projects with new goals. When man becomes unable to elaborate new projects or to set new goals, when he describes himself as "having nothing worthwhile to do," or when he compulsively repeats his behavior patterns, these are taken as symptoms of a serious behavior disorder or, more properly, a disturbed personality.

---

[7]Note that persons are not always clearly aware of the projects and plans they are implementing. Cognitive elaboration of needs does not necessarily imply clear awareness (see Leeper, 1953).

To summarize, human behavior will not be fully understood by psychologists until the conception of a personality constructively interacting with its environment is taken as the framework for theoretical analysis. Within this framework, the study of learning has the important role of seeking to establish how the organism employs its past experience in the constructive process — that is, of determining what are the learned residues of past experience and how those residues are acquired and used. Further, the two-way interaction between the personality and the learning process must be recognized. In one direction, the personality constructs its goals and projects from the learned residues of past experience; in the other, the personality directs the learning process toward acquiring information and skills (or reaction patterns) that will be useful in implementing projects to obtain new goals.

While the processes of learning and adaptation have been subject to abundant experimental study by psychologists, the constructive aspect of behavior — a combination of motivational and cognitive processes — correspondingly has been neglected. Our purpose in this chapter has been chiefly to indicate these neglected characteristics of behavior in order to provide an orientation for the needed research. The concept of open task, which will be elaborated later (see Chapter 5), represents a concrete operationalization of a situation in which the constructive aspects of behavior may be studied. Our research will employ learning tasks as a vehicle for studying the constructive aspects of behavior. It is via the conception of stimulus and response as integrated components in a project, or experimental task, that we will be able to shed some new light on human learning and performance.

LEARNING BEHAVIOR AND LEARNED BEHAVIOR

Let us elaborate a remark made in passing in the last section — that the learning process can be subordinated to a project or task. To learn to play tennis or to paint with oils, to learn to read or to write, etc., are learning activities subordinated to major projects of the personality. This intentional learning behavior will persist, with the characteristic repetitive practice of learning tasks, only so long as the directing goal or reward is not regularly obtained. When the goal is obtained and the project is completed, the learning behavior (repetitive practice, etc.) ceases and the learned behavior can be used, if needed, as a technique or tool applied to new tasks within new projects, pointing toward new goals. The tools (i.e., learned behavior) may be acquired at the level of motor performance or in the form of stored information at the cognitive level. Both types of learned material (for example, typing ability and scientific knowledge) are at the person's disposal for the construction of his future behavior. The writing of a book or delivering of a lecture, as well as a persuasive attempt to sell a friend a car, are coordinated sets of actions constructed with the aid of learned motor skills and information at the performer's disposal. The connections formed or strengthened by the learning process do not themselves elicit these sets of responses under the control of stimulating conditions; the inadequacy of this simple view was indicated by the research of Lewin as early as 1922. The basic product of learning is the acquisition of behavioral possibilities or capabilities at the performer's disposal. Only in special circumstances do stimuli automatically elicit responses, following the path of innate or learned connections. Such automatic behavior (conditioned reflexes) may also occur in the service of larger projects (such as driving an automobile). In this view, what is learned is identified chiefly as a capability for performance, a behavioral repertoire, rather than simply as progressively increasing numbers of habits under stimulus control. The motor and cognitive capabilities stored through intentional learning projects are considerably increased, in the course of normal experience, by accidentally learned information, attitudes, and skills. All such available equipment will come into play when needed in the construction of behavior for implementing projects.

It will be clear from the foregoing remarks that, in our opinion, cognitive and motivational factors are expected to play an important role in the construction of behavior. The problems to be investigated in the following chapters are related to some very specific questions in the field of learning theory. But as we noted at the outset, the phenomena to be explained ultimately are those of human behavior in its integrated complexity. Therefore, the framework sketched in this chapter should be useful to the reader in understanding the theoretical directions we will be taking in interpreting the results of the experiments to be reported in the following chapters. A more concrete hypothesis about the specific processes involved in the selective activation of learned behavior for use in implementing projects and performing at various tasks will be outlined (Chapter 8) after we have had opportunity to present the results of a number of relevant research programs.

•

CHAPTER 2

IMPRESSIONS OF SUCCESS AND FAILURE

THE PROBLEM

The present chapter is concerned primarily with the manner in which general impressions of success or failure are formed on the basis of experiences of reward and punishment. Since much previous research is at least indirectly relevant to this problem, let us examine some results that are already well established before proceeding to a consideration of our own findings.

Some of the earliest pertinent research dealt with the general problem of affective influences on memory (see Rapaport, 1942). In this context, the formation of impressions of success and failure was not directly studied, but there was considerable attention given to the possibility of differential tendencies to recall activities that led to success as compared to those that led to failure. Among Rosensweig's many experiments on this topic, there was one (Rosensweig & Mason, 1934) in which children were asked to assemble jigsaw puzzles depicting common objects. After having worked on a number of these puzzles over a period of 45 minutes, subjects were asked to recall as many as they could of the objects depicted on the puzzles. Substantial individual variation in the tendency to recall predominantly successfully completed or predominantly unsuccessful attempts was found. Rosensweig and Mason felt that the individual differences were systematic, reflecting basic personality variations among the children.

Another well-established and relevant area of research is concerned with the judgment of the degree of one's success at some performance. The judgment can be either an anticipatory estimate of success at some to-be-performed task, as in experiments on level of aspiration by Lewin and his co-workers (Dembo, 1931; Hoppe, 1930), or else an estimate of success at some just-completed task. In the latter case, the subject typically is not provided with any direct information about his actual success. In both kinds of experiments, it has generally been found that the correlation between judged success and actual success is rather low (see, among others, Hilgard & Sait, 1941). Such research has demonstrated (a) substantial individual differences in success estimates, possibly rooted in personality differences, as well as (b) various situational determinants of both recall of past success and judgment of past or future success.

Unlike these experiments on judgment of an uncommunicated outcome, our research in this chapter is concerned with clearly communicated successes and failures for a series of tasks. We shall seek both individual differences and situational factors influencing general impressions of the relative numbers of successes and failures obtained.

This problem of impression formation regarding success-failure is of interest to us because it bears (as we shall see in the next chapter) on problems raised in connection with research on Thorndike's law of effect. Moreover, the problem is important in itself in that it relates to the study of self-perception and interpersonal perception in general.

In our typical experiment, a subject is given a series of (say) 20 problems and told, for 10 of them, that his response was correct and, for the other 10, that it was incorrect. Immediately after having experienced this series of successes and failures, the subject is asked to give his general impression of whether the majority of his responses was correct or incorrect. He is invited to express this general impression in a quantitative way, judging how many out of the series of 20 tasks he answered correctly and how many he failed (that is, how many times he heard the experimenter say *right* and how many times *wrong*). In some of the experiments, the subject is additionally asked to judge his general satisfaction or dissatisfaction with his performance. In the next chapter, we shall proceed to consideration of the more specific problem of recall of success (reward) and failure (punishment) for performances of individual tasks within the series.

DISTORTIONS IN IMPRESSIONS OF SUCCESS

INDIVIDUAL DIFFERENCES (Experiments P_{1-4})

The experiments reported in this section were directed primarily at observation of the range of individual differences in impressions of success and failure.

Materials

Twenty cards, each 10 cm square, displayed irregular colored geometric figures. Each figure differed from others in both color and shape. Three additional cards, quite different from the 20 used in the main part of the experiment, were used for introductory demonstration purposes.

Procedure

The experimenter first told the subject that he would be shown a series of cards containing irregular geometric forms. For each card, the subject was to judge, to the nearest 5 cm², the area of the figure on the card. The subject was further told that his estimate should be made on the basis of a very quick inspection and that any time the guess was "sufficiently close" to the actual area of the figure, the experimenter would say *right*. If the guess were not within this criterion of accuracy (unspecified to the subject), the experimenter would say *wrong*.[1] The task was then illustrated with the three demonstration stimulus cards. On these practice trials, the subject received no information about his accuracy.

Rewards and punishments did not in fact depend on the accuracy of the subject's guesses but were rather given according to one of two prearranged schedules (A or B). The schedules, shown in Table 2.1, were random series of 10 successes and 10 failures with schedules A and B being mirror images of each other; any serial position rewarded in schedule A was punished in schedule B, and vice versa. As soon as the subject had completed his guesses for the 20 cards, the experimenter asked three questions in the form of an informal interview. First, the subject was asked to estimate whether he had obtained more successes (*rights*) than failures (*wrongs*), or vice versa. The second question sought a more precise estimate; the subject was told that there had been 20 cards and was asked on how many of them he had been *right* and on how many *wrong*. Finally, the subject was asked if he was satisfied with his performance in the experiment.

Subjects

The same procedure was replicated with four groups of subjects, designated as follows.[2]

---

[1]In the experiments reported in this volume, reward and punishment were usually conveyed by the French words *bien* and *mal* or *bonne* and *mauvaise*. The first pair of words will be translated as *right* and *wrong*, respectively, while the latter will be rendered as *good* and *bad*. [AGG]

[2]Throughout this volume, experiments are designated by the symbols used in the original French publication. These symbols consist of a letter or letters representing the basic paradigm [e.g., P = *perception;* S = *souvenir* (memory); RR = *renforcement réitéré* (repeated reinforcement); etc.], and subscript numbers indicating separate groups of subjects with whom the paradigm was used, either in exact replication or with minor variations. [AGG]

P_1: 16 males and females, average age 17
P_2: 16 females, average age 16
P_3: 24 males, aged 15 to 16
P_4: 15 males, aged 14 to 15

Results

The judged numbers of successes and failures for groups P_{1-4} are presented in Table 2.2. It is apparent that subjects generally tended to judge the series of 20 guesses as having resulted in more failures than successes, i.e., more *wrongs* than *rights*, while in fact the actual numbers of guesses of each type had been the same. The mean number of recalled successes for P_{1-4} (combined) was 9.11, significantly lower than the actual figure of 10.00 ($t = 3.44$, $p < .01$).

Results have not been presented separately for reward-punishment schedules A and B since, in general, the results for the two schedules were quite similar. We should draw attention to the fact that, despite

Table 2.1
SCHEDULES OF REWARD (+) AND PUNISHMENT (−)
(EXPERIMENTS P_{1-4})

Serial position	Series A	Series B
1	−	+
2	+	−
3	+	−
4	−	+
5	−	+
6	+	−
7	−	+
8	+	−
9	+	−
10	+	−
11	−	+
12	−	+
13	+	−
14	−	+
15	−	+
16	−	+
17	+	−
18	+	−
19	−	+
20	+	−

Table 2.2
DISTRIBUTION OF ESTIMATES OF NUMBER OF SUCCESSES
(EXPERIMENTS P_{1-4})

Experiment	N	Number of successes estimated									
		5	6	7	8	9	10	11	12	13	14	15
P_1	16		1	2	3	3	3		1		2	1
P_2	16	2	2	1	3	2	4		1	1		
P_3	24		2	4	9	2	4	1	1	1		
P_4	15		1		1	3	6		4			
Total	71	2	6	7	16	10	17	1	7	2	2	1

Note: Actual number of successes received was 10, in a series of 20 problems.

the general tendency for subjects to underestimate the proportion of their successes, it is apparent that a minority gave quite the reverse result. Inspection of Table 2.2 indicates that individual differences in impressions of success were substantial.

IMPRESSIONS OF SUCCESS AND SATISFACTION WITH PERFORMANCE

Responses to the question as to whether or not the subject was satisfied with his performance correlated strongly with the tendency to overestimate or underestimate success. The few subjects who overestimated their success generally indicated satisfaction with their performance in response to this question. Those who had the impression of equal numbers of successes and failures tended to be more satisfied than not, while those who underestimated their success tended not to be satisfied. There is no way of telling, of course, whether subjects were satisfied because they had over estimated their success, or if the tendency to exaggerate success was a function of subjects' general level of self-satisfaction.

CHILDREN'S IMPRESSIONS OF SUCCESS AND FAILURE
(Experiments P_{5-8})

The generality of the findings obtained in Experiments P_{1-4} was demonstrated in similar experiments with groups of younger subjects using somewhat different tasks.

In an experiment with 22 boys in the 10 to 12 age range (P_5), a series of 10 problems requiring guesses of the (unfolded) shape of a cutout in folded paper was used, 5 guesses being rewarded, 5 being punished. The direction of the results of P_{1-4} was confirmed, but not in a statistically significant manner. Ten subjects recalled more failures than successes, 5 recalled equal success and failure, and 7 recalled more successes.

A task appearing to be an intelligence test was used with three groups in the 7 to 8 age range (P_{6-8}). In this "intelligence" task, it was possible for subjects to be correct in an objective sense; nonetheless, the number of rewards and punishments administered could be controlled by constructing the series of 14 tasks with 7 very difficult ones and 7 very easy ones. When, by virtue of exceptional ability or inability, a subject did not perform according to plan, the remaining items in the series were modified by adding either easy or difficult ones, as necessary, in order to produce 7 successes and 7 failures.

This procedure was first used with 19 boys (P_6) and 20 girls (P_7) with the experimenter informing the subject *right* or *wrong* for each guess as it was made. P_6 and P_7 replicated the results of previous experiments in this series, i.e., subjects generally had the impression of more failures than successes. These results are given in Table 2.3. Combining the data of P_6 and P_7, we find that the mean number of recalled successes was 6.13, significantly lower than the actual figure of 7.00 ($t = 2.63$, $p < .02$).

Table 2.3

DISTRIBUTION OF ESTIMATES OF NUMBER OF SUCCESSES
(EXPERIMENTS P_{6-8})

| Experiment | N | \multicolumn{12}{c}{Number of successes estimated} |
		3	4	5	6	7	8	9	10	11	12	13	14
P_6	19	3	4	4	2	2	1	2			1		
P_7	20		3	2	5	5	3	1	1				
P_8	17	1	3	1	1	1	1		3	1	1	3	1

Note: Actual number of successes was 7, in a series of 14 problems.

Experiment P_8 was run with a group of 17 boys and girls of the same age used in P_6 and P_7 (7 to 8 years), using procedures identical to P_6 and P_7, except that the experimenter did not comment after each response as to whether it had been *right* or *wrong*. However, since the questions used were of such a nature that subjects could easily perceive whether they had been correct or not, each subject presumably was aware, during the experiment, of being correct seven times and incorrect seven times. In this situation, the discrepancy between subjects' judgments of the numbers of successes and failures and the actual numbers was generally greater than in the previous experiments (see Table 2.3). Further, this is the sole experiment in this series, to this point, in which the number of optimistic subjects exceeded the number of pessimists. That is, out of the 17 subjects, 10 recalled more successes than failures, whereas only 6 recalled fewer.

EXPERIMENTS WITH REDUCED OBJECTIVE PROPORTIONS OF FAILURE ($P_{9, 10}$)

In a few additional experiments, the number of actual failures in the experimental series of tasks was reduced to a rather small proportion. These experiments used a task of comparing the areas of two figures on a single card. The figures were identified by letters (e.g., A and B) and the subject's task was to estimate whether figure A was larger or smaller than figure B. This again was a task in which the experimenter could arbitrarily provide rewards and punishments that would be accepted without question by the subjects. In Experiment P_9, with 61 male subjects, average age 15, a series of 24 such cards was used with 3 incorrect outcomes inserted in a series of otherwise correct guesses. In Experiment P_{10}, with 64 male subjects between the ages of 13 and 14, the same task was used with 1 failure in a series of 8 guesses. While, in both of these experiments, more than half of the subjects recalled the number of incorrect guesses exactly, for those who were in error, there was a substantially greater number who overestimated the number of failures (see Table 2.4).

Table 2.4
DISTRIBUTION OF ESTIMATES OF NUMBER OF FAILURES
IN EXPERIMENTS WITH RELATIVELY FEW FAILURES

Experiment	N	Number of failures estimated		
		Less than actual number	Actual number	More than actual number
P_9 (3 failures)	61	10	35	16
P_{10} (1 failure)	62	1	50	11

Note: In each experiment, the ratio of failures to successes was 1:7.

CONCLUSION AND DISCUSSION

The results of P_{1-10} indicate that individuals vary considerably in their tendencies to perceive their performances as predominantly successful or unsuccessful and that, on the average, subjects tend to have the impression of a predominance of failure for the kind of task used here.[3] While the interpretation of this finding is not yet clear, it is undoubtedly of some significance. The tendency to recall past performances as having been predominantly successful or unsuccessful can have not only an immediate effect on the individual's mood, as demonstrated in fact by responses to our question assessing subjects' general satisfaction with their performance, but may also in the long run have an effect on personality traits (e.g., optimism-pessimism) related to impressions of one's own success or failure. Additionally, the tendency to recall past performance as predominantly successful or unsuccessful should be expected to affect the extent to which behavior in learning situations would vary over time. That is, the behavior of a person who felt that his performance was largely unsuccessful would be expected to change more upon repetition of the task than that of one who felt he was, overall, successful.

An additional six groups of subjects were used in variations of the paradigm of P_{1-10} in attempts to find systematic determinants of general impressions of success and failure. In the first of these experiments, distortions in impressions of a series of affectively neutral events were explored.

IMPRESSIONS OF A SERIES OF NEUTRAL EVENTS (Experiment P_{11})

Materials

Twenty subtraction and addition problems were used. Each was written on a card displaying two 2-digit numbers with either a + or − between them, e.g., $38 + 21$, $42 − 27$. In all cases, the problems could be solved fairly easily without pencil and paper. Two series of 20 problems were prepared. In each series, a given pair of numbers always appeared in the same serial position; however, problems that were addition problems in series A became subtraction problems in series B and vice versa. For example, the first problem of series A was $67 + 15$ while the first card of series B was $67 − 15$. The order of addition and subtraction problems in the two series is given in Table 2.5.

---

[3]There was some indication that the nature of the task may have been one of the factors responsible for this predominance of failure-impressions. In more recent experiments with different tasks the striking individual differences are maintained but there is no longer a tendency for a predominance of impressions of failure.

Table 2.5
SERIES OF ADDITION (+) AND SUBTRACTION (−) PROBLEMS
USED IN EXPERIMENT P_{11}

Serial position	Series A	Series B
1	+	−
2	−	+
3	+	−
4	+	−
5	−	+
6	+	−
7	−	+
8	−	+
9	+	−
10	−	+
11	−	+
12	+	−
13	−	+
14	−	+
15	+	−
16	−	+
17	+	−
18	+	−
19	−	+
20	+	−

Procedure

Subjects were instructed to perform the indicated addition or subtraction problem on each card and to write down the answer on a separate sheet. Also, subjects were instructed to place the cards for completed problems into separate piles for addition and subtraction problems, as each problem was completed. This ensured that subjects correctly identified the type of problem for each card. The experimenter gave no information about correctness or incorrectness for the problems, this information not being of any significance for the present experiment. After the 20 problems were completed, the experimenter first asked the subject whether the series contained, on the whole, more additions, subtractions, or the same number of each. After obtaining a response to this question, the experimenter remarked that there had been 20 problems in all and asked the subject to guess how many of them had been additions and how many subtractions. The subject was asked not to attempt to count the cards in the two piles but simply to give his impression of the number of each type.

Subjects

Twenty-six females between the ages of 17 and 18 participated in P_{11}. Half of these received series A, half received series B.

Results

The responses to the second question are presented separately in Table 2.6 for subjects who received series A and those who received series B. While it is apparent from the combined data that subjects generally recalled more additions than subtractions, this finding is of less importance than two others. First, as in previous experiments, it was apparent that there was substantial individual variation in impressions of the numbers of the two events. Whereas in our previous experiments, the two events had been success and failure, here the two events were neutral ones: addition and subtraction. More important, however, is the difference in results between the group that received series A and that which received series B. It is quite apparent that series A tended to produce the impression of a predominance of addition problems, whereas series B produced a slight tendency to recall a preponderance of subtraction problems. The mean estimated number of subtractions was 8.54 for series A, significantly lower than the mean of 10.46 for series B ($t = 2.32$, $p < .05$).

Table 2.6

DISTRIBUTION OF ESTIMATES OF NUMBER OF SUBTRACTION PROBLEMS FOR SERIES A AND B OF EXPERIMENT P_{11}

Series	N	Number of subtractions estimated								
		6	7	8	9	10	11	12	13	14
A	13	1	1	7	2			2		
B	13			3	2	1	2	4		1
Total	26	1	1	10	4	1	2	6	0	1

Note: Actual number of subtractions was 10, in a series of 20 problems.

While it is not possible to give a definitive interpretation of these results on the basis of a single experiment, there would seem to be little doubt that the result was due in some way to structural differences between series A and series B. Perhaps the most noticeable difference in structure (see Table 2.5) is the fact that series A starts and ends with a predominance of additions (considering the first six and last six problems) whereas series B, the mirror image, starts and ends with a predominance of subtractions. It would appear that the items at the ends of the list were prepotent in determining general impression of the content of the list. This problem will be considered further in another section of this chapter (see p. 27–31).

SUBJECT-VARIABLES AND IMPRESSIONS OF SUCCESS

We summarize briefly here the results of three experiments (P_{12-14}).

In Experiment P_{12}, 16 "optimists" and 14 "pessimists" were selected from 350 professional school students between the ages of 16 and 18. The selections were made by three teachers who had daily contact with the students. Detailed instructions were given to the teachers as to the behavioral criteria on which the judgments should be made; students were classified as optimist or pessimist only if they were independently so classified by all three judges.

Each of the subjects was given a series of 30 problems, 10 each of three different types. In all cases, the problems were of a nature such that the correctness or incorrectness of the subject's response could be arbitrarily specified by the experimenter. For all subjects, 15 responses were called *right* and 15 *wrong* according to a prearranged scheme.

When later asked to give their impressions as to the numbers of successes and failures, the pessimists clearly had the impression of more failures, while the optimists felt that failures and successes were about equal, on the average (see Table 2.7). Owing perhaps to the small number of subjects, the difference between the optimist and pessimist groups fell short of statistical significances ($X^2 = 2.46$, $p = .12$, $df = 1$).

Experiment P_{13} was conducted on a sample of 31 mental patients, 11 of whom had been classified as "manic," the other 20 as "depressive." It was considered that these manic and depressive patients would constitute an abnormal sample corresponding, respectively, to the normal optimists and pessimists of P_{12}. The experimental procedure was similar to that of P_{12} and it was found that the manic group tended to overestimate the number of successes, whereas the tendency among the depressives was to overestimate the number of failures (see Table 2.7). The difference between the two groups in P_{13} was statistically significant ($p < .05$ by Fisher exact test).

Table 2.7

IMPRESSIONS OF SUCCESS AND FAILURE
FOR NORMAL AND ABNORMAL SAMPLES
OF OPTIMISTS AND PESSIMISTS
(EXPERIMENTS P_{12} AND P_{13})

	Overall impressions		
Experiment	Overestimate failure	Overestimate success	Accurate
P_{12} (normals)			
Optimists ($N = 16$)	7	7	2
Pessimists ($N = 14$)	11	2	1
P_{13} (abnormals)			
Manics ($N = 11$)	1	6	4
Depressives ($N = 20$)	9	5	6

Note: Cell entries are numbers of subjects. Significance tests described in the text were conducted using only the data in columns labeled "Overestimate failure" and "Overestimate success."

The results of P_{12} and P_{13} demonstrate that distortions in general impressions of success or failure can be due to personality factors.

For Experiment P_{14}, two groups of female students, average age 17, were selected according to the extent of their ego-involvement in the study of music. Subjects were selected if two out of three teachers who served as judges classified them as "manifesting an interest and ability in music" ($N = 25$) or "without interest and ability" ($N = 16$). A series of 20 music questions was constructed in such a manner that it was possible to control the number of correct and incorrect responses given by each subject at 10 apiece, by use of very easy and very difficult questions (cf. P_{6-8}). Information about correctness was given by the experimenter after each response.

Those "with interest and ability" in music recalled their successes and failures fairly accurately, tending to judge them as equal in number on the average, while those "without interest and ability" greatly tended to overestimate their failures (see Table 2.8). The result was significant beyond the .05 level ($t = 2.4$, 39 df). This finding suggests that subjects tend to have a stronger impression of success for an activity in which they are ego-involved (i.e., one in which they feel they have ability and interest) than for one in which they are not ego-involved.

Table 2.8

OVERALL IMPRESSIONS OF SUCCESS AND FAILURE FOR
SUBJECTS "WITH INTEREST" AND "WITHOUT INTEREST"
IN THE EXPERIMENTAL TASK
(EXPERIMENT P_{14})

	Overall impressions		
Subgroup	Overestimate failure	Overestimate success	Accurate
With interest and ability in music ($N = 25$)	11	10	4
Without interest and ability in music ($N = 16$)	11	1	4

Note: Cell entries are numbers of subjects.

THE ROLE OF FIRST EXPERIENCES OF SUCCESS OR FAILURE IN THE FORMATION OF GENERAL IMPRESSIONS

The finding that the ordering of neutral events can influence the impression of overall composition of a series of such events (Experiment P_{11}) led to further experiments in which the ordering of successes and failures within a list was deliberately varied.

PRELIMINARY SUCCESS OR FAILURE (Experiment P_{15})

Materials and Procedure

The task was identical to that used for P_1, involving estimation of the area of a series of 20 irregular geometric forms, followed by questions on general impressions of success and failure and then requests for more precise judgments of numbers of successes and failures. Whereas, however, in Experiment P_1, subjects received no feedback about performance on three practice estimates, in the present experiment, the experimenter remarked *right* following each of the three practice responses for subjects in group A while subjects in group B were told *wrong* for the three practice problems.

After the three practice problems, the experimenter said: "These were only for practice; they won't count."

The three practice cards were then put aside and the experimenter said: "Now we'll start." Subjects in both groups then received 10 successes and 10 failures in the experimental series of 20 problems.

Subjects

Group A consisted of 34 male students, about 15 years in age, and group B consisted of 30 male students of the same age and school grade.

Results

The data are shown in Table 2.9. It is apparent that, whereas subjects in both groups A and B tended to overestimate the number of failures, this tendency was much greater for group B, in which subjects had received feedback of *wrong* for the three practice problems. The difference between groups A and B was significant at the .001 level ($X^2 = 10.82$, 1 df).

It should be noted that, when asking subjects to give their impressions of successes and failures, the experimenter took care to inform them that estimates were to be based solely on the 20 problems that followed the three practice tries and that performance on the practice problems was to be excluded.

When the results of P_{15} are considered together with those of P_{12} (see above), it appears possible that the initial success or failure on the practice task in P_{15} might act to create a temporary feeling of optimism or pessimism with regard to the task, these feelings then determining the overall impression of success or failure, respectively.

On the other hand, it is possible that the results of P_{15} were influenced by the preponderance of successes or failures in the total series of problems (i.e., the 23 problems including practice) and that subjects were unable to restrict their attention, as instructed, to the final 20 problems when giving their impressions of success and fail-

Table 2.9

OVERALL IMPRESSIONS OF SUCCESS AND FAILURE AS A
FUNCTION OF SUCCESS OR FAILURE ON PRACTICE TRIALS
(EXPERIMENT P_{15})

		Overall impressions		
Practice condition	N	Overestimate failure	Overestimate success	Accurate
Success (group A)	34	14	10	10
Failure (group B)	30	26	1	3

Note: Cell entries are numbers of subjects. The significance test described in the text was conducted using only the data in the columns labeled "Overestimate failure" and "Overestimate success."

ure. In consequence, an additional experiment (P_{16}) was conducted. In P_{16}, the total numbers of successes and failures received by each of two groups of subjects were identical and only their order within the experimental series was varied.

Materials and Procedure

The experimental task was the same as that used in P_5. This task involved the experimenter's taking a piece of paper, folded three or four times, giving it an irregular cut with a scissors, and asking the subject to indicate which of three alternative forms best corresponded to the figure that would result when the cut paper was unfolded. After one demonstration problem, for which no information about correctness was given, the experimental series of 10 problems was administered. The schedules of successes and failures used for groups A and B are presented in Table 2.10. It may be seen that group A was given feedback of *right* on four of the first five problems, whereas group B was told *wrong* for four of the first five problems. Since, for both groups, the numbers of successes and failures was constant at five apiece, it followed that the last five problems would consist predominantly of failures for group A and of successes for group B. With this design, it is possible to determine, if indeed any differential effect of the different temporal distributions of rewards is obtained, whether the outcomes of problems early in the list are more influential than others in determining the general impression of success or failure.

Table 2.10

SCHEDULES OF REWARD (+) AND PUNISHMENT (−)
(EXPERIMENT P_{16})

Serial position	Group A	Group B
1	+	−
2	+	−
3	−	+
4	+	−
5	+	−
6	−	+
7	−	+
8	−	+
9	+	−
10	−	+

Subjects

Thirty boys, between the ages of 9 and 12, participated in P_{16}. They were assigned randomly to groups A and B.

Results

The data of P_{16} are given in Table 2.11. It is apparent that subjects in group A tended to overestimate their successes whereas those in group B tended to overestimate their failures. The difference between groups A and B was significant beyond the .025 level by Fisher exact test.

Table 2.11
IMPRESSIONS OF SUCCESS WITH THREE SERIES OF
TASKS DIFFERING IN TEMPORAL DISTRIBUTIONS OF
FIVE REWARDS AND FIVE PUNISHMENTS
(EXPERIMENTS P_5 AND P_{16})

	Overall impressions		
Temporal distribution	Overestimate failure	Overestimate success	Accurate
Success at beginning (P_{16A}; $N = 15$)	3	12	0
Even distribution (P_5; $N = 22$)	10	7	5
Failure at beginning (P_{16B}; $N = 15$)	9	4	2

Note: Cell entries are numbers of subjects. Significance test described in text was based only on the data in the "Overestimate failure" and "Overestimate success" columns for the two groups of Experiment P_{16}.

These findings indicate that the predominance of either success or failure at the beginning of a series is important in establishing a corresponding general impression. Further, the data of P_{16} support those of P_{15} which, it will be recalled, showed that feedback for practice problems preceding a longer series of problems influenced general impressions of success or failure.

In Table 2.11, the data for the two groups of P_{16} are compared with those for all subjects in P_5, which was comparable to P_{16} both in subject sample and experimental task. In P_5, however, the distribution of successes and failures through the ten problems was fairly even. It may be seen in Table 2.11 that the results of P_5 fall midway between those of groups A and B of P_{16}, as would be expected on the assumption that successes and failures experienced at the beginning of a series are prepotent in determining overall impressions.

CONCLUSION

We have seen how a series of rewards and punishments experienced in the course of performing a series of related tasks can generate substantial individual differences in overall impressions of success or failure. More importantly, we have found three factors that reliably influence overall impressions of success or failure.

First, the existence of a predominance of either success or failure at the start of a series of related tasks works to establish an impression that the originally predominant outcome pervades the series. Second, general traits of optimism and pessimism seem to influence the tendency to perceive a given series of outcomes as predominantly successful or unsuccessful, respectively. Finally, the more ego-involved a subject is in the task he is performing, the more he tends to perceive his performance as successful.

This set of findings may be interpreted in terms of a need for consistency in self-perception. A person may perceive his successes and failures in the context of a preestablished conception of himself and of his behavior; he may tend to view his performance as confirming this preconception. The self-concept may be part of an enduring personality trait such as optimism or pessimism, a specific area of felt competence in which the person is ego-involved, or may be established only momentarily in the experimental situation itself by virtue of the feedback received for first performances at a new task.[4]

---

[4]In each chapter that presents research results, we will devote a concluding footnote to consideration of relevant literature, if any, that has appeared subsequent to the original publication of *Tâche, Réussite, et Échec*. The topic of the present chapter, formation of impressions of success and failure, is one that has not seen noteworthy research activity in the last several years. For this reason, the present conclusions cannot be amplified nor do they require amendment on the basis of more recent findings. The author (Nuttin), however, has been continuing research on this topic during recent years. He has extended the number of variables investigated; for example, the observation of other's successful and unsuccessful performances as a determinant of perception of one's own success or failure has been studied. The results of these more recent studies will be published in the near future. [AGG]

CHAPTER 3

•

RECALL OF REWARD AND PUNISHMENT

PROBLEM AND METHOD

With some notable exceptions (for example, Tolman, 1938; 1959), systematic behavior theories have not attributed an important role to the recall of past outcomes in the determination of future behavior. Rather, reward and punishment have typically been credited with automatic effects in the modification of behavior, independently of the learner's recall of them. It should be noted that the possible importance of outcome-recall has been ignored empirically, as well as theoretically. This inattention is surprising, in light of the seeming importance of outcome-recall in subjective interpretation of our own behavior. That is, we frequently have the feeling of choosing to do A rather than B, "because" we recall that A has been successful in the past while B has led only to failure.

It is a basic tenet of psychoanalytic theory that pleasure and pain tend to distort one's memory for the situations in which these affects have been experienced. In particular, psychoanalytic theory predicts that painful situations will be suppressed or repressed from memory. Many studies (summarized in Rapaport, 1942) have sought to analyze this phenomenon experimentally, with widely divergent results. While it is impossible to summarize these studies in terms of any comprehensive generalization, it does appear that a variety of personality and situational factors determine whether or not recall of pleasant experiences will be superior to recall of unpleasant ones. The present chapter is devoted to further research in this area. We shall not be concerned, however, with recall of the rewarded and punished activities. Rather, we wish to discover what determines whether one will accurately recall a previously received outcome (reward or punishment) when one is reminded of the activity for which the outcome was received.

The results of experiments reported in the previous chapter demonstrated systematic distortions in general impressions of success and failure. These findings lead us to expect comparable distortions in the recalled outcomes of specific performances.

Thorndike was convinced that the strengthening effect of reward applies not only to the S-R connection that is rewarded, but also has a more diffuse action on the preceding and following S-R connections (spread of effect). One could generalize this effect to predict that the diffuse action of reward might operate also on the connection between reward and the S-R unit for which it was received (that is, an S-R-reward connection). If this is the case, then rewarded items should be recalled as having been rewarded more accurately than punished items are recalled as having been punished.

GENERAL STATEMENT OF METHOD

The procedures of the experiments reported in this chapter are similar in general form to those of the previous chapter. Each subject is asked to perform a series of related tasks, i.e., to respond to each of a series of stimuli, each response being called *right* or *wrong* by the experimenter immediately upon its completion. Owing to the nature of the tasks used, the experimenter is free to present the outcomes entirely arbitrarily, independently of the subject's performance, without destroying the subjective character of real success or failure for each outcome. As previously stated in Chapter 1, we generally seek to establish conditions in which the experimenter's comments of *right* and *wrong* are perceived, by the subjects, as ego-involved successes and failures.

A prearranged schedule of successes and failures is employed for half the subjects, the remainder receiving an alternate schedule in which the *right* and *wrong* outcomes of the first schedule are interchanged.

The dependent data of outcome recall are obtained when, after a short time interval, the experimenter reinstates each of the stimulus situations encountered in the original series of tasks, asking the subject to recall for each one if his response had been called *right* or *wrong*.[1]

It is readily observable that with serial tasks such as those used in the present experiments, there is a good deal of interference generated by similarities among the individual problems in the series.

---

[1] The time interval prior to tests for outcome-recalls was generally devoted to assessing overall impressions of success and failure. These data, for several of the experiments reported in this chapter, have already been presented in Chapter 2.

As a result, there is a substantial amount of inaccurate outcome-recall that is perhaps untypical of outcome-recall in nonexperimental situations. Presumably, this deviation from nonexperimental reality would only have the effect of facilitating observation of those factors that systematically influence outcome-recall for distant past events.[2]

ACCURACY IN RECALL OF REWARD AND PUNISHMENT

EXPERIMENT S₁

Task

The subject was shown a drawing of a character (letter or number) and was asked to reproduce this drawing with an outline pencil drawing of his own. The stimulus characters were 22 letters and 8 digits, each with distinctive features, such as segments of varying thickness, length, and curvature. The subject saw each stimulus drawing for 4 seconds, following which he was to attempt to reproduce its distinctive features in his own drawing. The experiment was presented as one concerning the accuracy of form perception and the subject was not told exactly which features or dimensions of the drawings should be particularly attended to. About 20 seconds usually sufficed for the subject to make his drawing. After 15 seconds, the subject was advised that time was nearly up and care was taken to ensure that there was little variation in the amount of time spent on the different characters by a given subject. The subject was told that the aesthetic qualities of the drawings were irrelevant to the task.

A few of the unused letters of the alphabet served for practice trials on the task, given prior to the presentation of the 30 stimulus characters. Each of the subject's drawings for the 30 stimuli (but not for the practice ones) was appraised by the experimenter as soon as it was completed. The experimenter immediately transmitted his evaluation (*right* or *wrong*) to the subject, according to a prearranged schedule of 15 favorable and 15 unfavorable outcomes, and quickly proceeded to the 4-second exposure of the next stimulus character, leaving the subject little time to reflect upon the previous outcome.

---

[2]Nuttin's observation about the deviation of his procedures from everyday situations perhaps underestimates the similarities between his experimental situation and normal learning situations. His experimental situation is, for example, similar to that of the golfer who typically plays a long series of strokes from different "lies" and with different clubs, some successful, others not. Perhaps interference in outcome recall is a major part of the difficulty of such repetitive learning situations. [AGG]

Five minutes after completion of the original presentation of the 30 stimuli, the experimenter gave the following instructions.

"You will once again be shown the models for the characters you just drew. You are simply to tell me, for each character, if the drawing you made of it was satisfactory or not. In other words, you are to tell me if I said *right* or *wrong* for your drawing of each character. If you are unsure, say that your recall is doubtful."

Only the stimulus, or model, character was presented on the test series in order that the subject would not adopt the set of trying to evaluate the adequacy of his own actual drawings.

Subjects

Thirty university students participated in the experiment.

Results

A total of 900 responses was obtained (30 subjects × 30 drawings). Of these, about a third were labeled "doubtful." The remaining ("certain") judgments were classified as accurate or inaccurate outcome-recalls. The data are presented in Table 3.1.

Table 3.1

Percentages of Accurate and Inaccurate Outcome-
Recalls for Rewarded and Punished Responses
(Experiment S₁)

Outcome recalled	Outcome received (%)	
	Reward	Punishment
Reward	**36**	34
Punishment	27	**35**
Doubtful recalls	37	31
Total	100	100

Note: Figures printed in boldface indicate accurate outcome-recalls. Doubtful recalls have not been categorized in terms of accuracy in this table. Each column is based on 15 recalls for each of 30 subjects.

Only 1% more rewarded than punished drawings had properly recalled outcomes (36% versus 35%) that were judged as "certain," indicating no basic difference in accuracy of recall of favorable and unfavorable outcomes. The fact that there were slightly fewer inaccurate outcome-recalls for rewarded performances may be attributed, not to superior accuracy in recall of rewards, but simply to the fact that subjects recalled *right* more frequently than *wrong*, in general.

In light of the fact that just slightly more than half of the outcomes that were presumably recalled with some degree of certainty in Experiment S_1, were, in fact, recalled accurately, it must be concluded that there was little memory for outcomes in that experiment. In order to achieve a better test of the relative strength of recall of favorable and unfavorable outcomes, it was desirable to obtain a greater overall level of outcome-recall. It was assumed that this could be done by using more meaningful and differentiated task materials, so that each stimulus could be better identified by the subjects.

Task

The materials consisted of 20 cards showing photographs of groups of objects (e.g., a collection of bicycles, a street lined with trees, a row of houses, a flock of sheep). The experimenter gave each subject the following instructions.

"I will show you a series of photographs such as this [a sample card was shown]. You are to look briefly at each and estimate the number of objects you see on it. For example, how many bicycles are on this one?

"You will see each card for only 4 seconds, so it will be impossible for you to count the objects. It is recommended that you make a rough estimate of the number of objects after a brief inspection and then express your estimate to the nearest multiple of 5. For example, 35 or 40, rather than 37 or 41.

"After each judgment, I will tell you if you were close or not by saying *right* or *wrong*, depending on how close you come to the number of objects in the photograph. Of course, it is understood that you will not be able to guess the number of objects on the cards exactly."

Immediately after the outcome (*right* or *wrong*) was announced for each judgment, the subject was shown the next photograph. In accordance with standard procedure in this series of experiments, a preestablished schedule of 10 rewards and punishments was employed, with half the subjects receiving a reversed schedule. Prior to the experiment proper, the subject was given three practice cards for which his guesses were neither rewarded nor punished.

Five minutes after completing his judgments, the subject was asked to recall, for each photograph, whether his response had been called *right* or *wrong*. In this recall task, the stimuli were not presented a second time. The experimenter, rather, simply reminded the subject of the various photographs by asking, for example, "Was your judgment of the number of bicycles *right* or *wrong?*" It was found, in preliminary experiments, that these reminders were sufficient to evoke, in the subjects, very clear representations (images) of each photograph. The reminders were presented in the same order as that of original presentation of photographs. This procedure of reminding, rather than re-presenting stimuli, was used to eliminate any interference due to tendencies to reevaluate the stimuli on a second presentation; that is, subjects might second guess, then realize that the second guess was the same or different from the first and, on this basis, judge that the original guess was *right* or *wrong*, respectively.

For each outcome-recall, the subject was asked to indicate whether the outcome was recalled with "certainty" or was "doubtful."

Subjects

Thirty-eight university students participated in the experiment.

Results

Table 3.2 summarizes the results for 760 outcome-recalls (38 subjects × 20 stimuli). It may be noted that the experiment was successful in its primary aim of increasing the accuracy of outcome-recall; not only was the percentage of accurate outcome-recalls increased, but also the proportion of recalls qualified as "doubtful" was noticeably decreased.

The most notable result was the larger number of accurate recalls

Table 3.2

PERCENTAGES OF ACCURATE AND INACCURATE OUTCOME-
RECALLS FOR REWARDED AND PUNISHED RESPONSES
(EXPERIMENT S₂)

Outcome recalled	Outcome received (%)	
	Reward	Punishment
Reward	**58**	17
Punishment	25	**66**
Doubtful recalls	17	17
Total	100	100

Note: Figures in boldface indicate accurate outcome-recalls. Doubtful recalls have not been categorized in terms of accuracy in this table. Each column is based on 10 recalls for each of 38 subjects.

of the negative outcome. While there were significantly more accurate recalls of negative than of positive outcomes ($t = 2.2$, $p < .05$), it should be noted that this finding can be attributed entirely to the larger number of recalls (both accurate and inaccurate) of the negative outcome (55% of all judgments given with certainty). In fact, since 75% of the certain judgments were accurate, one would expect that an even greater proportion (68% rather than 66%) of the punished outcomes should have been accurately recalled, on the assumption of no difference in ease of recall for rewarded and punished outcomes.

CONCLUSION

The results of Experiments S_1 and S_2 provide no basis for assuming that favorable outcomes are more accurately recalled than unfavorable ones. Differences in accuracy of outcome-recalls in both experiments were attributable entirely to differences in tendencies to recall exaggerated proportions of one or the other type of outcome.[3] It remains possible that there are systematic determinants of accuracy of outcome recall, but the positive or negative character of the outcome itself does not seem to be one of these. The next section of this chapter will explore such possible systematic influences.

DETERMINANTS OF OUTCOME-RECALL

In unpublished research conducted at the Louvain Psychology Laboratory, Donceel (1934) noted a tendency for his subjects to recall some categories of items as *right*, independently of whether or not they had actually been rewarded. On the basis of some characteristics of these experiments, which cannot be fully described here, the following hypothesis was formulated: When, in a series of poorly differentiated stimulus-response items, some items are better recognized (i.e., more familiar) than others on the test presentation of the series, such items will elicit an exaggerated proportion of positive outcome-recalls. In the following experiments, we attempted to explore and refine this hypothesis by designing procedures in which recognition of situations (stimuli) was systematically varied.

---

[3]These tendencies in Experiments S_1 and S_2 are probably to be explained in terms of such subjective factors as the general impression of success or failure (see Chapter 2).

SITUATION RECOGNITION AND OUTCOME-RECALL (EXPERIMENT S₃)

In order to test the hypothesis that better-recognized situations tend to produce outcome-recall of success, each subject was familiarized, prior to the experiment, with a subset of the task-stimuli used in the experiment proper. Presumably, the familiarization procedure would enhance the subsequent recognizability of these subtask stimuli. If the hypothesis is correct, this should result in a greater tendency to recall the outcome of success for familiarized than for nonfamiliarized task-stimuli.

Task

Experimental materials consisted of a number of cards (10 cm square) on which were drawn irregular, colored forms. The designs might be compared to colored Rorschach forms, differing in the use of greater variety and intensity of color and a black outline for each form.

For the familiarization procedure, the experimenter said: "I am going to show you a series of cards. Later, these cards will be mixed with others containing different designs. It will be your task to recognize the ones you see now in the larger set you will see later."

Each of a set of 24 stimulus cards of the type described above was then shown for 4 seconds, during which time the experimenter was silent. After this presentation, the 24 cards were mixed, face up on the surface of a large table, with 30 others of the same general type. When the cards were well mixed, the subject was asked to select, from all those on the table, only those that he had seen earlier. During this task, the experimenter actively aided the subject. That is, when the subject selected a card that he had actually not seen before, he was asked to put it aside on the table; also when he could not recognize cards he had seen before, they were pointed out to him from the ones remaining on the table. While this familiarization procedure could not be expected to enable subjects to recognize perfectly all the cards that had been familiarized, certainly it made them more identifiable than nonfamiliarized cards.

Next, the experimenter drew up a set of 48 cards, including the 24 familiarized ones and 24 entirely new ones (i.e., ones not used in the above sorting task) of the same general type. This set of cards was then used for the area estimation task previously used in Experiments P_{1-4} (see Chapter 2). In this task, the subject was to guess the area of the form on each card, to the nearest 5 cm², and was given feedback of *right* or *wrong* according to a prearranged schedule. In this case, half of the responses to each subset of 24 cards (familiarized and non-familiarized) were rewarded and half were punished. As usual, two forms of the prearranged schedule, one the reverse of the other, were used. During this area estimation task, no indication was given to the subject as to which of the cards were the familiarized ones, or even that some of the cards were familiar.

Five minutes after completion of the series of area estimations, the subject was asked, in the manner of Experiment S_1, to view the stimulus cards and to judge, for each, whether his area estimate had been called *right* or *wrong*, and to qualify as doubtful those cards for which his recall of outcome was uncertain.

Subjects

Forty university students participated in S_3.

Results

In Table 3.3, the outcome-recall results of S_3 are presented separately for familiarized and nonfamiliarized cards. These data can be condensed to test three hypotheses. First, let us consider overall accuracy (combined over familiarization levels) of outcome-recall for rewarded versus punished responses. We find 49.5 % of rewarded responses and 50.5 % of punished responses with accurate outcome-recall. Not only does this indicate no difference between outcome-recall accuracy for reward and punishment, it indicates essentially chance level of accuracy in outcome-recall, i.e., outcome-recall was at best a very difficult task under the conditions of experiment S_3.

Second, we may determine whether outcome-recall was more accurate for familiarized than for nonfamiliarized cards. We find that there was accurate outcome-recall for 51 % of familiarized cards and 49 % of unfamiliarized cards in Experiment S_3. Again, we have little evidence of any accuracy in outcome-recall, since performance deviates little from the chance level even for the familiarized cards.

Finally, we may consider whether, as hypothesized, there was a tendency for subjects to recall more responses as rewarded for familiarized than for nonfamiliarized cards. In this comparison, we find that 54 % of familiarized cards were recalled as having had rewarded responses, compared to only 45 % for nonfamiliarized cards.

Conclusion

The only clear result of Experiment S_3 was a greater proportion of

Table 3.3

ACCURACY OF OUTCOME-RECALLS FOR
FAMILIARIZED AND NONFAMILIARIZED STIMULI
(EXPERIMENT S_3)

| | Level of familiarization and outcome received | | | |
| | Nonfamiliarized | | Familiarized | |
Outcome recalled	Reward	Punishment	Reward	Punishment
Reward	44 (%)	46	**55**	53
Punishment	56	**54**	45	**47**
Total (%)	100	100	100	100

Note: Figures printed in boldface indicate accurate outcome-recalls. Each column is based on 12 recalls for each of 40 subjects.

positive outcome-recalls for the familiarized cards than for the non-familiarized ones. Some reservations on the potential generality of this finding may be noted. First, the result was obtained in an experiment in which, overall, the accuracy of outcome-recall was poor; the recognition or familiarization factor might be less important as accuracy of outcome-recall improves. Second, the present experiment obtained an effect of contrast between familiarized and nonfamiliarized situations (i.e., familiarity level was a within-subjects variable). It may therefore be that relative familiarity rather than absolute familiarity is a determinant of recall of predominantly successful outcomes. This observation is supported by comparison with the results of S_1 and S_2. It will be recalled that S_2 was specifically designed so that the stimulus materials would be better recognizable (i.e., more meaningful) than those of S_1. As a result, it follows that the stimulus situations of S_2 were more familiar than those of S_1 when the subject was reminded of the stimuli and asked to recall outcomes. The fact that subjects in S_2 recalled an exaggerated proportion of punished outcomes is thus clearly contrary to a general relationship between absolute familiarity level and tendency to positive outcome-recall. It appears therefore that the finding of S_3 should be confined to cases in which different levels of familiarity are experienced by a single subject, the result then being interpreted as due in some manner to the contrast between the more and less familiar stimuli.

RECALL OF RESPONSE AND OUTCOME-RECALL (Experiments S_{4-7})

It seemed likely that when a subject was able to recall properly the response given to a particular stimulus, there might simultaneously be superior recall of the outcome received for that response. Four experiments in which this possibility was examined experimentally will be summarized here. We shall not elaborate the procedural details of these experiments since procedures used in several of the previous experiments were again employed.

The basic situation was one in which, as usual, subjects were asked to perform a series of related tasks for which their responses were called *right* or *wrong* according to a prearranged scheme. Subjects were next shown the task stimuli a second time and asked to reproduce the response originally given for each stimulus as it was re-presented. (They had not been led to expect this kind of recall test.) At the same time, the subject was asked to recall whether the (recalled) response had been called *right* or *wrong*.

The results of the four experiments are presented, combined, in Table 3.4; subjects' outcome-recalls have been categorized in terms of the outcome actually received and according to whether or not the response for which the outcome was given had been properly recalled.

Table 3.4

ACCURACY OF OUTCOME-RECALLS AS A FUNCTION
OF RESPONSE-RECALL ACCURACY
(COMBINED DATA OF EXPERIMENTS S_{4-7})

Outcome-recalls	Accuracy of response-recall (%)		Diff. (%)	CR	p
	Accurate	Inaccurate			
Correct recalls					
Reward	22.0	12.0	−10.0	8.47	<.001
Punishment	41.5	51.0	+ 9.5	5.94	<.001
Incorrect recalls					
Reward	20.5	17.0	− 3.5	2.80	<.01
Punishment	16.0	20.0	+ 4.0	3.20	<.001
Total	100.0	100.0			

Note: A total of 148 subjects were involved in Experiments S_{4-7}. Of their response recalls, 2196 were accurate and 1704 were inaccurate. In these experimental tasks, more punishments than rewards were actually administered, explaining why there were more accurate punishment-recalls than reward-recalls.

A finding apparent in Table 3.4 is that recalls of reward were more frequent following accurate, as opposed to inaccurate, reproduction of the response. This was true no matter whether the response had originally been rewarded or punished. In other words, accurate recall of response did not generally increase accuracy of outcome-recall. Rather, it produced a systematic bias toward recall of positive outcomes. In the summary and conclusion section of this chapter, we shall consider the possibility of a relationship between this finding and that of bias toward recall of reward when the stimulus is relatively familiar (Experiment S_3).

SUBJECTIVE CERTAINTY AND OUTCOME-RECALL (Experiments $S_{8, 9}$)

It is possible to examine the content of outcome-recalls as a function of the degree of subjective certainty expressed by the subject in stating the recalled outcome. In Table 3.5, the data for two experiments (S_8 and S_9) of the same type described earlier in this chapter are given separately for outcome-recalls labeled "certain" and "doubtful" by subjects. Only the data for inaccurate outcome-recalls are given in Table 3.5 so that we may confine our attention to recalls not explainable in terms of response-outcome connections actually formed during performance of the experimental tasks. For recalls judged certain, 53.5% were recalls of a favorable outcome, while for those judged

Table 3.5

CONTENT OF INACCURATE OUTCOME-RECALLS AS A FUNCTION OF
SUBJECTS' FELT CERTAINTY OF OUTCOME-RECALL
(EXPERIMENTS S_8 AND S_9)

Experiment	Percentage of incorrect recalls of reward for	
	Doubtful judgments	Certain judgments
S_8	47.1	56.2
S_9	46.7	52.6
Weighted mean (%)	46.8	53.5

Note: These data are based on a total of 433 erroneous recalls from 30 subjects in Experiment S_8, including 157 doubtful and 176 certain judgments; and 1512 erroneous recalls from 62 subjects in Experiment S_9, including 766 doubtful and 746 certain judgments.

doubtful, only 46.8% were of success. The difference between these proportions was statistically significant ($t = 2.95$, $p < .02$).

GENERAL IMPRESSION OF SUCCESS OR FAILURE IN RELATION TO RECALL OF SPECIFIC OUTCOMES (Experiments S_{10-15})

In Chapter 2, we examined individual differences in general impressions of success and failure for performance at series of tasks such as those used in the present experiments. It will be recalled that, in, experiments in which equal numbers of rewards and punishments were administered, subjects varied considerably in terms of recollection of a predominance of reward or punishment. In the case of several of these experiments, after collection of the general impression data, we proceeded to collect data on recall of specific outcomes as in other experiments described in the present chapter. That is, after subjects had been asked to estimate the numbers of rewards and punishments they had received, we proceeded to re-present the specific stimuli used and to ask for recalls of the outcome received for the response to each.

It is far from a trivial question to ask if general impressions of outcomes are related to specific outcome-recalls. When the subject is attempting to recall outcomes for specific stimuli, he need not respond at all in terms of a general impression but may respond simply in terms of specific memories.[4] While it is intuitively reasonable that general impressions and specific recalls be related, the operations for determining these two types of recollection of success and failure are decidedly distinct and it remains an empirical question to determine their interrelationship. The pertinent data for six experiments are presented in Table 3.6.

It is apparent that there was a significant tendency to recall specific outcomes as being in accord with the general impression of success or failure. In the six experiments combined, the mean percentage of recalled punishments was 55.7% for subjects having an overall impression of a predominance of failures, as compared to 39.4% for subjects with the predominant impression of success. (For this difference, $t = 6.34$, $p < .001$.) The data in Table 3.6 are combined for accurate and inaccurate outcome-recalls; it may be noted that the observed

---

[4]It is interesting to note that some subjects spontaneously expressed a feeling of contradiction between the fact that they had a general impression of, say, more punishments, and that, during re-presentation of the subtasks, a preponderance of them evoked the impression of having been rewarded.

Table 3.6

PERCENTAGES OF SPECIFIC OUTCOMES RECALLED AS
FAILURES AS A FUNCTION OF SUBJECTS' OVERALL
IMPRESSIONS OF SUCCESS-FAILURE
(EXPERIMENTS S_{10-15})

| Experiment | Subject's overall impression | | | |
| | Success | | Failure | |
	N	Percent	N	Percent
S_{10}	4	43	9	56
S_{11}	2	49	10	60
S_{12}	3	44	17	52
S_{13}	7	30	10	49
S_{14}	10	38	14	59
S_{15}	1	45	26	56
Weighted mean (%)		39.4		55.7

Note: Percentages are based on 20 outcome-recalls for each subject indicated, with the exception of Experiment S_{13}, for which there were 10 outcome-recalls per subject. It is interesting to note that the young children who were subjects in S_{13} generally recalled fewer failures than older subjects (see Chapter 5, Experiment Re, for further discussion of developmental differences in success-failure effects).

relationship between general impressions and specific outcome-recalls held for both of these categories.

EFFECTS OF VARYING THE OBJECTIVE PROPORTIONS OF SUCCESS AND FAILURE (Experiments $S_{16, 17}$)

In Chapter 2, we saw that when subjects received equal numbers of rewards and punishments, they tended not to deviate far from recalling, on the average, equal numbers of the two types of outcome. In similar experiments in the present chapter, it has been apparent that, despite relatively poor recall of specific outcomes, the average proportions of recalled rewards and punishments have remained relatively near the 50:50 ratio actually received.

It is of some importance to consider whether these observations can be attributed to a general tendency for subjects to divide their guesses approximately evenly between the two outcomes, irrespective of objective frequencies of the outcomes, or rather to divide their guesses in proportion to the objective frequencies received. It is of course impossible to decide between these alternatives on the basis of experiments in which the objective frequencies of success and failure were equal. In Experiments S_{16} and S_{17}, data appropriate to this question were obtained by administering rewards and punishments in unequal proportions.

The experimental tasks used in S_{16} and S_{17} were similar to those previously described and need not be of present concern. In S_{16}, 35 15-year-old students performed a series of 40 related tasks of which 14 (35%) were rewarded. In S_{17}, 30 17-year-old students received 12 rewards in a series of 50 related problems (24%). In accordance with the typical procedure of experiments reported in this chapter, all subjects were subsequently re-presented with the full series of stimuli and were asked to recall the outcome for the response to each. At no time in these experiments were subjects asked to give an overall estimate of success or failure in the series of tasks.

The results indicating mean proportions of recalled rewards and punishments are given in Table 3.7. It should be remarked that, in general, accuracy of outcome-recall in these experiments was quite poor. Nonetheless, as shown in Table 3.7, in their recalls of specific outcomes for each stimulus, subjects were apparently guided by the objective frequencies experienced. In both experiments, the mean percentage of recalled rewards was decidedly below 50% and the differences between the two experiments corresponded to the objective differences between them in outcome frequencies. It may be concluded that, despite the generally poor learning of actual outcomes in S_{16} and S_{17}, outcome-recalls were nonetheless influenced by those actually received. This influence took the form of a fairly close correspondence between the proportion of rewards received and the proportion guessed.

Table 3.7

PERCENTAGES OF OUTCOME-RECALLS OF REWARD AS A
FUNCTION OF OBJECTIVE PROPORTIONS OF REWARD

	Experiment	
	S_{16}	S_{17}
Objective proportion of reward (%)	35	24
Number of subjects	35	30
Number of outcome-recalls per subject	40	50
Proportion of outcome-recalls of reward (%)	40	25

SUMMARY AND CONCLUSION

The experiments reported in this chapter have demonstrated that recall of a favorable or unfavorable outcome for a response is dependent on several factors other than the outcome actually received. While this has been best established for situations in which the general level of outcome-recall is rather poor (as it has been in most of the experiments in the present series), there is indication from Experiment S_2 that comparable influences are to be found with superior levels of recall. At the moment, it is possible to designate five sources of systematic distortion in recalling response outcomes.

1. The greater the relative familiarity of the stimulus, the more likely is the response to be recalled as having been successful (Experiment S_3).

2. Accurately recalled responses are more likely to be recalled as successful than are inaccurately recalled responses (Experiments S_{4-7}).

3. The greater the subjective certainty of recall of a specific outcome, the more likely that outcome is to be recalled as favorable (Experiments $S_{8, 9}$).

4. The recall of a specific outcome tends to be distorted in a manner consistent with the individual's general impression of success or failure at a series of tasks (Experiments S_{10-15}).

5. The probability of recalling a specific outcome as favorable or unfavorable is directly proportional to the objective proportions of favorable and unfavorable outcomes received (Experiments $S_{16, 17}$).

The first three of these findings may be considered as evidence for the occurrence of *affective transfer* in the process of outcome-recall. That is, the recognition of a stimulus as familiar, the accurate recall of a response, and the feeling of certainty of recall are likely associated with affective states more positive than the opposed situations of unfamiliarity, inaccurate recall, and feeling of doubt. The affective state thus aroused may transfer to the outcome-recall task as a systematic determinant of the affective content of the recalled outcome. The remaining two findings may be classified as cognitive determinants of outcome-recall, although finding (4) appears to represent some mixture of cognitive and affective influence.

It remains to consider the relevance of these conclusions to understanding the effects of reward and punishment in trial-and-error learning. In this respect, Thorndike (1935) has considered rewards to be effective in producing a "confirming reaction" that automatically strengthens recently activated stimulus-response connections. Thorndike also mentioned an "informative influence" for reinforcing events described as follows.

> When the [stimulus] word recurs in the next trial of the series, and the subject considers what [response] number he shall say for that word, the thought of the number which was rewarded will be more likely to make him think of "Right" and less likely to make him think of "Wrong" than the thought of one of the other numbers; and the thought of "Right" along with the thought of that number for that word will more or less validate that choice, and incline him toward it. (1935, pp. 28 and 29)

In the present chapter, we have seen several factors other than reward (which is the only factor mentioned by Thorndike) that may prompt a subject to recall a response as having been rewarded. To the extent that an "informative influence" is important in trial-and-error learning, these factors will influence learning data independently of any automatic "confirming reaction" such as that proposed by Thorndike in his law of effect. Although Thorndike (1935) attached little importance to the informative influence, it remains an empirical question to determine whether such cognitive processes play an important role in trial-and-error learning. It is interesting, in this respect, to note that Thorndike interpreted the repetition of punished responses near in series to a reward (spread of effect) as evidence for automatic effects of rewards. It is alternatively conceivable that such repetition of punished responses could be due to an informative influence coupled with distorted outcome-recall. Some suggestive evidence on this topic will be considered in the next chapter.

•

CHAPTER 4

A RECONSIDERATION OF THE SPREAD OF EFFECT

THE PROBLEM

It may commonly be observed that a single experience of success or failure has an effect that touches on more than just the rewarded or punished action itself. The terms "elation" and "depression" describe such potentially pervasive effects of reward and punishment. The extent of this type of diffusion of success and failure may be a function of personality characteristics. For example, success or failure by a student at a simple multiplication task may have little pervasive effect, may influence general attitudes toward multiplication problems, or, in more extreme cases, might affect the student's general attraction to the discipline of mathematics. Cartwright (1942), for example, obtained experimental evidence demonstrating attitudinal effects that extended to activities related to the specific rewarded or punished ones.

In the present chapter, we shall be concerned with the diffusion of effects of rewards and punishments within relatively homogeneous series of experimental tasks. Thorndike (1933) has experimented extensively on one aspect of such phenomena as they pertain to reward and has used the term "spread of effect" to describe his findings. The spread of effect, as is well known, consists of a tendency to repeat punished responses increasingly as a function of their proximity, within a series, to rewarded ones. It is also well known that Thorndike has interpreted the spread of effect in terms of a diffusion of automatic reinforcing effects of reward to stimulus-response connections occurring temporally near a reward.

The behavior of a subject who manifests a spread of effect may be described in terms of his "acting as if" a punished response near a rewarded one had, in fact, been rewarded. In the last chapter, we uncovered several situational influences that could cause a subject to recall a punished response as having actually been rewarded (or vice versa); it was also noted that subjects' recalls of outcomes were frequently in error and that a substantial degree of subjective certainty was frequently attached to erroneous outcome-recalls.

In this chapter, we shall give serious consideration to the possibility that the spread of effect may be interpretable in terms of erroneous outcome-recalls rather than in terms of diffusion of automatic effects of rewards, as proposed by Thorndike. In particular, we shall examine the possibility that the spread of effect may be due to a tendency for subjects to recall punished responses as rewarded as a function of their proximity in series to a reward. Two types of evidence will be brought to bear on this problem: First, we shall directly examine errors in outcome-recall as a function of serial proximity to reward; second, we shall look at strengths of stimulus-response associations as a function of serial proximity to reward. A diffusion effect obtained with the former type of data would be consistent with an interpretation in terms of erroneous outcome-recalls; a diffusion effect with the latter type of data would be consistent with Thorndike's interpretation in terms of spread of automatic reward effects.

EXPERIMENTAL EVIDENCE

SPREAD IN RECALL OF SUCCESS (EXPERIMENTS C_{1-11})

Procedure

Subjects were given the task of learning the correct translation in a "foreign language" for each of 40 common words. The 40 stimulus words were listed down the left side of a printed sheet. Next to each were five two-syllable words of the "foreign language" (actually nonsense words). For example:

| HAND | kos-var | em-sos | den-sok | ger-sem | al-nok |
| PEN | nos-ga | tin-so | ves-kor | hur-sis | ab-tar |

The subject was told that only one of the five response words was the exact translation of the stimulus word. The translation was to be learned by reading aloud the stimulus word and then one of the response words. The experimenter would then say *right* or *wrong* and the subject would proceed to the next row on the sheet. The subject was told that the task of guessing one response word for each stimulus word would be repeated until the correct response was learned for each of the 40 stimulus words. After a few practice items, used to ensure that the subject understood the instructions, one trial through the entire list was conducted at the rate of about one line every 5 seconds.

The experimental design called for distributing rewards and punishments according to a prearranged schedule, irrespective of the response chosen by the subject for any specific stimulus word. After completion of the first presentation of the whole series, the subject's task was unexpectedly changed. He was now asked to reproduce for each stimulus word, as he read it for the second time, both the response he had given the first time (regardless of whether it was called *right* or *wrong*) and the outcome received (*right* or *wrong*).

Subjects and Reinforcement Patterns

The procedure just described was employed with 11 groups of subjects (C_{1-11}) using three different reinforcement patterns. The reinforcement patterns for these experiments and for some to be presented later in this chapter are given in Table 4.1. Table 4.2 summarizes the constitution of the subject groups for Experiments C_{1-11}. It should be noted that, in all the patterns used, a minority of responses was rewarded. This was necessary in order to have usable data for punishments situated at list positions of more than one or two steps from reward. Further, the specific positions rewarded were varied across the three reinforcement schemes in order that no fortuitous differences among items be allowed to influence the results systematically.

Table 4.1

REINFORCEMENT PATTERNS OF EXPERIMENTS C_{1-11}
AND Ci_{1-5} IN TERMS OF NUMBERS OF PUNISHED
RESPONSES AT VARIOUS DISTANCES FROM NEAREST
REWARDED RESPONSE

Distance from nearest reward	Experiments			
	C_{1-2}	C_{3-6}	C_{7-11}	Ci_{1-5}
Between two rewards	8	1	1	6
One step before or after	9	13	13	9
Two steps before or after	7	8	10	8
Three steps before or after	2	5	5	6
Four steps before or after	0	3	2	5
Five or six steps before or after	0	2	1	4
For comparison: number of rewarded responses	14	8	8	12
Total responses	40	40	40	50

Table 4.2

SUBJECT GROUPS IN EXPERIMENTS C_{1-11}

Experiment	N	Mean age
C_1	35	15
C_2	37	16
C_3	13	17
C_4	14	18
C_5	19	16
C_6	40	18
C_7	40	15
C_8	40	16
C_9	40	18
C_{10}	40	19
C_{11}	40	20

Note: Subjects samples included both males and females, except for Experiment C_1 which employed an all-male sample.

Results

For the present, we shall be concerned only with the outcome-recall data of Experiments C_{1-11}. (Response-recall data will be considered later in this chapter.) In Table 4.3, the percentages of responses recalled as *right* are presented in terms of the list-position distance of responses from the nearest rewarded response. Since no systematic difference was found between items preceding and those following reward, the data in Table 4.3 are categorized only in terms of absolute distance from the nearest reward.

It is apparent that, similar to results reported in the last chapter, there were many errors in outcome-recall. Further, there were systematic trends in these errors as a function of list-position distance from the nearest reward. Punished responses were more likely to be recalled as having been rewarded the greater their proximity to reward. The most marked effect occurred in the case of punished responses situated between two rewarded ones; these were recalled as *right* about as often as actually-rewarded responses. Punished responses one step from reward were slightly more likely to be recalled as rewarded than those two or three steps from reward which, in turn, were more likely to be recalled as rewarded than those four or more steps from reward.

Table 4.3

PERCENTAGES OF RESPONSES RECALLED AS REWARDED
AS A FUNCTION OF PROXIMITY TO NEAREST REWARD
(EXPERIMENTS C_{1-11})

Experiment	Number of steps removed from nearest reward						Rewarded responses (%)
	Between 2	1	2	3	4	5 or 6	
C_1	39.3 (%)	35.5	33.9	31.4	–	–	46.7
C_2	40.5	32.1	29.3	36.5	–	–	56.9
C_3	30.8	14.8	23.9	13.9	12.8	15.4	20.2
C_4	57.1	23.6	26.8	24.3	16.7	7.1	27.7
C_5	31.6	22.7	23.7	24.2	19.3	10.5	21.1
C_6	15.0	22.5	19.4	20.5	15.0	12.5	32.2
C_7	27.5	17.6	24.2	20.6	19.0	22.5	28.5
C_8	30.0	25.9	24.5	25.6	22.0	22.5	34.7
C_9	45.0	24.8	25.0	15.6	21.0	20.0	29.7
C_{10}	25.0	20.4	15.5	20.0	16.0	20.0	25.9
C_{11}	30.0	29.1	20.0	23.9	17.0	25.0	31.9
Weighted mean (C_{1-11})(%)	32.3	25.1	23.9	23.7	–	–	33.8
Weighted mean (C_{3-11})(%)	30.4	23.0	22.0	21.1	18.1	18.9	29.3

Discussion

On the basis of these results, we may conclude that there was a "spread" in the recall of success. This phenomenon should not be identified with Thorndike's spread of effect because the interpretation offered by Thorndike for the spread of effect cannot be used to account for the present data. Thorndike's spread of effect was conceived as a strengthening of neighboring connections due to diffusion of an automatic effect of reward (the "confirming reaction"). If reward indeed strengthens neighboring connections, one should expect the connection between a stimulus-response pair and its outcome [e.g., (HAND-den-sok) – wrong] to be strengthened as a function of proximity to reward. That is, the memory of the outcome should be more accurate as a function of proximity to reward. It is obvious that the outcome-recall data just reported are not consistent with this interpretation since outcome-recalls were less accurate with increasing proximity to reward.

While it is appropriate to reject the notion of diffusion of an automatic strengthening effect of reward as the explanation for the Table 4.3 data, it is not immediately clear what the source of the spread of recall phenomenon is. Let us turn to a second series of experiments designed to clarify the interpretation of our results.

FURTHER ANALYSIS OF THE SPREAD OF RECALL (EXPERIMENTS Ci_{1-5})

Our spread-of-recall data might be attributable to some diffuse effect of reward on the learning of outcomes. If so, this would be an effect of proximity to reward on the first, or learning, trial of our experiment. On the other hand, the data might result from a vagueness in the subjects' recollections of the positions at which rewards occurred in the list. If so, subjects ought to tend to recall connections as rewarded if their positions on the second, or test, trial are near originally rewarded positions, irrespective of proximity to reward on the learning trial. The relative value of these two explanations could be explored rather easily by altering positions of specific punished items between the two trials; this alteration, of course, would have to be done without the subject's knowledge.

Procedure

The materials were similar to those of Experiments C_{1-11}. The list length was changed to 50, rather than 40, stimuli and there were four response alternatives per stimulus rather than five. The distribution of outcomes is summarized in the rightmost column of Table 4.1. The procedure used for the first presentation of the list, i.e., the learning trial, was identical to that used in C_{1-11}. While the subject was being given instructions for the (unexpected) tests for recall of original responses and outcomes, i.e., the second list presentation, the original sheet of stimuli and responses was inconspicuously set down out of his sight by the experimenter. When the experimenter finished these instructions, he picked up a new list but said: "Here is your list again. You may start now." While the subject was thus led to believe he was seeing the same list again, he actually received one that had been altered in the following ways:

a. Punished items originally between two rewarded items were interchanged with items originally four, five, or six positions removed from reward.

b. Punished items one position before or after reward were switched with ones three or four positions removed.

c. Rewarded items and punished items two positions removed from reward were left unchanged in position. Also the first two items of

Table 4.4

PERCENTAGES OF PUNISHED RESPONSES RECALLED AS REWARDED AFTER
CHANGE IN THEIR POSITIONS RELATIVE TO REWARD
(EXPERIMENTS Ci_{1-5})

Experiment	Distance from reward of punished responses on second presentation			For comparison	
	One step[a]	Three steps or more	Difference	Rewarded responses	Punished responses at two steps
Ci_1	24.9 (%)	21.8	+3.1	33.9	20.0
Ci_2	26.0	21.2	+4.8	34.1	25.8
Ci_3	27.2	15.0	+12.2	35.6	19.3
Ci_4	27.7	22.6	+5.1	31.1	27.8
Ci_5	33.7	27.7	+6.0	32.1	25.6
Weighted mean (%)	27.5	21.5	+6.0[b]	33.3	23.8

[a] Includes responses one step before reward, one step after reward, or between two rewards on the second list presentation.
[b] $s_{diff} = 1.5$; $t_{diff} = 4.0$, $p < .001$.

the series were unchanged, to prevent subjects from suspecting that changes were made.

No subjects were observed to become aware of the alterations in the list. The five subject groups used with these procedures were as follows.

Ci_1: 30 male students, aged 16 to 17
Ci_2: 32 male students, aged 16 to 18
Ci_3: 31 male students, aged 15 to 17
Ci_4: 31 male students, aged 13 to 15
Ci_5: 20 male students, aged 14 to 16

Results

The data for the five groups are given in Table 4.4 in terms of four categories of proximity to reward on the second, or test, trial. The category of items labeled "one step" distant from reward includes those between two rewarded items on the test trial: it will be recalled that these items were four, five, or six steps distant from reward on the first, or learning, trial. The column labeled "three steps or more" distant from reward includes items originally either between two rewards or one position before or after a reward. It may be seen that punished responses close to reward on the test trial were more likely to be recalled as rewarded than were those close to reward on the learning trial.

These findings are not consistent with the supposition that the spread of recall is due to any diffusion of reward effects during the learning trial. Rather, they support the interpretation that subjects remember only the approximate serial positions of rewards and that the spread phenomenon is simply the concomitant of frequently erroneous recalls.

RECALL OF RESPONSE AND PROXIMITY TO REWARD
(Additional Data of C_{1-11} and Ci_{1-5})[1]

It will be recalled that subjects in the preceding experiments were asked on the test trial to recall the response given for each stimulus at the same time as being asked to recall the outcome received for that response. We shall presently consider the response-recall data since these, also, are pertinent to the understanding of the spread of effect. For Experiments C_{1-11}, response-recall data are given in Table 4.5, while in Table 4.6 the corresponding data for Ci_{1-5} are given.

[1]These data were originally presented in Appendix I of *Tâche, Réussite, et Échec.*

Table 4.5
PERCENTAGES OF PUNISHED RESPONSES ACCURATELY RECALLED
AS A FUNCTION OF PROXIMITY TO REWARD ON ACQUISITION TRIAL
(EXPERIMENTS C_{1-11})

Experiment	Number of steps from reward on acquisition trial					
	Between 2	1	2	3	4	5 or 6
C_1	52.1 (%)	56.5	52.3	52.9	–	–
C_2	53.0	55.2	60.6	55.4	–	–
C_3	46.2	47.3	47.1	50.8	46.2	50.0
C_4	35.7	41.8	41.1	31.4	47.6	28.6
C_5	68.4	43.7	48.0	45.3	50.9	42.1
C_6	55.0	54.8	53.4	50.0	51.7	57.5
C_7	60.0	50.4	50.5	48.3	40.0	40.0
C_8	40.0	51.1	52.1	42.2	51.0	55.0
C_9	40.0	51.1	48.2	47.8	47.0	42.5
C_{10}	35.0	48.3	44.7	41.7	39.0	35.0
C_{11}	47.5	48.3	48.2	46.1	56.0	42.5
Weighted mean $(C_{1-11})(\%)$	48.3	50.9	50.4	47.2	–	–
Weighted mean $(C_{3-11})(\%)$	47.2	49.6	48.9	45.5	47.6	44.6

Table 4.6
PERCENTAGES OF PUNISHED RESPONSES ACCURATELY RECALLED AS A
FUNCTION OF PROXIMITY TO REWARD ON ACQUISITION TRIAL
(EXPERIMENTS Ci_{1-5})

Experiment	Number of steps from reward on acquisition trial					
	Between 2	1	2	3	4	5 or 6
Ci_1	47.8 (%)	48.3	53.3	52.8	44.0	53.3
Ci_2	51.6	47.6	53.1	58.8	51.9	50.0
Ci_3	43.0	44.9	50.5	55.6	50.0	51.0
Ci_4	51.6	50.0	55.7	52.6	51.3	45.0
Ci_5	37.5	47.8	51.2	41.7	46.0	41.2
Weighted mean (%)	47.2	47.9	53.0	53.0	48.8	48.5

It will be recalled that the order of presentation of stimuli was
altered on the test trial for Ci_{1-5}. While in Table 4.4 the outcome-recall
data for Ci_{1-5} were presented in terms of proximity to reward on the

test trial, in Table 4.6 we have the response-recall data from the same experiments presented in terms of proximity to reward on the first, or learning, trial. This format is used because our present interest is in evaluating a learning effect that would have occurred, in accordance with Thorndike's interpretation, as a function of proximity to reward on the learning trial.

With the response-recall data, a spread of effect in Thorndike's sense of automatic connection-strengthening would appear as an increased ability to recall the original response (i.e., an increased S-R associative strength) as a function of proximity to reward on the learning trial.[2] The data in Table 4.5 show a trend in this direction, with greater recall of responses within two steps of reward as compared with recall of those three or more steps distant. However, this trend is not supported in Table 4.6. In interpreting Table 4.6, it must be recalled that positions of stimuli were altered on the test trial in groups Ci_{1-5}. The fact that stimuli two steps distant from reward were left unchanged may be responsible for superior recall for that position. If attention is restricted only to those positions that were altered between learning and test (all positions other than "two steps"), the data in Table 4.6 give no approximation to a spread of effect in response-recall; in fact, the trend is in the direction of greater response-recall with greater distance from the rewarded position. While it is possible that this trend may somehow be explainable in terms of the position-alteration procedure, it is not apparent how any such explanation could be consistent with Thorndike's spread-of-effect hypothesis.

SPREAD OF RECALL WITH PUNISHMENT (EXPERIMENT Ce)

Before drawing conclusions about theoretical implications of the results described in this chapter, it will be useful to consider data from an experiment in which outcome-recalls were observed following exposure to an isolated punishment in a series of tasks.

Procedure and Subjects

The experiment employed the "area comparison" task, briefly described earlier (Experiments $P_{9,10}$, Chapter 2). Each subject was

---

[2]It may not immediately be clear to the reader that the response-recall measure is appropriate as a measure of S-R associative strength. The basis for this assertion is developed in Chapter 5 (pp. 64—68), and further in the Appendix (pp. 148-152). [AGG]

presented with eight cards (each 15 × 15 cm) in succession. On each card were two thickly printed capital letters separated by a hyphen (T-J, Z-F, etc.). The subject was instructed to examine each card briefly as it was presented and estimate the relative area of the surfaces occupied by the two letters. He was then to respond, for example, "T is larger than J" or "T is smaller than J", always mentioning first the leftmost of the two letters on the card. The experiment was described to the subject as a study of the influence of shape on estimation of area.

Sixty-four male students, between the ages of 12 and 16, participated in the experiment. For each subject, the first five and last two responses were called *right*, while the sixth was called *wrong*. To avoid any systematic influence of the particular letter-pair rewarded, the 64 subjects were divided into eight sub-groups ($N = 8$ each), in each of which a different letter-pair was in the sixth position.

After the series of eight cards was completed, the subject was given the unanticipated task of recalling for each card whether his estimate about the relative size of the letters had been called *right* or *wrong*. This test was conducted by presenting, in their original order, the leftmost letters on each card. The subject first was asked to recall the second letter on the card and, then, to recall the outcome received for his response to that card.[3]

Results

The frequencies of recall of *wrong* as the outcome received are given in Table 4.7 for each of the eight serial positions and separately for the eight subgroups of subjects. It is apparent that a spread of recall of punishment was obtained with responses tending increasingly to be recalled as *wrong* as a function of their proximity to the actual punishment. The position immediately preceding the punished one was particularly favored in this regard, with 12 out of 64 subjects recalling that position as having been punished while, of course, it was actually rewarded. The difference between the proportion of recalls of *wrong* at the two positions adjacent to the sixth position, as compared with that for all nonpunished positions, was statistically significant (CR = 4.02, $p < .001$).

After completion of the experiment, subjects were invited to comment introspectively on their performance at the experimental task.

[3]The associative learning data for this experiment are presented later in this volume; see Experiment IR$_1$, Chapter 7.

Table 4.7

OUTCOME-RECALLS OF PUNISHMENT AS A FUNCTION
OF LIST POSITION FOR EIGHT SUBGROUPS OF
EXPERIMENT Ce

	Serial position of response							
Subgroup[a]	1	2	3	4	5	6[b]	7	8
Ce_1	0	1	0	0	1	4	0	0
Ce_2	0	1	0	1	2	2	2	0
Ce_3	0	0	1	0	4	4	1	1
Ce_4	0	0	0	0	2	5	1	0
Ce_5	0	0	0	0	0	6	3	0
Ce_6	0	0	0	1	2	7	0	0
Ce_7	0	0	0	1	0	7	0	1
Ce_8	0	0	0	0	1	5	0	1
Total	0	2	1	3	12	40	7	3
Percent	0.0	3.1	1.6	4.7	18.8	62.5	10.9	4.7

[a] $N = 8$ per subgroup. Table entries are numbers of subjects recalling punishment at each position.

[b] Only the response in the sixth position was actually punished.

The following comment was typical: "In the beginning, I made several correct estimates but, near the end [others say: "in the middle"] I made one mistake." Most of the subjects accurately recalled that they had made only one mistake in the series.

THEORETICAL IMPLICATIONS –
A RECONSIDERATION OF THE SPREAD OF EFFECT

The outcome-recall data presented in this chapter have established the spread of recall as a reliable finding. This phenomenon may be summarized as a tendency to err in recall of outcomes, but with a certain degree of accuracy preserved in the erroneous recalls; punished responses are more likely to be recalled as rewarded the greater their proximity to an actual reward, while rewarded responses are more likely to be recalled as punished the greater their proximity to an actual punishment.

Table 4.3 indicated that the probability of recalling a *wrong* response as *right* if it was close to a *right* one (i.e., either between two *rights* or adjacent to a *right*) was about the same as the probability of correctly recalling that the *right* response was *right*. In other words, accuracy in outcome-recall was generally quite poor; this finding was also noted in Chapter 3, it will be recalled.

At the same time, the original (punished) response made to each stimulus was recalled relatively accurately in these experiments. For either the case of choosing a response from five or four alternatives (Tables 4.5 and 4.6, respectively), recall accuracy was in the neighborhood of 50%, substantially above chance.

In summary, subjects recalled their original responses with some accuracy, but were rather poor at recalling the outcome received for each response. In an experiment employing learning tasks such as the present ones the subject is therefore likely to be confronted relatively frequently with a situation in which he recalls his response but is less certain about whether it was *right* or *wrong*. Let us make the reasonable assumption that a subject is more likely to repeat a recalled response when he guesses it to be *right* than when he guesses it to be *wrong*. Coupling this assumption with the spread of recall phenomenon, we would anticipate that repetition of punished responses in the neighborhood of a relatively isolated reward would tend to increase as a function of proximity to the actual reward. Such a prediction is, of course, a statement of Thorndike's spread of effect, but the prediction is made with no reference to diffusion of automatic effects of rewards.

Our "reasonable" assumption, that subjects will tend to repeat responses they recall as having been *right*, may be recognized as what Thorndike (1935) called the "informative influence" of reward (cf. p. 48, above). In commenting further on this process, Thorndike said:

> The informative influence of a reward would not be expected to spread or scatter to strengthen neighboring wrong connections. . . . A secondary image or idea of "Right" derived from the informative influence of a reward would have not only to get loose from the "word-number-Right" sequence to which it was attached, but also to knock out the third member of some "word-number-Wrong" sequence and take its place (1935, pp. 29 and 30).

The data of the present chapter suggest that Thorndike underestimated the importance of the informative effect of rewards. It presently appears that the "informative influence" can offer an interpretation of spread of effect data, stated in terms of cognitive, rather than automatic, effects of rewards. The present findings, however, do not stand as proof of this contention. In further research on the spread of effect, it will be necessary to guarantee that obtained spreads of repetition of punished responses near a reward are not the product simply of a spread of recall.

The response-recall results reported in this chapter also bear on the spread of effect. If strengths of punished connections occurring near a reward are indeed increased by diffusion of automatic reward effects, we should have found increased response-recall as a function of proximity to reward in Experiments C_{1-11} and Ci_{1-5}. This finding was not clearly obtained; the data of C_{1-11} showed a tendency in the expected direction, but Ci_{1-5} showed a tendency in the reverse direction.

CONCLUSION

The present chapter has contributed to our understanding of outcome-recall phenomena. We have found a spread of recall of outcomes and interpreted it in terms of a tendency for subjects to recall approximate, but fequently inexact, locations of rewards or punishments in a series of related tasks. This finding may be seen as a continuation of the research described in Chapter 3, in which we began to explore systematic determinants of errors in outcome-recall. The potential significance of the spread of recall finding is greatly enhanced, however, by virtue of its bearing on Thorndike's law of effect. In that the spread of effect gave evidence for automatic connection-strengthening effects of rewards, it was considered by Thorndike (e.g., 1933) as one of the empirical cornerstones for his law of effect. In that the data of the present chapter provide grounds for questioning the validity of the spread of effect, they also provide grounds for questioning the "automatic action" clause of Thorndike's law of effect.[4]

---

[4]The precise interpretation of the spread-of-effect phenomenon remains in doubt, even considering the most recent pertinent publications on the topic. Marx (1956), in a comprehensive review, has suggested that some spread-of-effect experiments have adequately controlled for the "spread-of-recall" source of artifact. It has subsequently been argued (Greenwald, 1966), however, that even the studies referred to by Marx must be regarded as inconclusive. The original spread-of-effect experiments opened a Pandora's box of methodological problems that are still in the process of being worked out. Postman (1962) provides the most recent review of progress that has been made in resolving these problems. While Postman draws the conclusion that the balance of evidence currently favors the legitimacy of Thorndike's original hypothesis of a scatter of automatic effects of reward, we feel that the experimentation needed to provide definitive support for that conclusion remains to be done.

Both Marx (1967) and Postman (1966) have questioned the appropriateness of the response-recall procedure in tests of the spread of effect. As we have already mentioned in an earlier footnote, more detailed considerations of this point are given in Chapter 5 and the Appendix of this volume. [AGG]

CHAPTER 5

•

DOES REWARD STRENGTHEN CONNECTIONS?

PROBLEM AND METHOD

Thorndike (1911, 1932) asserted that a "satisfying state of affairs," following a response, strengthens the connection of the response to stimuli in whose presence it was performed. Hull (1943) restated Thorndike's law of effect only slightly by declaring that "need reduction" had such connection-strengthening properties. The concern of the present chapter is to evaluate the accuracy of these and related assertions. We shall not take a position on the definition of reward as as "satisfying state of affairs" or "need reduction," etc. Rather, we shall make the noncontroversial assumption that certain events (for example, the words *right* or *good*) are generally agreed on as rewards. We shall then examine learning under experimental conditions designed to determine whether such events have any inherent connection-strengthening properties.

The observed data of many experiments by Thorndike have been taken in support of his postulated connection-strengthening property of rewards. In a typical procedure, he commented:

> We provide . . . a long series of situations to each of which several responses are possible, one of which is arbitrarily followed by a reward, any other being followed by a punishment. For example, a series of words is said by the experimenter to each of which the subject may respond by any number from 1 to 10. If he says the number that has been chosen to be "right" he is rewarded; if he says any other, he is punished. So we have a long sequence of connections and after-effects, in the form Word 1 → number, reward or punishment; Word 2 → number, reward or punishment; Word 3 → number, reward or punishment . . . and so on (Thorndike, 1933, p. 2).

Findings in such experiments typically show that about 50% of rewarded (*right*) numbers are repeated in response to subsequent presentation of the stimulus word, while the repetition figure for punished (*wrong*) numbers is in the neighborhood of 20 − 25 % (Thorndike, 1933, p. 4). Is the observed superior repetition frequency of rewarded responses due, as Thorndike claims, to strengthening of connections by reward? Or are other explanations of the increased repetition frequency equally (or more) reasonable?

63

One might object to Thorndike's conclusion since, in his paradigm, in which the subject has an explicit learning task, the obtained elevated probability of repeating rewarded responses may be interpreted in terms of subjects' recalling their responses and the outcomes (*right* or *wrong*) received for them, then selectively repeating responses recalled as *right*. In commenting on this possibility, Thorndike (1935, p. 29) observed that, in his procedures, stimulus item< succeeded each other with sufficient rapidity that subjects normall would not take the strategy of attempting to recall previous response. and outcomes. Presumably, subjects responded by giving the firs number that occurred to them upon presentation of the stimulu word. Thorndike thus opposed a conscious cognitive process inter pretation of learning not only for his experiments on "learning withou awareness" and "spread of effect" (which are not of present concer but also for those in which the subject was given an explicit lear ing task.

Our present concern is to obtain clear evidence pertinent to t manner of operation of rewards in human learning. We may start noting that we hold no argument with the accuracy of the facts dem strated in Thorndike's experiments and in many others. Human a animal subjects certainly tend to repeat rewarded responses and avoid repetition of punished or nonrewarded ones. We do not, ho ever, take these repetition data as proof that stimulus-response (S- connections are being differentially strengthened (in some structur sense) by reward and punishment. As a preliminary to consideration of our own experiments, we must first settle on some appropriate means of assessing structural changes in the strength of S-R connections.

MEASUREMENT OF CONNECTION STRENGTH

One may distinguish two senses in which the phrase "connection strength" is used. First, connection S_1-R_1 may be said to be stronger than S_1-R_2 when it is observed that R_1 is given more frequently than R_2 as a response to S_1. In this sense, connection strength carries no meaning beyond the observable dimension of repetition probability.

The second sense in which connection strength is used implies an explanation of the process or mechanism underlying observed variations in repetition probability. This process is usually thought to involve some structural change in the nervous system of the learning organism. In the theories of Thorndike or Hull, reward is assumed to produce automatically such a structural change with the result that repetition probability is increased.

Thorndike's (e.g., 1932) experimental data clearly warrant the conclusion that reward strengthens S-R connections in the first sense described above. It is not clear that the same conclusion is warranted when it is the second sense of connection strength that is intended. One reason for this doubt is that subject's motivations to perform rewarded and punished responses are far from identical. Subjects wish to repeat rewarded responses and to avoid repetition of others. Thus, differences in repetition probability could result from these motivational differences in addition to or instead of structural associative differences (i.e., differences in connection strength in the second sense).

In order to test more strenuously Thorndike's and Hull's theory about reward-produced structural changes, it is desirable to ensure that motivations to repeat rewarded and punished responses are equated. Although this would generally be difficult, if not impossible, with animal subjects, it may be accomplished readily enough with human subjects simply by instructing them to repeat all responses that they have previously given, i.e., to repeat punished responses as well as rewarded ones. If reward genuinely produces automatic structural changes that differ in strength from those produced by punishment, subjects should not be able to reproduce punished responses as well as rewarded ones, even when motivations to repeat them are identical.

This procedural suggestion for testing structural changes in S-R strength should be acceptable even to those students of stimulus-response theory who do not commonly make a distinction between learning without intent to learn (Thorndike, 1932, pp. 209ff.), subjects stimulus-response theory viewpoint, for assuming that the procedure of equating motivation should obscure differences in connection strength previously established by reward and punishment. In fact, the particular approach of Hull and his students would seem to demand that such motivation-controlling procedures be in force in order to remove from "reaction potential" any systematic effects other than those due to differences in "habit strength." [In Hull's (1943) theory, habit strength is the construct that corresponds to S-R connection strength in Thorndike's theory.] In other words, a rewarded connection can be said to be structurally stronger than a punished one when the subject is not able to reproduce the punished connection as well as the rewarded one. This "being able to reproduce" aspect of a punished (or rewarded) connection can be operationally defined in terms of actual reproduction of the punished (or rewarded) response when the subject is motivated to do so, upon presentation of its stimulus.

The reader may not be aware that a procedure of the type suggested here for equating motivation to repeat different classes of responses was used in some of Thorndike's own research. In *The Fundamentals of Learning*, Thorndike (1932, p. 70) set out to demonstrate the importance of what he called stimulus-response "belonging" in connection formation. This research problem demanded a measurement of the strength of connections between the second member of a given word-number pair (pair 1) and the first member of the immediately following pair (pair 2). This measurement required asking subjects to attempt to recall the first member of pair 2 when the second member of pair 1 was presented. This was, of course, a use of new motivating instructions for the purposes of testing connection strength. Rather than merely presenting the second member of pair 1 and allowing the subject to give whatever response occurred spontaneously to him, Thorndike felt it necessary to change instructions in order to obtain a test of connection strength.

Our typical procedure in the experiments to be reported in this chapter will be to ask subjects, during a test period, to repeat all responses originally made during an acquisition period. The subject will first have been rewarded for some and punished for others of these responses; the reproduction task will then be given without the subject having prior warning of it.

It is obvious that the motivation-changing procedures we shall use are inapplicable to infrahuman research; an animal cannot be instructed so as to equate incentives to repeat punished and rewarded responses. This is not to imply that our present analysis of reward effects may not be applicable in one or another way to the interpretation of animal learning data.

OPEN AND CLOSED TASKS[1]

In considering the validity of Hull's and Thorndike's interpretations of reward effects, a second methodological consideration must be raised. If we find that connections are indeed strengthened by re-

---

[1] It will be seen in the discussion in this section that the difference between open and closed tasks corresponds in part to that between intentional and incidental learning procedures and in part to that between imcompleted and completed tasks in the sense of Zeigarnik (1927). Since, however, neither of these latter distinctions fully reflects the open-closed distinction made in the present section and since English-language psychology does not contain more appropriate terms, we have adopted the solution of using literal translations for *tâche ouverte* (open task) and *tâche fermée* (closed task). [AGG]

ward, we must then be able to ask what aspect of reward is responsible for this reinforcement. Is it perhaps need reduction, as proposed by Hull? Is it a confirming reaction, as postulated by Thorndike? We suspect that it may be neither of these. A third factor not sufficiently explored by either Hull or Thorndike is the persistence of need (as opposed to the reduction of need) that typically characterizes a learning task. In learning tasks, subjects are characteristically (either explicitly or implicitly) instructed that it is of more importance for them to perform correctly on later trials than on early ones. This persisting task-tension, i.e., the need to perform correctly on later trials, is likely of greater motivational significance to subjects than the immediate need to be correct on early trials. Therefore, rewards and punishments may be of less significance for reducing present needs or producing present satisfaction than for their bearing on future need reduction or satisfaction. A reward thus serves to identify a response as one that will subsequently be of use in regard to the persisting task-tension while nonreward or punishment correspondingly indicates lack of future usefulness. The type of task in which rewards and punishments have such future significance will be referred to as an open task, to be distinguished from a closed task in which rewards and punishments are devoid of such future significance.[2]

The question to be asked in this chapter is: When rewards lack significance other than as immediate-need reducers or as momentary satisfiers, will they serve nonetheless to strengthen stimulus-response connections? If the interpretations of Hull and Thorndike are accurate, the answer to this question should be affirmative.

In order to answer this question, it is necessary to have an experimental situation that corresponds to what we have defined as a closed task. This requirement can be met by a variety of incidental learning experimental situations. In our closed-task paradigm, the subject is given a judgment task, for example, to estimate the area of a stimulus object, to guess the number of objects of a given type present in a photograph, etc. The experimenter remarks *right* or *wrong* after each judgment. Rewards of *right* provided in this context should certainly serve to provide immediate or momentary satisfaction. However, once the response to a given stimulus is made, the task with respect to that stimulus is finished; the subject is not expecting to have to respond again to it. This fulfills the definition of a closed task; the factors of need-reduction or satisfaction are present in reward, but

---

[2]A further discussion of open and closed tasks in terms of the future time perspective in human behavior is given in Nuttin (1964).

the significance of reward for future behavior is absent.[3] If need-reduction and/or satisfaction are crucial to connection-strengthening effects of reward, we should find learning effects in these closed-task experiments comparable to those obtained in typical open-task learning experiments. If such learning effects are not found, we must conclude that the connection-strengthening effectiveness of reward typically observed in learning experiments is not due to any inherent characteristics of reward. Rather, such effectiveness may be due to the persistence of need, or of task-tension, that characterizes open tasks.

SUMMARY

In this chapter we shall attempt to answer two questions:

1. In a learning (open) task, is the connection between a stimulus and a rewarded response made in its presence structurally strengthened?

2. Is it need-reduction or a confirming reaction or any other characteristic inherent in reward that causes whatever connection-strengthening property reward has?

To answer the second of these questions, we shall use the closed-task type of experiment and the method of assessing connection strength described in the preceding sections. More specifically, subjects will first be given a judgment task and will be led to believe that each stimulus will be seen only once. Subsequently, they will be asked (without prior warning) to reproduce both rewarded and punished responses as the judgment stimuli are re-presented.

ARE REWARDED CONNECTIONS STRENGTHENED
IN OPEN TASKS?

EXPERIMENTS Ro$_{1-9}$

Experiments reported in Chapter 4, in connection with our analysis of the spread of effect, are pertinent to the analysis of effects of reward in open-task situations. In these experiments, subjects were

[3]Rewards and punishments in such closed-task judgment situations may have future significance in regard to gross features of responding. For example, the subject may come to feel, on the basis of rewards and punishments received, that he generally overestimates (say) and he may therefore seek to avoid this error on future judgments. Even this type of future significance of rewards and punishments can be eliminated, as in the experiments to be described in this chapter, by using difficult judgment tasks and making the experimenter's comments of *right* and *wrong* entirely independent of the subject's accuracy of response.

given the (open) task of learning words in a "foreign language" by pronouncing one of several alternative "translations" of a common word. Later, they were asked to reproduce all of their first translation attempts while the stimulus words were being re-presented. Strengths of connections established by reward and punishment are indicated in Table 5.1 as percentages of responses accurately recalled. It may be noted that there was a consistent superiority of recall of rewarded responses, the average difference between recalls of rewarded and punished responses being 4.5%. On the basis of the data of Ro_{1-9} we shall accept the conclusion that reward is superior to punishment in strengthening connections in open-task situations.[4] We may proceed to a consideration of the more important question as to the source of this effectiveness of reward.

Table 5.1

PERCENTAGES OF ACCURATE REPRODUCTIONS OF REWARDED
AND PUNISHED RESPONSES IN OPEN TASKS
(EXPERIMENTS Ro_{1-9})

Experiment	N	Numbers of responses per subject		Percent accurate reproduction		Difference (%)
		Reward	Punishment	Reward	Punishment	
Ro_1	40	8	32	56.9	53.6	+ 3.3
Ro_2	40	8	32	56.6	55.4	+ 1.2
Ro_3	40	8	32	59.4	49.3	+10.1
Ro_4	40	8	32	51.9	49.9	+ 2.0
Ro_5	40	8	32	51.3	48.8	+ 2.5
Ro_6	40	8	32	48.1	44.8	+ 3.3
Ro_7	40	8	32	51.9	48.3	+ 3.6
Ro_8	35	14	26	58.6	53.6	+ 5.0
Ro_9	30	12	38	60.8	50.0	+10.8
Weighted means (%)				53.8	49.3	+ 4.5[a]

[a]Standard deviation of mean difference $= 1.02$, $t_{diff} = 4.40$, $p < .001$.

[4]To conclude from these data that reward strengthens connections more than punishment in the open-task situation may be premature. Additional data, to be considered later, on structural determinants of connection strength (see Chapter 7 of this volume) indicate that connections receiving an outcome that occurs relatively infrequently in a series tend to become stronger irrespective of whether reward or punishment was the infrequent outcome. It is therefore possible that the relative infrequency of reward in Experiments Ro_{1-9} may have been responsible for observed superior connection strength. More data pertinent to reward-punishment differences in open-task situations are given in the Appendix of this volume. [AGG]

ARE REWARDED CONNECTIONS STRENGTHENED IN CLOSED TASKS?

Two sets of experiments were conducted for the purpose of analyzing the involvement of need-reduction, satisfaction, or other inherent reward properties, in the connection-strengthening process. In the first set of experiments, subjects responded once to each judgment stimulus, the response being either rewarded or punished in a closed-task situation. Stimuli were then re-presented and subjects were asked to repeat or reproduce their original responses. The second set of experiments differed in that the procedures involved repeated presentation of the judgment stimuli while maintaining the closed-task situation.

EXPERIMENTS WITH RESPONSES REWARDED OR PUNISHED ONCE (R_{1-5})

The first series of experiments used the number-estimation task previously described in Chapter 3 (see Experiment S_2). It will be recalled that in this task the subject is shown a series of photographs (of groups of objects) for each of which he guesses, to the nearest five, the number of objects represented. In accordance with a preset scheme, the experimenter calls half of these guesses *right* and half *wrong*. Later, the subject is asked to reproduce all of his original guesses as the experimenter names the type of object in each photograph. This naming procedure, it will be recalled, assures that the subject will respond in terms of memory for his original response rather than by making a new estimate of the number of objects in the stimulus photograph.

Subjects

The same basic experiment was replicated with five groups of subjects. All were university students. The number of stimuli in the experimental series varied between 20 and 40 in different groups as indicated below.

R_1: 38 males; 20 stimulus cards
R_2: 63 males; 20 stimulus cards
R_3: 20 males; 40 stimulus cards
R_4: 100 females; 30 stimulus cards
R_5: 100 males; 30 stimulus cards

Results

Our main interest was in determining whether, under the closed-task conditions of Experiments R_{1-5}, subjects would be able to reproduce more of their rewarded than punished responses. In Table 5.2, the mean percent of rewarded and punished responses reproduced is indicated separately for the five experimental groups. These results indicate that, on the average, slightly fewer than 50% of both rewarded and punished responses were accurately reproduced. For the results of the experiments individually, only the difference in recalls for R_2 was statistically significant, and this was in the direction of superior recall of punished responses.

Table 5.2

PERCENTAGES OF ACCURATE REPRODUCTIONS OF REWARDED
AND PUNISHED RESPONSES IN CLOSED TASKS
(EXPERIMENTS R_{1-5})

Experiment	N	Percent accurate reproductions for		Difference (%)	$s_{diff.}$
		Reward	Punishment		
R_1	38	72.1	71.8	+0.3	3.25
R_2	63	61.1	67.6	−6.5	2.69
R_3	20	47.0	47.0	0.0	3.53
R_4	100	41.7	41.6	+0.1	1.80
R_5	100	43.3	41.3	+2.0	1.80
Weighted mean (%)		48.1	48.3	−0.2	

Note: Data are based on 20 responses per subject in R_1 and R_2, 40 responses per subject in R_3, and 30 responses per subject in R_4 and R_5. In all cases, half of these responses were rewarded and half punished.

In an additional analysis of the data of these five experiments, each subject, of the total of 321 who participated, was classified in terms of whether he reproduced correctly more rewarded responses, more punished responses, or equal numbers of the two categories. It was found that 39.9% of the subjects accurately reproduced more rewarded responses, 44.9% gave more punished responses correctly, and the remaining 15.2% reproduced equal numbers of rewarded and punished responses. While the preponderance was in the direction of more learning with punishment, the difference between the percentages falling in the first two categories did not approach statistical significance.

From these results, it appears that the ability to respond to a reinstated stimulus with one's original response to that stimulus is not facilitated by reward for the original response. On the basis of our earlier discussions about the appropriateness of the response-reproduction procedure as a measure of connection strength, we must therefore conclude that these findings are inconsistent with the theoretical interpretations of reward given by Thorndike and Hull.[5] Let us consider further evidence pertinent to this problem.

EXPERIMENTS WITH RESPONSES REWARDED OR PUNISHED MORE THAN ONCE (RR_{1-6})

It was conceivable that no facilitating effect of reward was obtained in Experiments R_{1-5} because, with each response rewarded or punished only once, differential effects of reward and punishment were of insufficient magnitude to be observable. It remains possible that such differential effects would emerge with repeated applications of reward and punishment. Somewhat of a methodological problem is generated by the need to present stimuli and elicit responses repeatedly while continuing to maintain the closed-task aspect of the present series of experiments. Our solution to this problem is described in the following procedures for Experiments RR_{1-6}.

Procedure

For the basic experiment, the material consisted of 144 cards, each showing two thickly painted capital letters separated by a hyphen, e.g., **R-B**. The two letters on each card were painted in black in such fashion that their surface areas were not discriminably different. Twelve different pairs of letters were used, each in 12 different printing styles, in a random order.

The task was the area comparison problem described earlier for Experiment Ce (Chapter 4). The subject first responded to each card by estimating the relative areas of the two letters and then saying, e.g., "R is larger than B" or "R is smaller than B," always mentioning first the letter displayed on the left side of the card. In the present version of this task, subjects' responses were always called *right* for six of the letter pairs, every time they appeared, while responses to

---

[5]Further consideration of the appropriateness of the equated-motivation response-recall measure is given in the Appendix of this volume. [AGG]

the other six pairs were always called *wrong*. In this fashion, the response of naming a given ordered pair of letters was rewarded 12 times for six pairs and punished 12 times for the other six pairs. Subsequently, the subjects were tested as if the experiment had been a paired-associate learning problem; this, of course, was an unanticipated test. The experimenter conducted the test by saying, for example, "R is larger than . . . " The subject was required to supply the letter which spontaneously came to mind as having appeared to the right of R on the previously seen cards. (Subjects were not explicitly informed that the same letter had appeared together with R on all of its previous presentations.) The experimenter used "is larger than" or "is smaller than" for each test letter by selecting the one of these phrases that had been given most frequently for the letter-pair in question by the subject during his original area-comparison judgments.

If reward has special connection-strengthening effectiveness in this closed-task situation, it should be found that subjects are able to reproduce the second letter of repeatedly rewarded pairs more frequently than the second letter of repeatedly punished pairs.

In that the subjects of these experiments are explicitly being rewarded only for the presumed accuracy of their area-comparison judgments, it is appropriate to consider whether Thorndike's interpretation of reward should be expected to predict selective strengthening of connections between the two letters in each rewarded pair. Examination of procedures used in support of his own analysis of reward indicates that Thorndike would predict connection-strengthening by reward in this situation. For example, in experiments on learning without intent to learn (Thorndike, 1932, pp. 209ff.), subjects were initially asked to respond by selecting a correct translation of a stimulus word from one of five alternative response words. The response alternatives were set up so that correct responses tended to be located at the right side of each set of five alternatives. Thorndike predicted, and found, that in subsequent tests on new words, subjects demonstrated a tendency to select responses located on the right, even though correct responses were no longer concentrated on that side. In this example, the actual response rewarded or punished was one of selecting a correct translation. The response that was acquired was a response position bias that was incidental to the subjects' task. By analogy, it seems appropriate to conclude that the letter-pairs used in the RR series of experiments would be expected (by Thorndike) to fall under the influence of rewards and punishments received for area-comparison judgments, even though the content of the pairs is incidental to the subjects' task.

Subjects

Experiment RR was conducted with six groups of subjects, with variations (mentioned below) in the number of different pairs in the series, the number of times each pair was repeated (in different printing variations) in the series, and whether pairs of letters of letter-number pairs were used. When letter-number pairs were used (RR_5 and RR_6), the second element of each pair was one of the digits, 2 through 9; in order to make up 16 pairs (RR_5), each digit was used as the second element for two different letters. The subject groups and procedural variations were as follows.

RR_1: 22 males, average age 17, using 12 letter pairs, each presented 12 times

RR_2: 30 males, average age 14, using 12 letter pairs, each presented 12 times

RR_3: 78 males, between 20 and 22 years, using 12 letter pairs, each presented 12 times

RR_4: 34 males, average age 18, using 16 letter pairs, each presented 6 times

RR_5: 140 females, between 16 and 18 years, using 16 letter-number pairs, each presented 6 times

RR_6: 140 females, between 15 and 16 years, using 14 letter-number pairs, each presented 4 times

In keeping with standard procedure for our experiments, the specific pairs that were consistently rewarded for half of the subjects in each group were consistently punished for the remainder, and vice versa.

Results

Data for the six groups of subjects are summarized in Table 5.3. It is immediately apparent that no group demonstrated a significant difference between the number of rewarded and punished responses correctly reproduced. When the results were averaged over the six groups, it happened that slightly more of the punished responses (42.0%) as compared to rewarded ones (40.4%) were correctly reproduced, but this difference was not significant. The young subjects (age 14) of group RR_2 were notable in reproducing 6.6% more rewarded than punished responses. While this was not a significant reward superiority, it is possible that the effect of reward in a closed task is different for young subjects than for older ones. This point is discussed further below in connection with some concrete observations of young subjects in Experiment Re (this chapter).

Table 5.3

PERCENTAGES OF CORRECT REPRODUCTIONS OF CONNECTIONS
REPEATEDLY REWARDED OR PUNISHED IN CLOSED-TASK SITUATIONS
(EXPERIMENTS RR_{1-6})

Experiment	N	Number of connections per subject	Percent accurate reproductions for			
			Reward	Punishment	Diff. (%)	$s_{diff.}$
RR_1	22	12	53.0	52.3	+0.7	6.15
RR_2	30	12	48.3	41.7	+6.6	5.23
RR_3	78	12	44.9	44.4	+0.5	3.25
RR_4	34	16	26.8	28.7	−1.9	3.84
RR_5	140	16	42.1	45.5	−3.4	2.10
RR_6	140	14	37.0	39.2	−2.2	2.19
Weighted mean (%)			40.4	42.0	−1.6 (ns)	

Note: In all six experiments, half of the connections were rewarded and half punished for each subject.

In a supplementary analysis, combining the data from all six groups, it was found that 35.4% of the subjects (total $N = 444$) accurately reproduced more rewarded than punished responses, 22.3% reproduced equal numbers of each, while 42.3% reproduced more punished than rewarded responses. Again, the difference between reward and punishment was nonsignificant and was in the direction of more accurate reproduction with punishment.

In conclusion, repeated rewards and punishments in a closed-task situation did not result in differential strengthening of rewarded as opposed to punished connections. These findings support the interpretation that "inherent reward properties" do not account for the effects of rewards typically observed in learning experiments, i.e., heightened repetition of rewarded as compared to punished responses. In other words, no evidence of an automatic connection-strengthening property of reward was found in the closed-task situation.

FURTHER EXPERIMENTS WITH REPEATED REWARDS AND PUNISHMENTS (RF_{1-4})

In experiments with an additional four groups of subjects, a variant of the area comparison task used in the preceding experiments was employed.

Materials and Procedure

The basic experimental task was to judge the relative sizes of two irregular geometric forms displayed side-by-side on cards similar to those used in Experiments RR_{1-6}. The areas of the two forms on each care were approximately equal so that the subject's task was objectively difficult and the experimenter could call judgments *right* or *wrong* according to a prearranged schedule without arousing suspicion. On each card, each of the two forms was labeled with a 1-inch-high capital letter, these letters being used by the subject to identify each form. The subject expressed each judgment in exactly the same manner used for Experiments RR_{1-6}. That is, the figure on the left was declared to be larger than, or smaller than, the one on the right. If, for example, the figure on the left was designated R, the one on the right B, and the subject judged the one on the right to be the larger, his response would be: "R is smaller than B." A total of 144 cards was used in Experiment RF_1. Twelve different letter-pairs were used, each appearing on 12 cards with varying geometric forms. For each subject the responses to cards with 6 of the 12 pairs were consistently rewarded, while those to the cards with the other 6 pairs were punished on each appearance. In sum, the experimental task differed from that of Experiments RR_{1-6} only in that the areas compared were of geometric forms identified by letters, rather than areas of the letters themselves.

After completing their area-comparison judgments for the full set of stimuli, subjects received the same type of response-reproduction test used in RR_{1-6}, given without prior warning.

Experiments RF_{2-4} differed only slightly from RF_1, using a reduced set of materials in which each of 8 letter-pairs appeared on 12 different cards, i.e., a total series of 96 cards. The four groups of subjects used in RF_{1-4} were generally comparable to those used in RR_{1-6}.

Results

Table 5.4 summarizes the results for the four groups. Two aspects of the results are noteworthy. First, and consistent with the results of other closed-task experiments reported in this chapter, no significant differences between effects of reward and punishment were obtained. Second, the overall level of learning was poor by comparison with Experiments RR_{1-6}. In regard to the latter finding, it may be noted that the letter-pairs and age, sex, and intelligence levels of subjects in RR_1 and RF_1 were equivalent; the only difference between these two experiments was that the areas compared in the former experiment were of the letter-pairs themselves, while the letters only served to identify the area-pairs in the latter. Comparing Table 5.3 with Table 5.4, we find the overall level of associative learning in RR_1 to be over 50%, compared with less than 5% in RF_1. It may be concluded that the single procedural difference between the experiments was responsible for an impressive difference in the degree of strengthening of connections between the elements of letter-pairs. In fact, in RF_1 there was no evidence of any connection-strengthening; the overall level of accuracy was slightly lower than would be expected if the subjects guessed randomly from the 12 letters that appeared on the right sides of the stimulus cards.

Table 5.4

FURTHER DATA ON REPEATED REWARDS AND PUNISHMENTS
IN CLOSED TASKS
(EXPERIMENTS RF_{1-4})

| Experiment | N | Percent accurate reproductions for | | Total (%) |
		Reward	Punishment	
RF_1	16	2.1	7.3	4.7
RF_2	16	12.5	7.8	10.1
RF_3	20	12.5	10.0	11.2
RF_4	66	20.7	19.4	20.1
Weighted mean (%)		16.0	15.2	15.6

Note: In Experiment RF_1, there were six rewarded and six punished connections, each repeated 12 times. In RF_{2-4}, four rewarded and four punished connections were repeated 12 times.

The levels of accuracy on learning tests in RF_2, RF_3, and RF_4 were generally higher than that for RF_1. This may be partly attributed to the fact that only eight letter-pairs were used in RF_{2-4}, increasing the level of accuracy to be expected if subjects guessed randomly only from those letters that appeared on the right sides of stimulus cards. In RF_2 and RF_3 the overall accuracy rate did not exceed this chance expectation.[6] In RF_4 accuracy was greater than chance, and this may

[6]It is certainly somewhat inaccurate to calculate a chance baseline by assuming that subjects guessed only from those letters that were actually used as second members of pairs. In fact, subjects would on occasion guess unused letters, indicating that the chance baseline was somewhat lower than that derived from our assumption. Nonetheless, this assumption may be useful in estimating comparative baselines for experiments using varying numbers of pairs, as in comparing RF_1 with RF_{2-4}.

be attributable to a minor procedural variation that was introduced in RF$_4$; a different method of original presentation of cards for the area comparison task had the effect of slowing down the rate of presentation, this likely being responsible for the increased learning obtained.[7]

Conclusion

Again, it was found that the administration of reward in the context of a closed-task situation did not have any special effect in strengthening connections. Somewhat more surprising was the fact that 12 spoken repetitions of each letter-pair had little effect on strengthening connections between the elements of each pair. One would infer from results of RF$_{1-4}$ that the factor primarily responsible for the relatively high levels of learning obtained in RR$_{1-6}$ was the perceptual organization of the pairs used in the earlier experiments. The degree of belonging together and of perceptual unity of the letters in each pair is greater when the letters themselves had to be compared than when the letters only served to label the comparison forms. In other words, it would appear that the opportunity for subjects to organize the elements of each letter-pair into a perceptual unit was more important for connection-strengthening than (a) spoken contiguity of the elements, (b) repetition of such contiguity, or (c) reward.

A CLOSED-TASK EXPERIMENT WITH CHILDREN (EXPERIMENT Re)

It is of interest to give the problem of connection-strengthening by reward some developmental perspective. We have already had some indications (Experiment RR$_2$; Experiment S$_{13}$, Chapter 3) that reward may have effects for children that it does not have for adults (see also Marks, 1951). For this reason, we report the results of an experiment using a closed-task procedure with 12-year-old children.

Procedure

The materials consisted of a set of 10 cards, on each of which was a picture of a familiar object, e.g., a chair, a door, etc. At first, each of these cards was presented in succession, with the child being instructed simply to name the object shown on each card. Following this, the child was informed that each card had a different identifying number, between 1 and 10, and that the next task would be to try to guess the proper identifying number for each card. This was pre-

---

[7]Experiment RF$_4$ has been described in greater detail in Nuttin (1947b).

sented, in terms of our classification developed at the beginning of this chapter, as a closed task, in that subjects were not led to expect that the task of guessing the identifying numbers would be repeated. On this number-guessing task, half of the responses were called *right* according to a prearranged schedule, the remainder called *wrong*. Although the objective probability of being correct on this task was 10%, none of the subjects seemed surprised that they were correct 50% of the time. In fact, many showed noticeable disappointment when they were incorrect.

While it might not be expected that the number-guessing task would hold adult subjects' attention, the 37 children who participated in Experiment Re were obviously interested, and were visibly pleased at correct guesses.[8] After a guess had been made for each card, the experimenter re-presented the cards and asked the subject to repeat the guess he had just made of the identifying number for each. The experimenter made certain that each subject understood he was to try to repeat each response, no matter whether it had been called *right* or *wrong*.

Results

We must preface the discussion of the results, shown in Table 5.5, by noting that some of the children participating in Experiment Re apparently treated the task as a learning task in the sense of school-work. This was apparent from their answers to questions asked after completion of the experiment, and it is not clear what effect, if any, this may have had in producing differential attitudes toward rewarded and punished items. In any case, there was no significant difference between ability to recall rewarded and punished responses, although the small observed difference was in the direction of better recall with reward. Fourteen of the 37 subjects accurately recalled more rewarded than punished responses, as compared with 11 recalling more punished responses, and 12 recalling equal numbers of each.

An interesting observation concerned the behavioral reactions of the young subjects in Experiment Re to the rewards and punishments administered. When a reward was received, subjects were frequently observed to leave their attention fixed on the card for which their response was rewarded; on the other hand, a punishment typically resulted in an immediate direction of attention to the next card in the

---

[8]This kind of task, however, can hold adults' attention when it is described as a test of extra sensory perception; cf. Wallach and Henle (1941) or Postman and Adams (1954). [AGG]

Table 5.5

PERCENTAGES OF ACCURATE REPRODUCTIONS OF REWARDED AND PUNISHED
RESPONSES BY YOUNG CHILDREN IN A CLOSED TASK
(EXPERIMENT Re)

N	Percent accurate reproductions for		Difference (%)	$s_{diff.}$
	Reward	Punishment		
37	37.8	33.5	+4.3	5.12

Note: Each subject experienced five rewarded and five punished connections.

series. It seems possible that these reactions to the reinforcements might be responsible for the small reward-punishment differences generally found in our experiments with children.

SUMMARY AND CONCLUSIONS

At the beginning of this chapter, we set out to answer two questions pertinent to the interpretation of the law of effect. First, is the increased frequency of repetition of rewarded responses in learning experiments due to a strengthening of stimulus-response connections under the influence of reward? An answer to this question was obtained by motivating subjects equally to repeat rewarded and punished responses after giving typical learning-task instructions, i.e., that only rewarded responses were eventually to be repeated. Under these circumstances (Experiments Ro_{1-9}), evidence of greater connection-strengthening with reward than with punishment was indeed obtained. Our conclusion was that, when instructions generate an open-task attitude for the subject, reward facilitates the strengthening of connections.

Our second question was directed at determining whether properties inherent in reward were responsible for connection-strengthening observed in learning tasks. In a variety of experiments, a closed-task procedure served to eliminate any effects of reward that might be due to its serving as a signal that a specific response would be subsequently useful in regard to the subject's persisting learning task. When this attribute of reward was eliminated, it was consistently found that reward no longer had any special effectiveness in strengthening stimulus-response connections.

We may conclude that, although reward does strengthen stimulus-response connections in open-task situations (i.e., typical learning tasks), this strengthening is not an automatic product of any inherent reward quality. Our hypothesis is that the connection-strengthening effect must be attributed to a maintenance of psychological tension created by the open-task situation, together with the fact that reward informs the learner that the specific response just made is one that the learner will later be called on to make. It would therefore appear that persistence of need, or task tension, is of greater importance for strengthening stimulus-response connections in experiments of the kind reported here than is reduction of need, in the sense proposed by Hull. This hypothesis will be tested in the next chapter.[9]

[9]The assertion that there are no differences in connection-strengthening effects of reward and punishment in closed-task, or incidental learning, situations has been contested. The results of studies by Postman and Adams (1954, 1955) and Porter (1957) support the contrary assertion that reward has enhanced connection-strengthening properties even in the absence of a persisting task. It is certainly difficult to reconcile the Postman-Adams and Porter findings with those reported in this chapter. The Postman-Adams and Porter experiments were presented to subjects as tests of extra-sensory perception (ESP). The subjects' task was to guess the correct number from 1 to 10 for each of a set of stimuli. The present experiments, of course, were presented as judgment tasks. It is possible that being correct on an ESP task, especially one that has a relatively low (10%) probability of success, may be an event that has significant properties other than its reward properties; this particular type of success may act to draw the subject's attention to his response more than being correct on other types of tasks. In Chapter 7 of this volume, we shall see that relatively infrequent outcomes increase connection-strengthening no matter whether the infrequent outcome is reward or punishment. In the studies by Postman and Adams (1954) and Porter (1957), the rewards did occur relatively infrequently, making the alternative interpretation just mentioned quite plausible. In the second Postman-Adams (1955) study, reward frequency was increased to the point at which it no longer was relatively infrequent. The alternative explanation can be applied to this study only if it is assumed that an event that is inherently infrequent (such as being correct on the ESP task) preserves some of the connection-enhancing properties of infrequency even when it occurs relatively frequently. An additional and possibly significant aspect of the Postman-Adams (1955) procedures was that subjects had been "informed that responses called 'right' on the first trial *might or might not* be correct on the next trial (Postman & Adams, 1955, p. 98, italics added)." If a minority of subjects inferred from this instruction that there was a reasonable possibility that first-trial *right* responses would or might continue to be *right*, then resulting conscious attempts to repeat successes but not errors would have been sufficient to produce the obtained reward-punishment differences. That is, the ESP task may not have been devoid of open-task properties. [AGG]

CHAPTER 6

•

TASK TENSION AND LEARNING

HYPOTHESIS

In the preceding chapter, we saw that rewarded connections are strengthened in the course of learning but, on the other hand, that no inherent reward property was responsible for this strengthening. In the present chapter, we shall present further experimental analysis of this strengthening effect, making particular use of procedures for generating open- and closed-task situations.

Our hypothesis is as follows. When a task remains to be performed, there exists for the performer a cognitive state that may be called "task tension." Each component of the task participates in this state of tension as long as the subject perceives it as part of the to-be-performed task. In the case of a learning task, the fact that a response is successful, or rewarded, results in the perceptual inclusion of the response in the to-be-performed task. The unsuccessful response is correspondingly excluded. Thus, correct responses may be considered as becoming incorporated in a task-tension system from which incorrect responses are excluded. The experiments of the present chapter will be oriented around this hypothesis, that incorporation in a task-tension system is the essence of the connection-strengthening property of rewards.

Before presenting original experiments, let us consider some earlier findings that are consistent with this hypothesis. First, there are the data obtained by students of Lewin (Ovsiankina, 1928; Zeigarnik, 1927) using the interrupted-task method. In their experiments and many subsequent ones (see review by Alper, 1952), it was found that maintenance of a task-tension system by interruption of tasks prior to their completion resulted in better subsequent recall of the content of the interrupted tasks as opposed to comparable completed tasks.

Some data obtained by Aall (1912, 1913) prior to the work of Lewin's students, and less well-known, are perhaps even more pertinent. Two of his classes of students were studying the same topic. With one of

82

these groups, the topic was presented as one that was to be covered in detail on a subsequent exam, but that would be of no use to the students after the exam. The second group was instead told that the same information would be of substantial use after the exam. The two groups demonstrated equivalent command of the material on the examination. Several weeks later, both groups were given an unexpected retest on the information in question. The second group showed superior retention, consistent with the proposal that maintenance of a continuing task-tension system facilitates retention of learned material. Their superiority could not be explained, it was later ascertained, in terms of additional study of the material subsequent to the exam.

Our own experiments, presented in the following sections of this chapter, will be directed at theoretical interpretation of the respective roles of persisting task tensions and reward in learning experiments. If our hypothesis as formulated above is correct, then connections that are incorporated in a persisting task will be more readily reproducible (when the subject is motivated to reproduce them) than will be nonincorporated connections.

STRENGTHENING OF CONNECTIONS BY INCORPORATION IN A TASK-TENSION SYSTEM (EXPERIMENTS T_{1-3})

The first experiments we shall consider employ a variant of the interrupted-task method. In each of these, two groups are given the same task, up to a point at which one group is led to believe that part of the task remains to be completed at some future time while the other group is given a sense of task completion. Difference in retention of material learned during the original task will constitute an estimate of the importance of persisting task tension for the retention of learned connections.

Experiments T_{1-3} shared approximately the same procedure. Whereas T_1 was performed with subjects run individually, T_2 and T_3 employed groups of subjects run simultaneously. We shall describe the procedure of T_1, later noting those respects in which T_2 and T_3 differed.

Procedure

The subjects were all native Dutch speakers who were students at the same curricular level in a French course. Each subject was first shown a passage of about 15 lines in French and informed that it was to be used for measuring the subject's ability to translate from French to Dutch. The experimenter said:

"I know there are words in this passage that you have not yet learned and do not understand. Each time you encounter such a word, rather than translate it incorrectly, simply ask me for the meaning . . . by speaking aloud the word that troubles you."

With the aid of the students' French professor, the passage was designed with half a dozen words that could be expected to be incomprehensible to nearly all of the subjects and that could not be defined by inference from context. In order to ensure that subjects would read only so far as desired, they were instructed to write their translations in sentence-by-sentence order and to use a blank sheet to obscure the untranslated remainder of the passage from view as they worked.

Subjects in the Completed-Task condition were allowed to continue their translating through to the end of the passage. Those in the Interrupted-Task condition were interrupted three lines from the end of the passage by the experimenter, under the pretext of requiring the subject's help with another problem. The Completed-Task subjects also were asked to help the experimenter with the same task which involved cataloguing a set of library books. All subjects were occupied with this task for an interval of 5 minutes after either completion or interruption of the translating task.

After the 5-minute interval, each subject was given a sheet of paper on which were written all of the French words for which he had requested a translation. The subject was asked to translate them again. Although the content of this test varied somewhat from subject to subject, depending on his earlier translation performance, nonetheless for most subjects the intended difficult words did in fact appear on this test.

We may summarize the procedure in terms of the difference between the Completed- and Interrupted-Task conditions. This was that Interrupted-Task subjects started on the 5-minute "filler" task prior to completion of the translation of the last three lines of the 15-line French passage while the Completed-Task subjects first finished the translation. It may be added that the passage was in fact a coherent and interesting short story, the last three lines of which presented a denouement to which the earlier lines were leading. The selection of this interruption point, it was hoped, would serve to generate a substantial and genuine persisting tension connected with the translation task.

All the intended difficult words were in the first 12 lines of the passage. It should further be noted that, for the Interrupted-Task group, task tension was not attached to the difficult words themselves. None of these words was expected to reappear in the remaining portion of the task (the last three lines) and, in any case, translations for them were always available on the sheet of paper with the already completed portion of the task. This point represents an important difference between Zeigarnik's experiment and the present one. The items recalled by subjects in Zeigarnik's experiment were the completed or interrupted tasks themselves. In the present experiment, the French-Dutch translations for which subjects were to be tested were instead only associated with a completed or interrupted translation task. The critical translation items were, in fact, completed by all subjects in both conditions. The purpose of the experiment was, then, to determine whether or not the incorporation of a connection in a general persisting task-tension system would facilitate retention of that connection, independently of any expectation that the connection would be part of the remaining task.

In Experiments T_2 and T_3, similar procedures were used, modified to allow for group administration and use of longer intervals between the initial translation task and the later test for retention of translations. Subjects were run in groups of 12 students, and the experiment was conducted under the guise of a translation examination by their French instructor. For this test, there were 10 to-be-translated sentences printed on the upper half of each of two sheets, i.e., a total of 20 sentences. The 10 sentences on the first page of the test employed six extremely difficult words which, one could be quite sure, were not known to the subjects and could not be guessed from context. Subjects were to write translations of the 10 sentences on the lower half of the sheet; translations of the six difficult words were provided as footnotes on the bottom of the first test page. For all subjects, the first sheet was collected as soon as it was completed and work was started on the second. For Completed-Task groups, subjects were allowed to complete work on the second sheet, which required no further difficult translations. The Interrupted-Task groups were interrupted during work on the second sheet of translations. The pretext for the interruption was that the second set of translations required some knowledge of grammar that had not yet been taught; the instructor collected the second sheets for Interrupted-Task groups with the understanding that work would later be resumed.

To this point Experiments T_2 and T_3 were conducted identically. A difference was now introduced in order to obtain different delay periods between original learning of the translations and retention test. In T_2, the retention test was conducted at the end of an hour-long grammar lesson; the test consisted simply of a request for the translations of the six words that had been defined in the footnotes of the first translation sheet. The same test was used in T_3, but it was administered at the beginning of the next day's class, i.e., after an interval of 24 hours. For Interrupted-Task groups in T_3, the maintenance of task tension during the 24-hour interval was facilitated by distributing the second sheets as if to resume the test at the end of the first day's lesson, but then collecting them because the class hour was over; it was announced that the test would be resumed at the beginning of the next day's lesson.

Subjects

In all cases, subjects assigned to the Completed-Task and Interrupted-Task conditions were equivalent in age, intelligence, and proficiency in French. There were 71 males, aged 14 to 16, in Experiment T_1; 48 males, aged 15 to 17 in T_2; 70 males, aged 15 to 16, in T_3.

Results

The data for T_{1-3} are summarized in Table 6.1, in terms of an index based on the number of correctly translated responses on the test divided by the number of test words.[1] It is apparent that, in each of the three experiments, the mean value of this index was significantly greater for the Interrupted-Task condition than for the Completed-Task condition. These findings strongly indicate that incorporation of a connection in a task-tension system facilitates retention and reproduction of that connection while the task tension persists.

It should be noted that two further variants on the procedure of T_1 were conducted, but with negative results; that is, the proportion of retained translations in interrupted-task conditions was not significantly higher than that for completed-task conditions. These additional experiments employed the same procedures as T_1, with the sole variation that the time interval spent on the intervening task of sorting and cataloguing books was increased from 5 minutes to 15 minutes or 1 hour, respectively. Observational data indicated that this particular intervening task was sufficiently involving so as to

---

[1] For T_2 and T_3, there were exactly 6 test words per subject, it being assumed in effect that no subject originally knew the definition of any of the 6 difficult words. For T_1, all but 2 of the 71 subjects received between 3 and 7 test words (depending on the number of words for which they had requested definitions), with the great majority having 4, 5, or 6; the mean number of test words was 4.8. The two exceptional cases were students who requested definitions for 2 and 8 words, respectively.

Table 6.1

PERCENTAGES OF TRANSLATIONS LEARNED FOR COMPLETED-
TASK (COMP) AND INCOMPLETED-TASK (INC) CONDITIONS
(EXPERIMENTS T_{1-3})

Experiment	Interval between learning and test	Mean percent of translations learned				Difference (%)	t_{diff}
		Comp	(N)	Inc	(N)		
T_1	5 minutes	47	(35)	77	(36)	30	6.00[a]
T_2	1 hour	29	(24)	51	(24)	22	4.15[a]
T_3	24 hours	38	(36)	58	(34)	20	4.25[a]

[a] $p < .001$.

dissipate persisting task tension from the previous translation problem when the intervening task duration was 15 minutes or more. In fact, it was observed that at the end of the 15 minutes some subjects had forgotten their interrupted task. It was for this reason that the procedures of T_2 and T_3 were designed to create a stronger persisting task tension for the interrupted-task conditions; this was done by presenting the original translation problem as an examination of some importance. We should observe that, even with these stronger experimental procedures, we were quite surprised to find that the Interrupted-Task subjects tested after a delay of 24 hours (Experiment T_3) showed as strong a retention-facilitation as was obtained with the shorter interval in Experiment T_2.

THE INTEGRATIVE FUNCTION OF REWARD
(EXPERIMENTS Ti_{1-5})

The problem to which we turn now is to consider how and why rewarded responses are incorporated in a task-tension system while punished responses are not. It may be assumed that the subject generally wishes to perform his experimental task competently. At the moment of generating a response to a new task stimulus, the subject is ignorant as to whether or not the response he is performing is one that he will want to repeat on subsequent re-presentation of the stimulus situation. It is only at the moment of the experimenter's comment of *right* or *wrong* that he receives this information.

To this point, our analysis is not much different from that of Thorndike who remarked, of a response that has been rewarded, that the subject "seems to accept it, say 'yes' or 'OK' to it, endue it with acceptability" (1932, p. 316).

What is the function of the "OK reaction"? Taken in the context of the open-task attitude, in which the subject is oriented more toward what remains to be done than toward what has already been done, a reward serves to indicate that what has just been done must be done again later. In other words, the favorable outcome in conjunction with the open-task attitude serves to incorporate or integrate the rewarded response in a task-tension system in which the rewarded response participates as a means of accomplishing the persisting task's goal. Thus, the strengthening of reward or of the OK reaction, instead of being automatic, as Thorndike proposed, may be due rather to its service as a signal for a response to be cognitively integrated into a task-tension system. A punishment, by contrast, may usually serve to exclude a response from such a tension system.

According to our thesis, reward serves a double function in learning experiments: (a) It provides a successful outcome for the response just given, and in this sense, it has a need-reducing or satisfying effect. (b) At the same time, it informs the learner that the response just given is useful for further task accomplishment and, hence, further need reduction or satisfaction. Given the open-task attitude of the subject, this informative function serves to incorporate or integrate the rewarded connection in the persisting task-tension system. This very fact of being incorporated in a persisting task-tension system is what strengthens a connection and makes it more available for subsequent performance.

Two points of this thesis have already been demonstrated: (a) that the need-reducing aspect of reward is not the factor responsible for the strengthening effect in the type of experiment with which we are concerned; and (b) that connections incorporated in a task-tension system are in fact retained better than nonincorporated ones. It remains to be shown that information about the usefulness of specific responses for further task accomplishment is the factor responsible for connection-strengthening.

Our present aim then is to isolate the informative aspect of reward. The research strategy employed in this section will be to provide subjects with an open task and with feedback that is strictly informative, rather than satisfying, in function. The information provided will indicate simply whether a response just made is going to be of use subsequently or not. This feedback should serve, respectively, to include or exclude the response from the tension system of the experimental task.

We shall first consider the data of two experiments conducted by J. Donceel, under the direction of A. Michotte, as part of a research project conducted independently of our inquiry into the integrative function of reward.[2]

EXPERIMENTS Ti_1 AND Ti_2

Unlike the experiments of the preceding chapter, which employed closed tasks with reward and punishment, the present experiments used an open task but without reward and punishment, for the reasons just mentioned.

Procedure for Ti_1

A memory drum was used to present 100 arbitrarily constructed pairs of words. Each pair was displayed for 2.5 seconds followed by a .25-second interval in which either the word *good* or *bad* appeared in the memory drum window, followed by a new word pair, etc.

The subject was instructed to read each pair aloud as it was presented and was advised that subsequently he would be tested for ability to recall the second word of each pair following which *good* had appeared, but not for pairs followed by *bad*. The later tests, the subject was told, were to be conducted by re-presenting the first word of each of the pairs that had been designated *good*. Further instructions advised the subject not to rehearse any of the pairs after the signal word was presented, but rather to proceed immediately· to pronounce the next pair of words. It was stressed that there would be no subsequent use for the pairs that had been labeled *bad*.

After complete presentation of the 100 word pairs, half followed by the signal *good*, half by *bad*, subjects were tested, contrary to expectation, for ability to provide the second word for all 100 pairs.

Tryouts of this procedure prior to the actual experiment indicated that the brief time intervals and instructions rendered it a virtual impossibility for subjects to engage in covert rehearsal of the *good* pairs.

Procedure for Ti_2

Experiment Ti_2 varied from Ti_1 in the following respects. The materials were 200 pairs of words, the second of each of which was a nonsense syllable described as a "foreign-language translation" of the first member of the pair. Further, four memory-drum presenta-

[2]The two following experiments, Ti_1 and Ti_2, are part of an unpublished thesis. We thank Professors Michotte and Donceel for their kind authorization to use these data.

tions of the entire set of 200 pairs were given, following each of which the subject was tested for ability to produce the second word (nonsense syllable) for a different subset of 50 of the 200 stimulus words, including 25 that had been labeled *good* and 25 labeled *bad*. This procedure was designed to determine differential effects of the two signals with repeated exposure to word pairs.

Subjects

Experiment Ti_1 was done with 30 subjects; word pairs labeled *good* for 15 of these were labeled *bad* for the other 15. Ti_2 was done with 10 subjects. For both experiments, all subjects were male students, about 20 years old.

Discussion of the Procedures

Experiments Ti_1 and Ti_2 differed from Thorndike's typical law of effect experiments in several ways. Most importantly, there was no trial and error feature to Ti_1 and Ti_2. That is, subjects did not generate their own responses to stimuli; rather, they pronounced the response word for each stimulus as it was presented in the memory drum, as is typical in paired associate-learning experiments. Further, the information provided after each response word was not intended to serve as a reward or punishment in the customary sense. Unfortunately, as it turned out, the signals were probably not entirely lacking in affective value for the subjects. Subjects on occasion showed apparent displeasure or chagrin when *bad* appeared and relief or satisfaction when *good* appeared. This was most likely due to the fact that, in being conscientious at their assigned task, subjects made an effort to remember each pair as it was presented. The signals *good* and *bad* therefore may have occasioned satisfaction and disappointment, respectively, by serving to indicate whether or not the effort of memory was well spent or wasted.

Results

The data for the two experiments are given in Table 6.2. In Ti_1, there was a significant difference between the effects of the two signals after only one application to each word pair. In Ti_2, the effect was not significant after one application, largely because the overall level of learning was much lower when nonsense syllables were used as the second element of word pairs. The effect became significant starting with the second trial of Ti_2 and increased thereafter.

These data tentatively support the interpretation that incorporation

Table 6.2

PERCENTAGES OF ACCURATE REPRODUCTIONS OF PAIRED
ASSOCIATES FOLLOWED BY SIGNALS INDICATING LATER
TEST OR NO TEST
(EXPERIMENTS Ti_{1-2})

| Experiment | N | Mean percent accurate reproductions when signal indicated | | Difference ($\%$) |
		Later test	No test	
Ti_1	30	32.3	24.8	7.5
Ti_2	10			
Trial 1		8.0	6.8	1.2
Trial 2		35.2	18.4	16.8
Trial 3		56.5	35.2	21.3
Trial 4		93.6	50.0	43.6

Note: In Experiment Ti_1, each subject was tested on 50 pairs for each signal; in Ti_2, each subject was tested on a different set of 25 pairs for each signal on each of the four trials.

in a system of persisting task tension is sufficient to produce connection-strengthening in learning experiments. It may be objected, however, that the signal of later test or no test served simply as a signal for the subject to rehearse a given word pair or not, and that, therefore, the observed differences should properly be attributed to differences in rehearsal. We feel this interpretation can be ruled out, since the conditions required subjects to attend immediately to the next-presented stimulus after the .25-second *good* or *bad* signal was presented. Observation of subjects' reactions to the two signals, as we have already noted, indicated that whatever rehearsal occurred took place prior to the test or no-test signal, with the signal then serving only to indicate whether or not this rehearsal was wasted. In considering the possibility of a differential rehearsal explanation, we should bear in mind that differential rehearsal could not possibly account for the differences between Completed-Task and Interrupted-Task conditions in Experiments T_{1-3}, presented earlier, since no subjects in those experiments had any indication of a later test.

It was unfortunate that the signals used to indicate later test or no test on a word pair did not appear to be entirely devoid of reward-punishment properties. It must be recalled, in this regard, that Experiments Ti_1 and Ti_2 were not originally designed by Donceel to test the hypotheses we are presently considering. In any case, this problem was avoided in Experiments Ti_{3-5}, to be considered next, in which reward-punishment properties were entirely absent from information used to establish or to remove persisting task tensions.

EXPERIMENTS Ti_{3-5}

Procedure

These experiments employed the "number estimation" task previously described (see, e.g., S_2 in Chapter 3 or R_{1-5} in Chapter 5). The subject's basic task, it will be recalled, was to guess to the nearest five the number of objects shown in photographs of groups of objects, such as houses, trees, bicycles, etc. In the present experiments, the subject first made guesses for a series of 40 such photographs, after having been instructed that the actual experiment would be conducted later with a selected subset of these 40 cards. The subject proceeded then to make number estimations for the entire set of 40 stimuli. Following each guess, the experimenter gave no indication of the accuracy of the subject's estimate, but did comment on whether or not the same stimulus would be part of the later test series. The experimenter said, for 10 of the 40 stimuli, "this is included," and for the remaining 30, "this is not." (After a few items this was abbreviated to one word, viz., "included" or "not.") Following either of these remarks, the next card in the series was immediately presented, in order not to allow subjects to attend differentially to the two sets of stimuli.

The instructions were explicit on the point that selection of a card for later test was in no way dependent on the accuracy of the original response made to it. The 10 stimuli that were supposedly for later testing were conspicuously placed in a pile separate from the other 30 as they were used during the preliminary estimation task.

When the preliminary task was completed, the experimenter named the type of object displayed in each of the 40 stimuli and asked the subject to recall the number he had estimated for the photograph showing a group of that type of object. This test was done, as in previous experiments using this task, without actually re-presenting the stimuli in order that the subject would not adopt the strategy of making new number estimates.

Subjects

The same procedure was employed with three groups of subjects. In Experiment Ti_3, 40 boys between the ages of 12 and 13 participated; Ti_4 was done with 20 males, average age 16; and Ti_5 with 40 females, average age 16.

Results

A clearly apparent result in all three groups of subjects (see Table 6.3) was that responses to stimuli designated as included in the actual experiment were better recalled than were responses to stimuli supposedly not to be later used. Over the three groups of subjects combined, this result was highly significant ($t = 5.36$, $p <.001$). These findings are consistent with the hypothesis that incorporation of a stimulus-response connection in a system of persisting task tension facilitates strengthening of that connection.

Table 6.3

PERCENTAGES OF ACCURATE REPRODUCTIONS OF RESPONSES
AS A FUNCTION OF THEIR INCLUSION IN OR EXCLUSION FROM
A PERSISTING TASK
(EXPERIMENTS Ti_{3-5})

Experiment	N	Mean percent accurate reproductions for		Difference (%)
		Included responses	Excluded responses	
Ti_3	40	40.2	30.0	10.2
Ti_4	20	48.5	38.5	10.0
Ti_5	40	44.8	36.0	8.8
Weighted mean (%)		43.7	34.1	9.6[a]

Note: In each experiment, 10 stimuli were designated as included in the persisting task, while 30 stimuli were designated as excluded.

[a] $s_{diff} = 1.79$, $t_{diff} = 5.36$, $p < .001$.

In Experiments Ti_{3-5}, as well as in T_{1-3}, the responses made by subjects in open-task situations were not ones that had to be remembered in order for the subject to perform whatever task he later was led to expect (as part of the open-task instruction). Nonetheless, these responses were better retained than comparable ones for which instructions established a closed-task situation. These findings were of sufficient magnitude to provide support not only for (a) our speculation that part of the connection-strengthening property of reward is due to its property of incorporating a response in a persisting task-tension system, but also for (b) the more extreme suggestion that possibly all of the connection-strengthening property of reward may be due to this informative or integrative attribute. In the next section, we shall attempt to determine whether the integrative effect of reward plays an equally important role in connection-strengthening by reward in a nonverbal (i.e., motor) learning situation.

THE ROLE OF OPEN-TASK ATTITUDES IN MOTOR LEARNING

The reader may have the impression that the theoretical analysis of reward and punishment, as it has been presented in this and the preceding chapter, is applicable only to the domain of verbal behavior. We have demonstrated the inefficacy of reward per se (i.e., need reduction, satisfaction, etc.) and the importance of persisting task tension in strengthening stimulus-response connections only with reference to human verbal behavior. It is, however, our opinion that the response modality (verbal or nonverbal) is not of primary importance; rather, we feel that the human cognitive apparatus would process the information of success or failure for nonverbal behavior in essentially the same fashion that we find for verbal behavior.[3] Take, for example, the motor learning involved in a sport such as tennis. We do not feel that the reward of winning a point with a well-hit ball acts primarily in an automatic fashion toward strengthening the stimulus-response connections involved in the winning stroke. Rather, we feel that the good stroke is incorporated in a system of persisting task tension, and the bad one excluded, essentially in the same manner we have described and demonstrated for verbal responses.[4]

It is, of course, of great interest to subject these speculations to experimental test. For such a purpose, the problem was stated in the following fashion: Will a rewarded motor response be better learned

---

[3]For the reader who may be interested in the analysis of animal behavior, it should be noted that the present cognitive analysis of reward-punishment effects is not intended necessarily to apply to the behavior of infrahuman species. Since we feel that this cognitive analysis requires an organism with a highly developed information-processing (cognitive) apparatus, it is reasonable to expect it to apply only to organisms relatively high on the phylogenetic scale. We have had indications, in fact, that the cognitive analysis may be less applicable to children than it is to adults (see Experiment Re, Chapter 5).

[4]Thorndike (1932, p. 182) has written: "In learning acts of skill there is a tendency to try to hold in mind the 'feel' of an act which is rewarded." We do not, however, exclude some direct strengthening of connections by reward as a slower-working process in less cognitively elaborated learning (see our discussion of *canalization* in Chapter 8).

when it occurs in the context of a persisting task than when it does not? The following experiment was conceived to test this proposition.

EXPERIMENT T$_m$

Apparatus

The movements to be learned were performed with the aid of a kinesthesiometer. This is a device on which a blindfolded subject rests his right forearm and initiates movements of his hand in a clockwise arc in the horizontal plane, pivoted at the elbow, always starting from a fixed initial position. The effort of making such arc movements is kept minimal with the aid of a low-friction bearing under the elbow. Therefore, the (blindfolded) subject's perception of the extent of his movement is limited virtually entirely to the kinesthetic sense modality.

The kinesthesiometer was equipped with an adjustable stop so that a movement initiated by the subject could be prevented from going beyond the point at which the stop was set. The experimenter could measure the extent of any movement made by the subject by reading a scale along which a pointer (attached to the pivoting arm-rest) moved.

Procedure

The instructions were intended to create a closed-task attitude for group A and an open-task attitude for group B, while having both groups perform essentially the same responses. The instructions were given before the subjects were blindfolded.

Group A subjects were told that the experiment would consist of a series of trials, each consisting of two steps. First, a sample response would be made by starting from the fixed starting position and moving slowly clockwise until the (adjustable) stop prevented further movement. At this point the experimenter would rapidly reset the subject's arm to the starting position and remove the adjustable stop. The subject's task was then to make a test response of the same amplitude as the sample one, i.e., to bring his arm to a rest at the point at which the sample response had been stopped. The experimenter would then inform the subject whether his test response was accurate or not; the subject was told that his response would be called *good* if it was within a degree on either side of the point at which the stop had been set, and *bad* if it was outside this two-degree range. The task would then proceed, the subject was told, with the setting of the adjustable stop at a new position, according to a prearranged scheme, and making of the sample and test responses, etc. One practice trial was conducted with the subject's eyes open. Then he was blindfolded and the experimental series of 50 sample and test responses was conducted.

For group B the instructions were identical, with one major exception. The subject was instructed that the stop would be in the same position for the sample response on every trial, and that the task was to learn to make this one response accurately.

In fact, the procedure for both groups was that which had been described accurately to the group B subjects; that is, the sample response was exactly the same for all 50 trials.

Let us review how these procedures established a closed-task situation for group A, but an open-task situation for group B. For group A, the subject believes that the response rewarded on one trial is of little or no use in helping him to perform his task on a subsequent trial, because the next sample response is expected to be different. On the other hand, a reward for a response by a group B subject is perceived as giving information that is of future use; the subject says to himself, in effect, that this is the response he should try to duplicate on the next test trial. These differences in perceptions of reward (and corresponding differences in perception of punishment) correspond to the distinctions we have previously defined as closed-task versus open-task attitudes.

One difficulty in the procedure had to do with the numbers of rewards and punishments received by subjects. It was desired that all subjects receive approximately the same number of rewards over the course of the 50 trials. In order to achieve this end, it was necessary to set different tolerances on the reward category for different subjects, as a function of their accuracy of performance. Thus, for those subjects whose early test responses were relatively inaccurate, the range of responses to be rewarded was extended to two degrees on either side of the correct point.

Subjects

Thirty-six students between 15 and 16 years old participated in Experiment T_m. These were divided equally between groups A and B. Because of experimenter's error in the procedure, data for three of the group A subjects were excluded from analysis.

Results

The sample response for all 50 trials for all subjects was an arc of 105°. For each test response, the subject's deviation from a 105° arc was recorded to the nearest tenth of a degree. The test performance for each subject was summarized into a single score by totaling these deviations over the 50 trials. If our analysis of the role of reward in learning is correct, we should find superior performance, i.e., smaller total deviation, in group B, for which the instructions generated an open-task attitude. The results are given in Table 6.4. It may be seen that group B was indeed superior in performance to group A ($t = 4.43$, $p < .001$).

Table 6.4

SUMS OF ERRORS (IN DEGREES) IN REPRODUCING A STANDARD
MOVEMENT UNDER OPEN- AND CLOSED-TASK CONDITIONS
(EXPERIMENT T_m)

Subjects	Task condition	
	Closed (group A)	Open (group B)
1	50.0	30.7
2	62.3	42.7
3	67.3	43.0
4	69.0	47.0
5	70.0	48.6
6	74.3	49.1
7	80.0	53.6
8	82.2	56.0
9	83.1	59.2
10	86.0	59.7
11	90.7	62.0
12	94.0	67.2
13	97.5	67.3
14	101.6	70.3
15	107.1	71.0
16	–	72.7
17	–	74.6
18	–	83.2
Mean[a]	81.0	58.8

[a]Mean difference $= 22.2°$; $s_{diff} = 5.01$; $t_{diff} = 4.43$, $p < .001$.

Since the group A subjects had inferior performance, on the average, it followed that, in general, they would have received rewards for less accurate responses than did subjects in group B. It is reasonable to ask whether the obtained results might not, in some way, have been produced as an artifact of this procedural difference. In regard to this point, we may note that since poor performance was a prior condition on which extension of the reward range was based, it is illogical to argue that the procedural difference was a cause of the performance difference. Moreover, it seems likely that the difference between the conditions might have been even larger had the reward range not been extended for those subjects whose performance was relatively inaccurate.[5]

Observation of behavior of subjects in group B indicated that, for some, the effect of a punishment was to produce a hasty return of the arm to the starting position while a reward provided the occasion for hesitation before return. This recalls to mind the quotation from Thorndike noted earlier, about subjects trying to hold "in mind" the "feel of an act which is rewarded." In our terms, this hesitation represents a behavioral counterpart of the process of cognitive incorporation of a response in a persisting task-tension system.

Conclusion

In Experiment T_m, subjects in two conditions performed at the same task of duplicating a sample movement on the kinesthesiometer. The only difference between the two conditions was in subjects' cognitive orientation toward the task, being either an open- or closed-task orientation. Since this difference was found to produce a significant superiority in performance for the open-task orientation condition, we may conclude that the effect of reward on a human motor skill, as on verbal behavior, may be analyzed in terms of the role of reward in incorporating a response in a persisting task-tension system.

THE INTEGRATIVE FUNCTION OF PUNISHMENT

Our analysis of reward has some interesting implications concerning effects of punishment. As a result, it is possible to obtain additional evidence relevant to our cognitive analysis of reinforcement by means of experiments testing these implications for punishment.

We may imagine a situation in which reward for a response carries no future significance for the subject, whereas punishment does. If our overall analysis is correct, it should follow that, in such a situa-

---

[5]Some data obtained by Greenwald (see Experiments 8 and 9 in the Appendix of this volume), in a task in which subjects tried to draw lines of a specified length when blindfolded, are pertinent to this suggestion. It was found that performance was relatively poor when the reward range (i.e., the range of inaccuracy within which a response would still be called *right* for the subject) was made sufficiently narrow so that subjects got less than half of their responses within that range. [AGG]

tion, the punished response would become better incorporated into the persisting task-tension system than would a rewarded one. The last three experiments to be reported in this chapter are tests of this prediction.

EXPERIMENTS E_{1-3}

In this series of experiments, we have sought to introduce a situation diametrically opposed to that of standard learning experiments. In these experiments, a punishment indicates a response that is of significance for the learner's future performance while a reward indicates a response of no future significance.

Procedure

The following instructions were given to each subject by the experimenter:

"I will show you a series of cards, on the front of each of which will be a letter of the alphabet and, on the back, one of the numbers between two and nine. You are to guess, for each card as it is shown, the number on the back. Do this by pronouncing first the letter on the front and then guessing the number. For instance, for this card (one with an X) you would say "X-5" or "X-2," etc. If your guess is correct, I will say *good*. If not, I will turn over the card so that you can see yourself that you were mistaken. When you see the back of the card, you should pronounce both the letter and the correct number; for example "X-4." Then we will proceed to the next card and do the same thing.

"The purpose of the experiment is to see how many times you must see the cards before you can guess all the numbers correctly once. Whenever you guess a correct number, I will set that card aside and you will not be tested on it again. When you guess a wrong number, I will show you the correct number on the reverse side; you will be tested again on cards for which you were wrong at first. We will see how many times it will be necessary to present the cards until you have gotten all of them right once. The numbers are assigned at random to the cards and more than one card may have the same number on its back. Therefore, you can do no better than simply to guess at random for your first guesses."

In order to ensure that subjects understood these instructions properly (and thereby achieved the desired task attitude), the instructed procedure was carried out first with a practice series of cards.

That is, cards for which the subject guessed the correct number were set aside and, when incorrect guesses were made, the card was turned around to show the subject the correct number; then, retesting was continued until the correct number had been guessed once for each card.

Then a new set of 11 cards was brought out. On the first trial through this series, the subject's response was arbitrarily called *good* for a pre-arranged subset of 5 cards, and for the remaining 6, he was shown the number on the reverse side. Of course, a response could not be considered incorrect if the subject happened, by chance, to guess the number on the back; this was likely to happen 12.5% of the time by chance. As a result, the number of rewards varied slightly from subject to subject; while most subjects had just the intended 5 correct responses, some had 6 and, a few, 7. The cards for which responses were to be punished each had a different number between 2 and 7 on the back. As is customary in our procedures, the cards rewarded for half the subjects were punished for the others, and vice versa.

After the first trial with the experimental set of 11 cards, the subject was tested, contrary to expectation, for correct responses on all 11 cards. That is, for rewarded cards, the subject was to give his original response while, for punished ones, he was to give the number he saw on the back of the card after he made his incorrect guess. The test trial was conducted by re-presenting the entire set of cards, with the subject first reading the stimulus letter and then attempting to recall the correct response.

Discussion of Procedure

In typical learning experiments, a reward has two kinds of significance, as we have noted before. First, it is a satisfying event for the subject.[6] Second, it provides information designating a specific response as being of future significance for the further attainment of satisfaction. In the present experiment, this typical situation is decidedly altered. A reward is presumably still satisfying, but carries no future significance since the task is completed for a given card when the first reward is obtained. On the other hand, the subject receives information designating a specific response as being of future significance in the context of a punishment, i.e., he receives it when the card is turned over, showing him the correct number that he has not

---

[6]Cf. Thorndike (1943, pp. 31 and 32), addressing an audience of students at Harvard University: "I know from many experiments that the majority of even so sophisticated a group as this have an appreciable satisfaction at being right in even so unimportant a matter as learning the number belonging to a word."

guessed. If our analysis is correct, it should happen that the response of future significance is better learned than the rewarded one even though it occurs in the context of a punishment and even though the task is complicated for the subject by possible interference from the incorrect response he has already made.

Variation of Procedure in E_3

The procedure of E_1 and E_2 was just as described above. E_3 was varied in the treatment of incorrect responses. The experimental series was extended to 20 cards and the subject was told *good* for a prearranged subset of 10 and *bad* for the others, without being shown the correct number on the reverse side. Again, the subject expected retests only on those cards for which he had originally been incorrect. In this procedure, there was nothing for the subject to remember after a wrong response other than the incorrect response itself. On the retest trial in this experiment the subject was tested for his ability to recall his original response for all 20 cards, not just for the 10 wrong ones for which he was expecting a retest.

Subjects

Experiment E_1 was done with 16 male university students; E_2 with 186 males and females between the ages of 16 and 19; and E_3 with 62 university students.

Results

The data for E_{1-3} are summarized in Table 6.5. In all three experiments, the differences in recall in favor of responses for cards that were originally punished were approximately of the same order of

Table 6.5

PERCENTAGES OF ACCURATE REPRODUCTIONS OF REWARDED AND PUNISHED
RESPONSES WHEN PUNISHMENT INDICATES RELEVANCE TO THE PERSISTING TASK
(EXPERIMENTS E_{1-3})

Experiment	N	Mean percent accurate reproductions for		Diff (%)	s_{diff}	t	p
		Reward	Punishment				
E_1	16	29.0	37.4	8.4	7.10	1.18	ns
E_2	186	26.1	31.6	5.5	2.00	2.75	<.01
E_3	62	28.1	37.2	9.1	2.65	3.43	<.01

Note: In each experiment, approximately half of each subject's responses were rewarded and half punished.

magnitude. In E_1, this difference did not reach significance because of the small number of subjects involved, while in both E_2 and E_3 the difference was significant beyond the two-tailed .01 level. As has been the case in experiments previously reported in this chapter, the results again indicated that incorporation of a response in a persisting task-tension system is of more importance to connection-strengthening than is the immediate satisfying aspect of reward.

CONCLUSIONS

All of the experimental results presented in the last two chapters have confirmed our hypothesis that, in human learning, retention of a stimulus-response connection is enhanced when it is acquired in the context of a persisting task, i.e., when the response is one of significance for the learner's future reward-attainment. Reward or punishment, insofar as they pertain only to the just-performed response and are not of future significance, have not been found to play an important role in connection-strengthening. Our theoretical interpretation of these findings is that integration of a connection into a system of persisting task tension is the essential mechanism of human learning.

The persisting task tension explanation allows substantial reconciliation among seemingly disparate results obtained by the Lewinian school and stimulus-response theorists. The fact that interrupted or unsuccessful responses are frequently found to be better recalled than completed or rewarded ones (in the former case) can be reconciled with the fact that rewarded responses are found more likely to be repeated (in the latter) when the typical experiments of each school are analyzed in terms of the persisting task orientation of the learner. In experiments of the Lewinian school, it is the interrupted or failed task that is generally of greatest future significance while, in those of the S-R school, it is generally the rewarded response that guides the learner to future successful performance.

It is not our intention to assert that the integration mechanism described here is the only mechanism by which learning occurs with human subjects. Another mechanism to which we shall address ourselves in the next chapter is designated by the broad heading of structural determinants of learning.[7]

---

[7]Weiner (1966) has recently reviewed literature on the role of motivation in learning and retention. His conclusion, " . . . that motivation influences the storage and retrieval of memory traces . . . " is quite consistent with the conclusions of the studies reported in this chapter. [AGG]

CHAPTER 7

•

STRUCTURAL ISOLATION AND LEARNING

THE PROBLEM

In daily experience, a relatively small number of events stands out from the background of the totality of incoming stimuli. In terms of Gestalt principles of perception, this selectivity of attention may be attributed, in part, to affectivity and need relevance of the incoming stimuli, but also to their structural or formal properties. In the preceding chapters, we have examined the role of affectivity or need relevance of outcomes on learning; we will now turn to a consideration of the role of structural or formal properties of outcomes in the connection-strengthening process.

Some existing research on learning bears on this general problem. Köhler and von Restorff (1933), for example, found that when a pair of numbers was inserted into a paired-associate task involving learning of syllable pairs, the association between the two numbers was better retained than was a typical association between syllables. One may generalize from this and related findings to conclude that a stimulus which commands attention selectively due to structural separation from its background is also likely to have an enhanced position in memory.

To extend the conclusion further, it is possible that when a stimulus-response connection is structurally isolated from its background by means of a distinctive outcome, there may also be an enhancement of connection-strengthening for that pair. This enhancement would be independent of other strengthening effects that might be due to the outcome received. Such an effect would be expected to occur equally when an isolated punishment occurs amidst a series of rewards or when an isolated reward occurs amidst a series of punishments. In the present chapter, we shall concern ourselves with such effects as they may occur with an isolated punishment, since any enhancement of connection-strengthening in this case would not be attributed to a nonstructural connection-strengthening property of the outcome.[1]

In order to restrict our attention to purely structural aspects of the effects of isolated punishments, we shall observe these effects in a closed-task context. Thus, whatever learning occurs will not be attributable primarily to persisting task tensions of the sort with which we were concerned in Chapter 6. Before presenting our experiments on isolated punishments, we shall describe some preparatory studies on effects of structural isolation of materials on learning (as in the Köhler-von Restorff study), but in the closed-task situation. The purpose of these preliminary experiments (IM_{1-4}, IP) will be simply to establish that the Köhler-von Restorff isolation effect can be obtained in a closed-task situation.

STRUCTURAL ISOLATION IN THE CLOSED-TASK SITUATION

EXPERIMENTS IM_{1-4}

Procedures

The experimental task used was that of area comparison, used in several previous experiments (e.g., RR_{1-6}, Chapter 5). The series of tasks was composed of seven comparisons, each involving judgment of whether the area of the first of a pair of digits or letters sketched on a card was greater or smaller than that of the second. In the present experiments, subjects received no feedback about the correctness of their guesses. After completion of the series of seven judgments, the subject was given an unanticipated test for formation of associations between elements of each of the seven pairs. In this test, the experimenter provided the name of the first element of the pair and the subject was to reproduce the second.

This procedure was used in four experiments. In each, a structural isolation factor was introduced by constructing the series of seven area comparisons with five of one type (either letter pairs or digit pairs) and two of the other. Evidence for an effect of structural isolation on connection-strengthening would appear in each as superior ability to reproduce the second element for pairs of the type that had been in the minority in the series.

In IM_1 and IM_3, five pairs of digits and two pairs of letters were

---

[1]Extending this principle, we would predict that a severe punishment would have enhanced attention value if it occurs against a background of mild punishment, or that a small reward would command selective attention when it occurs in a series of larger ones. Our research, as presented in this chapter, has not explored these related cases.

used, while these proportions were reversed in IM_2 and IM_4. In IM_1 and IM_2, the isolated pairs were in the third and sixth positions in the series, while in IM_3 and IM_4 they were in the fourth and fifth positions. The specific pairs of letters and digits used were ones that, in pretests, appeared not to be especially easy to associate. As an added procedural precaution, four different series of items were used in each experiment; as a result, for the set of four experiments, each pair of letters or digits appeared equally often in each of the seven serial positions.

Subjects

A total of 160 subjects, aged 13 to 15, participated in IM_{1-4}, with 40 in each experiment.

Results

The dependent data consisted of correct or incorrect reproductions of the second element in each of the seven pairs of letters or numbers used in the area comparison task. These data are presented in summary form in Table 7.1, with the data for groups in which the third and sixth positions were isolated presented separately from those in which positions 4 and 5 were isolated. It may be seen readily that structural isolation strongly enhanced formation of a connection between elements of the isolated pairs. The mean level of accurate reproductions was 22.8% for nonisolated pairs (whether letters or numbers) compared to 71.3% for isolated pairs; the difference between these percentages was highly significant ($t = 13.5$, 159 df). Further evidence for the effect of structural isolation was obtained from comparison of the reproduction levels for the first and second

Table 7.1

PERCENTAGES OF ACCURATE REPRODUCTIONS OF SECOND
ELEMENTS OF PAIRS BY SERIAL POSITION
(EXPERIMENTS IM_{1-4})

Experiment	N	Percent accuracy in serial position						
		1	2	3	4	5	6	7
$IM_{1\ and\ 2}$	80	21.3	13.8	**72.5**	15.0	22.5	**62.5**	38.8
$IM_{3\ and\ 4}$	80	27.5	15.0	17.5	**85.0**	**66.3**	20.0	31.3

Note: The figures in boldface indicate levels of reproduction for isolated pairs. The isolated materials were letter pairs in IM_1 and IM_3 and were digit pairs in IM_2 and IM_4.

isolated pairs in each series. It should be predicted that the isolation effect would be greater for the first isolated pair since the second has lost some of its distinctiveness or isolation or surprise value simply by virtue of the prior occurrence of a similar pair. This prediction was borne out. The mean level of accuracy for first isolated pairs was 78.8%, compared to 64.1% for second pairs; the difference of 14.7% was significant beyond the .001 level ($t = 4.07$, 159 df).

THE SPREAD OF ISOLATION (EXPERIMENT IP)[2]

The effect of structural isolation in a closed-task situation was tested with one additional experiment in which the procedure varied only in minor respects from IM_{1-4}. In Experiment IP, a series of 11 area comparisons was used, all but the sixth involving comparison of the area of two letters; the sixth required comparison of two digits. A total of 100 subjects participated, being subdivided into 10 subgroups of 10 apiece; in the 10 subgroups, the positions of the 10 letter pairs were systematically rotated. As in IM_{1-4}, subjects were given no information concerning correctness of their guesses and were not led to expect a subsequent test for associations between elements of the 11 pairs. The results of the tests for reproduction of second elements are given in Table 7.2.

Table 7.2
PERCENTAGES OF ACCURATE REPRODUCTIONS OF SECOND
ELEMENTS OF PAIRS BY SERIAL POSITION
(EXPERIMENT IP)

Percent accuracy in serial position										
1	2	3	4	5	6	7	8	9	10	11
29	33	30	33	40	**99**	35	25	28	24	32

Note: An isolated digit pair was located at position 6; the level of accurate reproduction for this position is indicated in boldface. There were 100 subjects in Experiment IP.

The effect of structural isolation on associative strength was on the same order as observed in IM_{1-4}. The isolated pair was reproduced accurately by 99 out of 100 subjects, while nonisolated pairs were reproduced accurately 30.9% of the time, on the average. Although the magnitude of percentage difference was larger than in IM_{1-4}, in

[2]This experiment was originally reported in Appendix I of *Tâche, Réussite, et Échec*.

comparing the experiments one must take into account the fact that the isolated pair in IP was a digit pair. Since digit pairs were, in general (and for obvious reasons), more easily reproduced than letter pairs in IM_{1-4}, it is to be expected that the isolation of a digit pair would give the appearance of a stronger effect than the isolation of a letter pair.

The data of Experiment IP are of further interest. It has already been clearly established that structural isolation enhances formation of associations. We were also interested in observing whether this associative effect would spread to neighboring connections. The theoretical importance of this point is obvious. In spread-of-effect experiments, an isolated reward is assumed to have associative effects on neighboring connections. While these effects have been attributed to a spread of associative effects of reward, it is not unreasonable to hypothesize (cf. Zirkle, 1946) that, if indeed any associative effect is spreading (cf. Chapter 4), that the effect may be due to isolation rather than reward. For this reason, we were interested in seeing whether the letter pairs in positions 5 and 7 in Experiment IP (i.e., those adjacent to the isolated digit pair) would show any associative enhancement. The pertinent data are presented in Table 7.3. For each of the 10 letter pairs used in Experiment IP, we have compared its probability of accurate reproduction when in the fifth or seventh position with the corresponding figure when in other positions. The data support the spread of isolation hypothesis, there being an average of 8.7% more correct reproductions of pairs when neighboring the isolated one than when more distant; this percentage difference was statistically significant beyond the .05 level ($t = 2.79$, 9 df).[3]

Conclusion

Experiments IM_{1-4} and IP have conclusively supported the Köhler-von Restorff phenomenon of associative enhancement due to structural isolation. Further, they have extended the result to the case of a closed-task situation in which the subject does not have an explicit learning task.

The results of IP indicated that the effect of structural isolation is sufficiently powerful to have an effect on associations experienced near in time to the isolated one. As we have implied, this result will be of special interest if it turns out that an isolated outcome (e.g., a

---

[3]Originally, this comparison was reported as nonsignificant in *Tâche, Réussite, et Échec* (Nuttin, 1953, p. 480). However, recomputation revealed that the difference did reach an acceptable significance level.

Table 7.3

PERCENTAGES OF ACCURATE REPRODUCTION FOR LETTER PAIRS
WHEN LOCATED ADJACENT TO OR DISTANT FROM THE ISOLATED
DIGIT PAIR
(EXPERIMENT IP)

| Letter pair | Percent accurate repro- duction when located | | Difference (%) |
	Adjacent	Distant	
P-L	40.0	22.0	+18.0
I-C	35.0	25.5	+ 9.5
K-N	30.0	27.5	+ 2.5
V-D	40.0	27.5	+12.5
E-A	20.0	23.7	− 3.7
G-S	35.0	22.0	+13.0
Z-F	15.0	10.0	+ 5.0
T-J	35.0	18.7	+16.3
R-B	50.0	58.7	− 8.7
H-X	75.0	52.0	+23.0
Average (%)	28.8	37.5	+ 8.7[a]

Note: Each letter pair was employed 20 times in a position adjacent to the isolated digit pair and 80 times in a more distant position.

[a] $s_{diff} = 3.14$, $t_{diff} = 2.79$, 9 df, $p < .05$.

single punishment against a background of rewards) has an associative enhancing effect similar to that of isolated task materials. We shall now turn our attention to a series of experiments in which we shall have the opportunity to observe associative effects of isolated outcomes.

THE EFFECTS OF ISOLATED PUNISHMENTS

EXPERIMENTS IR$_{1-3}$

Procedure

The area-comparison task was again used, the materials consisting of eight letter pairs of the type used in the previous experiments. As before, subjects made responses of the form: "L is (larger, smaller) than P," always mentioning first the letter positioned on the left side of the stimulus card. In these experiments, isolation was not achieved by insertion of distinctive materials, but rather by punishing the judgment for a single letter pair, while judgments for the remaining seven pairs were rewarded. As in the previous experiments, the subjects were not led to expect any kind of a retest on the area comparisons, but were nonetheless later tested for their ability to reproduce the second letter of each of the eight pairs when the first was provided by the experimenter.

Experiments IR_{1-3} differed from each other in relatively minor ways. In IR_1, a series of eight letter pairs was used, with the punished judgment occurring in the sixth position. In IR_2, a total of 24 area-comparison judgments was constructed from the eight letter pairs by using each pair in three printing variations on different cards; the judgment for one of the eight pairs was punished on all three occurrences of that pair, in positions 6, 14, and 22 of the series, respectively. In IR_3, the total series consisted of eight judgments, as in IR_1; however, the isolated punishment occurred in the second position of the series in order to eliminate the possible factor of surprise when (as in IR_1) a single punishment followed an uninterrupted series of five rewards.

Subjects

Sixty-four males, average age 14, participated in IR_1; in IR_2 and IR_3, there were 40 males, between 14 and 15 years in age, in each experiment. The subjects were divided into eight equal subgroups, in each of which a different one of the eight letter pairs was in the isolated (i.e., punished) position.

Results

The data for the three experiments are summarized in Table 7.4. It may be seen that in each experiment the level of accurate reproduction was higher for the letter pair in the position isolated by punishment than for those in the rewarded positions. The difference reached an acceptable significance level for IR_2 and IR_3. In IR_2, in which one letter pair was punished on each of its three repetitions, the finding of superior recall of the punished pair was strongest. Perhaps the result of IR_3 is most interesting, however. There, the pair isolated by punishment was significantly superior in association strength even though the punishment was not an isolated event when it occurred; it became isolated only by virtue of consistent reward for the six guesses after the punished one.

Discussion

An accessory observation in the experiments just described was that the second letter of the punished pair tended to intrude as an

Table 7.4

PERCENTAGES OF ACCURATE REPRODUCTIONS OF LETTER PAIRS BY
SERIAL POSITIONS IN EXPERIMENTS WITH ISOLATED PUNISHMENTS
(EXPERIMENTS IR$_{1-3}$)

Experiment	N	Percent accuracy in serial position								Mean for 7 pairs rewarded (%)	Diff (%)	t_{diff}
		1	2	3	4	5	6	7	8			
IR$_1$	64	15.6	25.0	20.3	17.2	15.6	**32.8**	10.9	29.7	19.2	13.6	2.21[a]
IR$_2$	40	27.5	22.5	15.0	21.6	20.0	**50.8**	24.1	28.3	22.7	28.1	5.97[b]
IR$_3$	40	10.0	**50.0**	17.5	15.0	35.0	25.0	22.5	25.0	21.4	28.6	3.39[c]

Note: The level of accurate reproduction for the position isolated by punishment is indicated in boldface for each experiment. In Experiment IR$_2$, the series of eight letter pairs was repeated three times in different printing variations; the results for these three series are combined into a single series in this table.

[a] $p < .05$.
[b] $p < .001$.
[c] $p < .01$.

error in response to the first letter of rewarded pairs. More precisely, in IR_1 and IR_2, the second letter of a punished pair intruded as an error about one and a half times as often as the typical second letter of a rewarded pair, while there was no such general tendency in IR_3. This extent of intrusion is not sufficient to support the interpretation that the superior reproduction of punished pairs was simply an artifact of a generally exaggerated tendency to give the second letter of the punished pair as a response; the magnitude of superior reproduction was too large to be explained in this manner. However, the observation is suggestive, indicating that the isolated punishment may have had effects other than those due to structural isolation.

It is possible that the isolated punishment may have produced, at least in some subjects, an open-task attitude in regard to the punished pair. To be more specific, the subject who found that his performance was near perfect may have identified his single error as the only thing keeping him from perfect performance. The single mistake may thereby have acquired some of the characteristics of a problem that remains to be solved, even though the subject was aware from instructions that he would not have another chance at that particular letter pair; the subject would like to "make up" for his single error, even though he does not expect to have the chance to do so. If this interpretation is accurate, the superior reproduction of letter pairs isolated by punishment should be attributed to some combination of a structural isolation effect and an effect of persisting task tension focused on the single error.

It would be useful if we could compare intrusions of the second letter of punished pairs in IR_{1-3} with similar intrusions of second elements of isolated pairs in IM_{1-4} and IP, in which isolation bore no relation to possible persisting task tensions. Such a comparison would enable us to determine whether the prominence of intrusion errors from the letter pairs isolated by punishment required an explanation in terms of persisting task tensions. Unfortunately, no such comparison was possible because of the manner in which isolation was accomplished in the earlier experiments. In those experiments, subjects could easily infer the rule that a pair either consisted of two digits or two letters, and not of one digit and one letter. Therefore, it is obvious that intrusions of the critical type would not be expected to occur in IM_{1-4} or IP.

EXPERIMENTS IR_{4-5}

Two additional experiments of the same general type presented thus far in this chapter, but with two punishments rather than a single isolated punishment, were conducted in order to compare the effect of the second isolated punishment with the first. (It will be recalled that a finding of IM_{1-4} was that the second of two isolated pairs did not show as stong an "isolation effect" as did the first of the two.)

Procedure

Experiment IR_4 used the same area-comparison task used in IR_{1-3}. Punishments occurred for responses to the fifth and sixth of a series of eight letter pairs. Forty subjects, average age 14, participated in this experiment.

Experiment IR_5 used the number-estimation task, previously described (e.g., Experiments R_{1-5}, Chapter 5; S_2, Chapter 3), in which we have generally found superior reproduction of original responses than in the area-comparison task. It will be recalled that, in the number-estimation task, the subject guesses for each of a series of photographs the number (to the nearest five) of objects represented on each. This task was employed in IR_5 with a series of 12 stimulus photographs, guesses for the fourth and ninth positions being called *wrong*; 50 males participated in this experiment.

Closed-task instructions were employed in IR_4 and IR_5, as in the previous experiments of the present chapter, in order that subjects would not anticipate the subsequent test in which they were asked to repeat their original guesses. In accordance with customary procedure, different subgroups within each experiment received different orders of presentation of stimuli so that results would not be influenced by fortuitous differences among the particular subtasks.

Results

The data of IR_4 and IR_5 are summarized in terms of serial positions in Tables 7.5 and 7.6. In each experiment, the average level of reproduction of the two letter pairs isolated by punishment was significantly greater than that for rewarded pairs (t's $= 5.21$ and 4.24, respectively, both $p < .001$). In both experiments, the first of the two punished pairs was better recalled than the second, as expected, but for neither experiment was this difference significant statistically. These findings support the conclusion of IR_{1-3} that stimulus-response connections isolated by virtue of a distinctive outcome acquire enhanced associative strength. The conclusion can now be extended, on the basis of IR_4 and IR_5, from isolation in the ratio of 1:7 to the higher ratios of 2:10 (IR_5) and 2:6 (IR_4).

We may take this opportunity to comment on another aspect of the

Table 7.5

PERCENTAGES OF ACCURATE REPRODUCTIONS OF LETTER PAIRS BY SERIAL
POSITIONS IN AN EXPERIMENT WITH TWO ISOLATED PUNISHMENTS
(EXPERIMENT IR$_4$)

Percent accuracy in serial position								Mean for 6 pairs rewarded (%)	Mean for 2 pairs punished (%)	Diff (%)
1	2	3	4	5	6	7	8			
15.0	2.5	15.0	15.0	**47.5**	**45.0**	25.0	17.5	15.0	46.25	31.25[a]

[a] $s_{diff} = 6.00$; $t_{diff} = 5.21$, $p < .001$.

Note: There were 40 subjects in this experiment. Boldface figures indicate the positions isolated by punishments.

Table 7.6

PERCENTAGES OF ACCURATE REPRODUCTIONS OF NUMBER-ESTIMATION
RESPONSES BY SERIAL POSITIONS IN AN EXPERIMENT WITH
TWO ISOLATED PUNISHMENTS
(EXPERIMENT IR$_5$)

Percent accuracy in serial position												Mean for 10 pairs rewarded (%)	Mean for 2 pairs punished (%)	Diff (%)
1	2	3	4	5	6	7	8	9	10	11	12			
38	38	40	**72**	38	46	52	38	**64**	48	61	64	46.4	68.0	21.6[a]

[a] $s_{diff} = 5.10$; $t_{diff} = 4.24$, $p < .001$.

Note: There were 50 subjects in this experiment. Boldface figures indicate the two positions isolated by punishments.

results of the present series of experiments, particularly noticeable in IR_5. That is the tendency for subjects to be more accurate in reproducing the last few nonisolated associations in each experiment than in reproducing earlier nonisolated associations. This tendency may be seen in the tabulated results of the experiments presented thus far in this chapter. It is perhaps particularly appropriate to compare the last few serial positions in each experiment with the first few, since it is typical in serial learning experiments for connections at each end of the list to become stronger than those nearer the middle. Such comparison indicates, as we have noted, a superior associative strength for connections at the finish of the lists. We may attribute this pattern to the fact that the unanticipated association test was administered shortly after completion of the initial series, thereby dispelling the closed-task attitude established by previous instructions. The task thus was changed from one of judgment to one of learning while the subject's last few responses were still relatively fresh in memory. We suggest the conclusion that the open-task attitude generated by the test instructions enabled superior reproduction of the last few connections in the series; this implies the assumption that an open-task attitude can be effective in facilitating retention even if it commences shortly after performance of the connection to be retained.

EFFECTS OF ISOLATED PUNISHMENTS IN LEARNING TASKS

To this point, our demonstration of associative enhancement by isolated punishments has been confined to closed-task situations. In these situations, for which we know from our other experiments (cf. Chapter 5) that reward has no special effectiveness in strengthening connections, we found that the isolation effect was sufficiently strong to raise the strength of association significantly above that for nonisolated rewarded connections. In the present section, we shall examine the effects of isolated punishments in ordinary learning (open-task) situations to determine how the effect of isolation-by-punishment on connection strength compares with that of (nonisolated) reward in the open-task situation.

EXPERIMENTS $IR_{6,7}$

Procedure

Experiment IR_6 employed the number-estimation task used in IR_5 as well as elsewhere in this volume. Sixteen stimulus photographs were employed, the responses to two (sixth and thirteenth positions) being called *wrong* while all other responses were called *right*. An open-task attitude was created by instructing subjects that their task was to learn the correct number for each photograph. After completion of the first series of guesses, subjects were tested again but, instead of being asked to give correct responses, they were instructed to reproduce their original responses for each stimulus no matter whether the response was called *right* or *wrong*. Sixty males and females, average age 16, participated in IR_6.

In IR_7, the area-comparison task was used (as in IR_2) with 24 cards made up of eight different letter pairs, each in three printing variations. Responses to one pair in each of its three occurrences (sixth, fourteenth, and twenty-second positions) were called *wrong*, the remainder being called *right*. Again the task was set up explicitly as one of learning correct judgments, but the subject was later tested for strength of association between the elements of each pair (cf. IM_{1-4}). The subjects in IR_7 were 40 males and females between the ages of 14 and 15.

In each experiment, the total group of subjects was divided into subgroups in which the specific isolated (punished) items were varied so as to avoid undue influence of chance differences among the subtasks.

Results

The data for IR_6 and IR_7 are summarized in terms of serial positions in Tables 7.7 and 7.8. It is apparent from these tables that an isolated punishment increased the associative strength of the isolated connection compared to nonisolated rewarded ones even in the context of a learning (i.e., open) task. The difference in favor of punishment was significant in both experiments (t's = 2.95, $p < .01$, and 6.99, $p < .001$, respectively). Further, the magnitude of obtained differences were not appreciably different from those in Experiments IR_2 and IR_5 which, respectively, were comparable to IR_6 and IR_7 except that the former experiments employed closed-task instructions.

The magnitude of the effect of isolated punishments in IR_6 and IR_7 was not anticipated since it was expected that establishment of an explicit learning task would elevate connection strength of rewarded connections relative to punished ones. However, postexperimental comments of some subjects suggested a reasonable interpretation of the obtained results. Avoiding the wrong response had been, according to these subjects, their main concern. When they found themselves performing at a high level of proficiency in the experimental task, they came to assume that they need not try to remember correct

Table 7.7
PERCENTAGES OF ACCURATE REPRODUCTIONS OF RESPONSES BY SERIAL
POSITIONS IN A LEARNING TASK WITH TWO ISOLATED PUNISHMENTS
(EXPERIMENT IR$_6$)

						Percent accuracy in serial position										Mean for 14 pairs rewarded (%)	Mean for 2 pairs punished (%)	Diff. (%)
1	2	3	4	5	6	7	8	9	10	11	12	13	14	15	16			
48.3	46.7	35.0	36.7	45.0	**55.0**	45.0	48.3	58.3	51.7	63.3	51.7	**70.0**	48.3	51.7	48.3	48.5	62.5	14.0[a]

[a] $s_{\text{diff}} = 4.74$; $t_{\text{diff}} = 2.95$, $p < .01$.
Note: There were 60 subjects in this experiment. Boldface figures indicate the positions isolated by punishments.

Table 7.8
PERCENTAGES OF ACCURATE REPRODUCTIONS OF LETTER PAIRS BY SERIAL
POSITIONS IN A LEARNING TASK WITH ISOLATED PUNISHMENT
(EXPERIMENT IR$_7$)

			Percent accuracy in serial position					Mean for 7 pairs rewarded (%)	Diff. (%)
1	2	3	4	5	6	7	8		
21.6	12.5	14.1	16.6	21.6	**50.8**	38.3	27.5	21.8	29.0[a]

[a] $s_{\text{diff}} = 4.15$; $t_{\text{diff}} = 6.99$, $p < .001$.
Note: There were 40 subjects in this experiment. The series of letter pairs was repeated three times in different printing variations with the sixth pair (data in boldface) punished each time; the results for these three series are combined into a single series in this table.

responses since they could perform successfully on later tests simply by using the same responding strategies they employed on the initial test. On the other hand, the receipt of a punishment was an occasion indicating failure of these strategies; in order to avoid repeating the error on a later test, it would be necessary to remember the stimulus involved (and the response) so as to be able to know later not to use the customary response strategy for that one. In other words, the integrative function of reward disappeared and the attitude of the subject became similar to that established in Experiments E_{1-3} (Chapter 5) by instructing subjects that they would be retested only on *wrong* responses.

The results of these two experiments have been very informative, indicating that factors of task attitude (open versus closed) cannot be separated fully from structural aspects of the task (specifically, the ratio of rewards to punishments). We know from our previous experiments that the open-task attitude typically facilitates retention of rewarded connections relative to punished ones. The present experiments indicated, however, that when punishments stand out as exceptional events against a background of consistent reward, such effects no longer obtain.

IMPLICATIONS FOR THE LAW OF EFFECT

Most of Thorndike's experiments (e.g., 1932, 1933) that have demonstrated superior connection-strengthening of reward relative to punishment have used series of tasks in which initially 25% or fewer of subjects' trial-and-error responses were rewarded, the remainder being punished. The previous results of this chapter alert us to the possibility that at least part of the effectiveness of reward in such situations might be attributable to isolation by virtue of a relatively infrequent outcome. In our final experiments, we will compare the effects of reward and punishment in a closed-task situation, while varying the ratio of reward to punishment. If the efficacy of reward is found to vary as a function of the reward-punishment ratio, we will have a basis for questioning the interpretation of a variety of experiments that have been cited as support for Thorndike's law of effect.

EXPERIMENTS $IR_{8,9}$

Procedure

Both experiments employed the number-estimation task used

several times previously. Each used 40 stimulus photographs for which the subject was to estimate the number, to the nearest five, of objects depicted. A closed-task attitude was established in that subjects expected no subsequent test for any of the stimulus photographs. After completion of the first round of estimates, however, subjects were asked to reproduce their original response to each stimulus regardless of whether the response had been called *right* or *wrong*. The recall test was conducted with the experimenter naming the type of object on each photograph, rather than re-presenting the actual stimuli, as cues for subjects' recalls. It will be recalled that this test procedure has typically been used with the number-estimation task in order not to allow subjects the opportunity to ignore the recall task in favor of the easier one of simply making new estimates for each stimulus. The only variation in procedure between the two experiments was that in IR_8 responses to a preselected set of 20 (50%) of the 40 stimuli were called *right*, while in IR_9 only 10 (25%) of the 40 responses were called *right*. All other responses were called *wrong*.

Subjects

Twenty university students participated in each experiment.[4]

Results

The results for the two experiments are given in Table 7.9, in terms of percentage of accurate reproductions of rewarded and punished responses. When reward and punishment were administered with equal frequencies (IR_8) there was no difference in the percentage of original rewarded and punished responses accurately reproduced. When reward was a relatively infrequent outcome (IR_9) there was a significantly superior reproduction of rewarded relative to punished responses. This finding is entirely consistent with those obtained previously in this chapter demonstrating superior recall of punished responses when punishment was a relatively infrequent outcome.

Discussion

The data presented in this chapter point unequivocally to the conclusion that connections receiving the more infrequent outcome (either reward or punishment) in a series of trial-and-error tasks are selectively strengthened. This conclusion is quite compatible with

[4]The data for IR_8 have been reported previously as Experiment R_3 (see Chapter 5). They are presented again here for comparison with the data of IR_9, which was conducted with a comparable group of subjects and used the same task, varying only the reward-punishment ratio.

Table 7.9

PERCENTAGES OF ACCURATE REPRODUCTIONS OF REWARDED
AND PUNISHED RESPONSES IN A CLOSED TASK WITH
VARYING REWARD-PUNISHMENT RATIO
(EXPERIMENTS IR_{8-9})

Experiment	Reward-Punishment Ratio	Mean Percent accurate reproductions for		Diff. (%)	s_{diff}	t_{diff}
		Reward	Punishment			
IR_8	20:20	47.0	47.0	0.0	3.53	0.00
IR_9	10:30	39.0	30.7	8.3	3.93	2.11[a]

[a] $p < .05$.

Note: There were 20 subjects in each experiment. The data for IR_8 have previously been reported as Experiment R_3 (Table 5.2).

findings that connections isolated by use of distinctive materials (Köhler & von Restorff, 1933) are selectively strengthened; also, it may be relevant to findings that connections marked by an emphatic (though not necessarily infrequent) outcome are selectively strenthened (Courts & Waggoner, 1938; Muenzinger, 1934; Tolman, Hall, & Bretnall, 1932). In sum, anything that selectively draws attention to a connection appears to result in increased strengthening. Occurrence of an infrequent outcome can be classed as one such procedure for drawing attention to a connection.

As we indicated in the preceding section, this conclusion has implications for much research pertinent to the law of effect in which reward has been a relatively infrequent outcome. Such studies must be interpreted with great caution as evidence for the effectiveness of reward (relative to punishment) since we can expect more connection-strengthening with reward in such experiments simply by virtue of its infrequency. By the same reasoning, we must look back at a few of our own conclusions which have been based on experiments with unequal outcome frequencies. In Chapter 5 (Experiments Ro_{1-9}), we drew the conclusion that reward was more effective than punishment in strengthening connections in open-task (i.e., typical learning) situations. In those experiments, the percentages of responses rewarded were 20% (Ro_{1-7}), 24% (Ro_9), or 35% (Ro_8). These percentages are for the most part in the range of infrequency that has been discovered, in the present chapter, to enable connection-strengthening regardless of whether the more infrequent outcome is reward or punishment. Thus, we would be firmer in our conclusion that reward normally is more effective than punishment in open-task situations if that conclusion had been based on experiments in which reward and punishment occurred in equal frequencies.[5]

The problem of outcome frequency applies also to a few of our experiments that did not directly concern reward and punishment. Specifically, in Chapter 6 (Experiments Ti_{3-5}) subjects were informed that they would be tested later on a specific subset of 25% of the stimuli on which they were originally tested (with no reward or punishment for their original responses). These experiments provided part of the basis for concluding that connections experienced in the context of an open (persisting) task are strengthened more than those experienced in a closed-task context. In this case, we feel that the conclusion is not damaged in the slightest by the fact that a

---

[5]Such experiments are presented in the Appendix of this volume. The results indicate that reward is not differentially effective in open-task situations in which reward and punishment occur equally often. [AGG]

minority of stimuli were singled out for later test; this confidence is based on the fact that other experiments ($Ti_{1 \text{ and } 2}$; E_{1-3}), in which the critical outcomes (reward or punishment; later test or no test) occurred equally often, supported the same conclusion.

The results of Experiment IP appeared to indicate that structural isolation effects might also have implications for spread-of-effect experiments. It will be recalled that we found enhanced association formation with letter pairs situated adjacent to the single (isolated) digit pair in the experimental series. This result, however, was not supported in any clear fashion by results of IR_{1-7} (see Tables 7.4 – 7.8), in which isolation was achieved by an infrequent outcome rather than by distinctive materials. Examination of the data for these experiments indicates that rewarded connections neighboring isolated punished ones were sometimes stronger and sometimes weaker than more distant ones; no regular pattern indicating spread of isolation was observed. In this connection, we may note that similar data pertaining to associative spread around isolated rewards were reported in Chapter 4; it will be recalled that some of these data indicated an associative spread (Table 4.5) while others (Table 4.6) did not. In summary of this collection of findings we may conclude that, while there may be an associative spread when isolation is accomplished by use of distinctive materials (Experiment IP), the same effect does not appear to occur when isolation is accomplished by a distinctive outcome; perhaps this is because the isolation by outcome is a weaker effect, to begin with, than isolation by materials. There is nonetheless an implication for spread-of-effect experiments here. We have shown that isolated outcomes (whether reward or punishment) produce an enhancement of connection-strengthening. Since spread-of-effect experiments necessarily involve the isolation of rewards in series of otherwise punished responses, it must be clear that a spread of effect cannot be operationally distinguished from a spread of isolation; in any experiment demonstrating a spread of effect, there is no reason for not referring to the outcome equally as a spread of isolation (cf. Zirkle, 1946).

Conclusions

The experiments reported in this chapter have done much to clarify the role of reward and punishment in learning situations. On the basis of experiments discussed in Chapters 5 and 6, we reached the conclusion that the subject's attitude (open versus closed) in regard to the experimental task was a strong determinant of retention of connections from the task. The present chapter has provided evidence supporting the importance of another factor, frequency (or isolation) of outcome, as a determinant of retention of connections. Perhaps most importantly, we have found that the two determinants, task attitude and frequency of outcome, do not operate independently. The frequency of an outcome was found, in Experiments IR_6 and IR_7, to affect task attitude in a manner contrary to the instructions that were explicitly given to subjects. Specifically, it was found that subjects attended selectively to responses that received an infrequent punishment despite instructions to learn only rewarded responses. Thus, the ratio of rewards to punishments in a series of tasks may be expected to affect learning (a) directly by virtue of an isolation effect in which the sheer infrequency of one type of outcome draws attention to the response that produced it, and (b) also indirectly in that the subject may find it more profitable, in regard to accomplishment of some persisting task, to focus attention on responses that receive the more infrequently occurring outcome. Consequently, the isolated outcome takes over what we have called the integrative function and the isolated connection becomes incorporated in a task-tension system.[6]

[6]A recent review of structural isolation effects on learning (Wallace, 1965) has suggested that the connection-strengthening effect of isolation in incidental learning (i.e., closed-task) situations is a relatively weak one. Several experiments in the present chapter, on the other hand, obtained clear and strong effects of isolation (either by materials or by outcome) in closed-task situations. This disagreement probably is no more than a concomitant of the differences between procedures used to establish a closed-task situation in the present experiments and incidental learning procedures used by other investigators. The findings reviewed by Wallace, we therefore feel, should not be interpreted as challenging the present conclusion that isolation enhances connection-strengthening in closed-task situations.

Wallace also reviewed several studies on the topic of spread of isolation, concluding that the spread of isolation was an unreliable effect, perhaps dependent on the extent to which the isolation procedure draws attention toward or away from items neighboring the isolated one. The present findings cannot add to this conclusion, especially in light of the fact that the spread of isolation was an unreliable phenomenon in the present series of experiments, obtained clearly only in Experiment IP.

The connection-strengthening effect of isolation by virtue of infrequent outcome (Experiments IR_{1-9}) was not obtained in a study by Postman and Adams (1955). As we have mentioned previously (Chapter 5, footnote 9), the results of this Postman-Adams study are difficult to reconcile with those of studies reported in this volume. We noted earlier that the disagreement in results possibly may be attributed to Postman and Adams' use of an ESP cover task for their experiment, and related instructions. Hopefully, further experimentation will resolve the apparent discrepancy among findings in this area.

In discussing Zirkle's "spread of isolation" explanation of the spread of effect (1946), Postman (1966, p. 387) commented: "Within the framework of the isolation hypothesis it becomes an internal contradiction . . . to predict superior retention of a given response and at the same time distortion of memory for the aftereffects of that response." In other words, if the associative-enhancing effect of isolation spreads so as to produce superior strength of neighboring associations, then it should also spread in the sense of producing superior memory for the fact that the neighboring associations were punished, thereby leading to reduced, not increased, levels of repetition. While it may be granted that this argument is plausible, it is nonetheless contrary to the facts of experimental data reported in this volume. Experiment IP demonstrated that associative effects of isolation could spread to neighboring connections; experiments reported in Chapter 4, above, indicated that erroneous recall of outcome was likely to increase as a function of proximity to an isolated one; and, most importantly, Experiments S_{4-7} (Chapter 3, above) demonstrated that accurately recalled punished responses tended to be recalled as rewarded (i.e. inaccurately) more often than inaccurately recalled punished responses (see Table 3.4, data for incorrect recalls of reward). Accordingly, Postman's rejection of Zirkle's hypothesis on "logical" grounds must be deemed premature. [AGG]

•

CHAPTER 8

ELEMENTS OF A BEHAVIOR THEORY

A THEORY OF LEARNING

In the empirical sections of this book, particularly in the last three chapters, we have analyzed the effects of some factors, specifically task orientation and task reward-punishment structure, that have not been considered important in previous theoretical analyses of learning in terms of reward (e.g., Thorndike) or need reduction (e.g., Hull). Before proceeding to draw theoretical conclusions, let us review briefly our major empirical findings.

SUMMARY OF THEORY-RELEVANT FINDINGS

1. Most of the archival experiments demonstrating or testing the law of effect have employed instructions creating higher levels of motivation for repetition of rewarded, as opposed to punished, responses on learning trials. It is possible, then, that fewer punished than rewarded connections are performed on test trials only because there is insufficient motivation to perform the former (cf. latent learning studies). In consequence, one of the present series of experiments (Ro_{1-9}, Chapter 5) employed learning tasks with test trial instructions creating equal levels of motivation for repetition of rewarded and punished connections. It was found, under these conditions, that punished connections were correctly reproduced less frequently than rewarded ones. This led us to conclude that the standard learning experimental situation produced not only superior repetition (performance) of rewarded associations relative to punished ones, but also superior stimulus-response association (learning). The present experiments, it should be noted, employed an operational definition of learning in terms of frequency of repetition of connections under conditions of equal motivation to repeat all previously practiced (i.e., rewarded and punished) connections.

2. The next phase in our empirical program was to determine whether superior learning of rewarded connections in learning ex-

periments was due to reward per se, rather than to other procedural aspects of the learning experiment. Our attention was particularly directed to the learner's task orientation as a basis for explaining superior learning of rewarded associations. That is, it was possible that reward and punishment produced different motivational attitudes in the subject with regard to the just-practiced association; this motivational orientation initiated during the learning trial, it should be noted, is conceptually separate from motivation to repeat rewarded rather than punished associations on the test trial, which was considered in the preceding paragraph. Specifically, our hypothesis was that reward for an association typically serves to generate an open-task orientation (or persisting task tension) with respect to that association, meaning that the subject is actively interested in preserving the rewarded association for use on a later test trial; punishment would not serve to create the open-task orientation, but rather a closed-task orientation, meaning that the subject expects little or no future usefulness for the punished association and hence does not try actively to retain it.

a. First, we examined the influence of reward on association formation in the absence of the open-task orientation, that is, employing closed-task procedures in which subjects expected no subsequent tests for either rewarded or punished associations. These experiments showed no superior association formation with reward, even when reward was repeated several times for the same connection (Experiments R_{1-5} and RR_{1-6}).[1]

b. The next series of experiments examined the effect of the open-task orientation in the absence of reward. It was found that associations practiced as part of an open task were better retained than those practiced in a closed-task orientation (Experiments T_{1-3} and T_m.

3. The preceding experiments suggested that the superior learning of rewarded connections in many learning experiments could be attributed to the different task orientation established by reward (open-task orientation) as opposed to punishment (closed). Reward, but not punishment, provides information indicating that the just-practiced association will subsequently be useful on a test trial and, thus, aids in incorporating or integrating the association in the persisting task orientation of the learning experiment. (This process may be called the informative or integrative function of reward.)

[1]An exception to these findings was that of Experiment Re (Chapter 5), in which young children formed stronger associations with reward than with punishment in the closed-task situation. We suspect that the closed-task orientation was not successfully established with these younger subjects.

a. This hypothesis was first tested in experiments in which some S-R connections were accompanied by a signal indicating their inclusion in a subsequent part of the experimental task, while others were accompanied by a signal indicating their exclusion from the remaining task. All connections were subsequently tested for learning and those designated as included in the remaining task were much better learned than those designated as excluded (Experiments Ti_{1-5}).

b. The hypothesis was also tested employing instructions creating an open-task orientation for punished associations, but not for rewarded ones. In this case, the hypothesis was supported when it was found that the punished associations were better retained than the rewarded ones (Experiments E_{1-3}). It may be noted that we found it difficult to establish the task orientation required for these experiments when young children were the subjects.

4. In the last portion of our research program, we examined the possible associative consequences of the fact that, in the archival learning experiments, typically only about 20−25% of practiced associations were rewarded, the remainder being punished. Our hypothesis was that rewarded associations might be better learned in such situations due to their relative structural isolation, rather than due to reward per se. This hypothesis was supported by the finding that punished connections were better learned than rewarded ones when the task reward-punishment structure was such that punished associations were in the minority (Experiments IR_{1-7}).

5. Another phase of the present research program, not involved directly in the sequence of theoretical problems just described, was a study of the determinants and consequences of accurate outcome recall (i.e., recall of success or failure for specific connections). This program of research, presented in Chapters 2, 3, and 4, explored several variables that affect the likelihood of recall of success for specific connections. The implications of these findings for the analysis of behavior rests on the validity of the assumption (not tested here) that subjects are more likely to repeat a response recalled as successful than one recalled as unsuccessful. In particular, it seemed likely that the influence of outcome recall on performance might be a contributor to the type of finding that Thorndike labeled "spread of effect."

ACQUISITION, RETENTION, AND PERFORMANCE PROCESSES IN LEARNING

Our understanding of the learning process will be clarified if we are careful to maintain a conceptual separation among three components of the learning process: (a) acquisition of associations; (b) retention, or preservation of learned associations; and (c) performance, the process by which retained associations, in conjunction with other variables, determine action.

Another distinction that seems warranted is to separate the performance process into two phases, a preparatory phase and an executive phase, the latter of which corresponds to overt behavior. Tolman (1938) has shown the possibility of observing the preparatory stage in the "vicarious trial and error" behavior of rats at maze choice points. This stage, in which the organism presumably anticipates the consequences of alternative response possibilities, must be regarded as especially important when one considers behavior at the human level. Corresponding to the preparatory-executive distinction, one may distinguish two categories of learned content: expectations (knowledge of "what leads to what") and behavioral skills. In effect, it is one thing to learn how to walk — a behavioral skill — and quite another to know how to get from the room one is in to the exit of a building — a set of expectations about relations among environmental events, that is, a cognitive map. (The indebtedness of the present analysis to the theorization of Tolman is obviously great.)

The acquisition of expectations may be described as cognitive learning. Expectations can be formalized as structures containing information about what will happen as the result of a given action operating on a given initial situation [cf. the formulation of expectations as $S_1R_1S_2$ structures by MacCorquodale and Meehl (1954) in their systematization of Tolman's theory.] The major problem for the theoretical analysis of cognitive learning is to know how, among the many $S_1R_1S_2$ sequences entering our perceptual world at any moment, some give rise to the effective acquisition of cognitive structures or associations, while others do not. It is to be expected that perceptual and motivational factors that affect the direction of attention will be important in explaining this selectivity of the cognitive learning process.

The acquisition of behavioral skills (including verbal ones) involves some combination of cognitive and motor learning that is presently not fully understood; the cognitive aspect of this learning consists of information received through proprioceptive channels.

The process of retention, or preservation of learned associations, has been the focus of our analysis of learning by incorporation of associations in task-tension systems. Here, theoretical interest focuses on the factors determining why some associations are more durable than others. The problem of preservation of learned connections over time was also an important focus of the theories and research programs of Thorndike and Hull. These authors postulated superior retention as a function of reward or need reduction, respectively. For Thorndike, we may note, the processes of learning and performance were not conceptually separate, so that his explanations of retention and of performance were identical. For subsequent theorists, the learning-performance distinction we make presently has been acknowledged in some form or other. In the case of human behavior, it is particularly evident that much of what is learned is not directly manifest in overt behavior, i.e., the executive phase of performance. For this reason, nonperformance of an S-R connection cannot be taken as a sign of no retention, unless there has been explicit provision (as is standard in our own experiments) of conditions producing equal motivation to perform all learned connections. In the realm of animal behavior, a similar necessity exists for conceptual separation of learning and performance, as is indicated by a variety of experimental findings, such as those summarized as demonstrating "latent learning" (cf. Thistlethwaite, 1951).

The interpretation of performance as activation of learned associations under suitable motivating conditions is satisfactory for interpretation of verbal learning experiments employing simple stimulus-response pairs in conjunction with reward and punishment. However, the explanation of behavior in nonlaboratory situations typically requires consideration of a larger number of interacting determinants of performance. In our view, performance must be analyzed in terms of the simultaneous contributions of expectations and behavioral skills, in the context of the human personality's interaction with its environment while implementing one of its major or minor projects (see discussion in Chapter 1). Our theoretical analysis of these processes will be presented later in this chapter.

LEARNING AND MOTIVATION

In our view, the psychological processes that facilitate acquisition and retention of either cognitive expectations or behavioral skills are essentially motivational in nature. The subject's motivational orientation is responsible not only for the fact that certain $S_1R_1S_2$ sequences are selectively perceived and acquired, but also for superior preservation of those expectations and skills that play a role in the projects and tasks at which the subject is performing.

The experiments reported in the several preceding chapters have demonstrated motivational influences on the acquisition and retention of verbal and motor S-R associations in learning tasks. In these experiments, subjects were able to judge which specific responses would, in specific stimulus situations, serve to achieve the goals of a persisting task. In our view, however, there is an additional learning process, not demonstrated in the present experiments, in which specific responses become motivationally integrated in a noncognitive fashion. This second process, canalization, occurs when a behavioral response functions as an outlet for a need.

Thus, while the present analysis of acquisition and retention appeals only to a single explanatory factor (i.e., motivational orientation), it acknowledges two different processes—one cognitive and one noncognitive—by which motivation may play a role in learning. These two processes will be discussed in detail in the following paragraphs.

LEARNING BY CANALIZATION OF NEEDS IN BEHAVIOR PATTERNS

In order to study the fundamental motives or needs of a given species, it is necessary to examine the species-typical patterns of interaction between organism and environment. The organism is said to be malfunctioning—either at a physical or behavioral level—when certain types of interaction characteristic of the species are absent or are disturbed. In such a state of malfunction, the organism is likely to be observed engaging in behavior apparently directed at reestablishing the absent or disturbed type of interaction. From such observations, it is sound to infer that certain types of interaction with the environment are required for healthy functioning of a typical organism of the species being observed. The required interactions occur significantly at two levels—biochemical and behavioral—and most of the required interactions involve both a biochemical and a behavioral phase. For example, obtaining nourishment from the environment involves both the biochemical phase of digesting food and the behavioral phase of obtaining food. The science of psychology is, of course, primarily interested in the behavioral aspect of required interactions between organism and environment. The basic frame of reference for psychological study is not the solitary organism, but rather the system of interrelationships between organism and environment; in this framework, organism and environment may be regarded as two parts of an integrated structure. The organism functionally consists of a system of biochemical and behavioral techniques for interacting with the surrounding environment. Needs may be defined as those organism-environment interactions that demonstrate the characteristic of requiredness, which manifests itself (a) by the existence of a coordinated hierarchy of activities within the organism's behavioral repertoire serving to maintain the required interaction, and (b) by the fact that the organism deteriorates physically or mentally if the relationships cannot be established or maintained. Needs are conceived here not merely as states of deficiency in the organism; the fundamental structure of a need includes the required interactions with the environment. Since a wide variety of the organism's activities function to ensure that the state of deficiency is never or, at best, rarely experienced, it seems appropriate to regard the deficiency state as only a phase in the total structure that constitutes the need.

The present view of needs as patterns of interaction with the environment, required for healthy functioning of the organism, is based on a conception of the living organism as an active insertion in the environment, i.e., a substructure in the organism-environment interaction system. Different species are different ways in which this insertion into the biochemical and social environment can be effected. The difference between a human personality and a protozoon can be conceived in terms of the very different interaction patterns which constitute these two forms of life.

Needs typically involve an object that the organism must obtain through the required type of interaction. Most of the time, a specific behavioral response to obtain a specific object is only one of many potential ways in which the interaction requirement could be satisfied. Therefore, the relation with the specific object is only required in a broad sense; this object typically may be replaced more or less satisfactorily by others belonging to the category that fulfills the required interaction; similarly, the specific behavior pattern may be replaced by others that serve to obtain objects in the required category.[2]

Some of the behavioral interactions required for the organism's healthy functioning are innately provided, while others remain to be progressively established (that is, learned). The most primitive level at which learning of the required interactions can occur is, in our conception, a process of canalization. Prior to the learning of behavioral interactions that satisfy need requirements, the need exists, it may be assumed, only as a vague state of tension. The vagueness of this state of tension can be conceptualized as the discrepancy between

[2]The present discussion of requiredness may be compared with those by Köhler (1938, pp. 327-340 and 363-368) and Heider (1960). Our conception of needs in terms of required relationships or interactions between the organism and the environment is known as the Interaction Theory of Needs; it has been more fully presented recently in Nuttin (1965, Chapter 8).

the required interaction structure and the one actually existing. This primitive need state is characterized by behavior giving the appearance of searching or trying out responses. A response that satisfies the required interaction (i.e., a rewarding response) can be said to provide an outlet for the need. The rewarding response, that is, may be conceived as the behavioral channel in which the vague state of tension finds concrete expression. In this way, the indefinite need for food becomes the urge to take a specific behavioral route to obtain a specific food object. The need for food is a designation for the dynamic aspect of this new behavioral pattern; a need for affection would be canalized in and, hence, identified by other sorts of behavioral exchange with environmental objects. In other words, the original vague, undifferentiated tension state gradually evolves through canalization of need-satisfying responses into specific types of interaction which can be identified as needs for the objects obtained by these interactions.

When the need is associated innately with one or more behavior patterns — in which case the term instinct is more appropriate than need — the occurrence of the need condition is synonymous with the occurrence of its associated behavior. When the response pattern must be acquired through learning, the integration of need state with behavior may become as close as in the case of instinct, although there usually remains the possibility for some flexibility in the response pattern or object obtained.

When a response does not meet the organismic demand (that is, does not obtain the required object) the organism's need condition will have no behavioral outlet; the need condition will not be canalized in this unsuccessful response and no integration of need and behavior pattern will take place.

In terms of the present theory of learning, stimulus-response units can be preserved or retained by their being integrated in a dynamic system by the canalization process. Canalization is a quite primitive mechanism by which a specific behavior pattern becomes integrated with a motivational state of the organism; the behavioral response is conceived as the channel through which a vague need for interaction with an environmental object finds outlet. It is, in fact, impossible to speak of a specific need until some canalization has occurred — i.e., until the organism has established a behavior pattern for extracting a specific object from its environment or, in other words, until the need tension has established a channel into a specific response. Nonrewarding responses, on the other hand, are those which are not able to serve as channels for the required type of environmental contact. Because these unsuccessful responses provide no outlet for the need tension, they are not integrated in the dynamic system of the need and, therefore, tend not to be preserved among the behavioral capabilities of the organism.

It should be clear from the foregoing that the canalization process is simultaneously a process of development of needs into concrete motives and development of behavioral reaction patterns (or learning). In this context, we may remind ourselves of Woodworth's (1918) and Allport's (1937) assertions that "mechanisms become drives." In fact, the canalized behavior patterns are nothing more than the concrete forms in which the needs of the living organism become manifest.

LEARNING BY INCORPORATION OF BEHAVIOR PATTERNS IN DYNAMIC ORIENTATIONS

The second process of learning—one that has been studied in the experiments reported in this volume and that applies especially to human learning—presupposes a cognitive elaboration of needs. We shall be able to be relatively brief in discussing this second category of learning, since we have already discussed the cognitive elaboration of human needs in the form of plans, projects, and tasks in Chapter 1, in connection with our discussion of the constructive character of human behavior.

In the study of human behavior, it is important not to treat motivational and cognitive processes as unrelated. The two constitute different aspects of the same behavioral processes and are closely interlaced with one another. We shall not discuss the fact that cognitive functions have their own dynamic basis (that is, that there exists a need to interact cognitively with the environment); but we must emphasize two important changes in motivation that follow from the fact of its coexistence with cognitive processes in an organism with highly developed mental abilities.

First, a given need—the need for food, say—does not interject itself into human behavior only as a pure and simple impulse to assuage hunger sensations. On the contrary, man works in a relatively continuous fashion to obtain the means of satisfying hunger even though hunger manifests itself as a need state only occasionally on a periodic basis. The need for food exists, for man, on a cognitive level even when it is not experienced in the form of hunger pangs. For this reason, the need for food, or any other human need, can elicit and direct behavior on a more or less continuous basis.[3]

[3]In cultures in which food is continuously present and in abundance, the hunger motive may not be extensively elaborated at the cognitive level.

Second, the cognitive elaboration of needs is manifest not only in the relatively continuous capacity of a need for direction of behavior, but also by virtue of the existence of means-end structures (projects, plans, tasks) organized in terms of the underlying need (see discussion in Chapter 1). These dynamic-cognitive structures typically are integrated with social phenomena such as economic organizations which play important roles in need satisfaction. Corresponding to human projects, such as to become a scientist, to get married, or to enjoy oneself as much as possible, there are areas of interest (laboratory research, eligible bachelors, or night clubs, for example) to which attention is directed by virtue of the specific cognitive elaboration that occurs. The consequences or outcomes of action are evaluated by the human actor in the framework of his unique set of projects and areas of interest. An outcome will be need-satisfying to the extent that it is successful in achieving a major goal or subgoal of a project. In the present analysis, it is emphasized that a successful outcome does not typically terminate the underlying need; the need, rather, persists by virtue of its cognitive elaboration in the form of continuing or evolving projects and areas of interest.

Thus, virtually all concrete expressions of human needs are in a form comparable to what we have designated as an open-task situation in our own experimental studies — that is, the underlying dynamism persists in a cognitive form beyond immediate need satisfaction, giving a future task-accomplishment orientation to need-relevant behavior. It is very rare in everyday life that actions and obtained outcomes cannot be related to some persisting project in which the actor is engaged. It is perhaps common only in experimental psychology laboratory situations that a subject engages in actions substantially unrelated to his cognitively elaborated needs. In such a context a persisting task orientation may be established briefly, but typically terminates at the end of the experimental session (and the subject can anticipate that it will end then), in contrast to the persisting projects of everyday life which can extend as far in the future as does the life of the actor. For this reason it is difficult to create, in the laboratory, conditions ideal for extended retention of learned associations and skills; on the other hand, a single experience occurring in the context of an important persisting task orientation in everyday life can have indefinitely retained effects. The nature of the materials typically used in laboratory learning experiments (usually serially presented verbal information with high interference potential) does not, of course, increase the likelihood of long-term retention.

The present conceptions of open task and incorporation in a persisting tension system of the open task in experimental situations would have to be formulated in more general terms to reflect the analogous processes as they occur in everyday life. We think the terms projects, plans, and areas of interest may successfully serve for discussion of nonlaboratory situations. The present analysis can be extended to the understanding of states of alertness and arousal which, in many cases, can be considered states of activation rooted in underlying persisting dynamic orientations. Situations and actions that become the focus of attention, i.e., that arouse the organism to an alert state, probably do so because of their relevance to persisting motivational orientations. The acquisition phase of learning is undoubtedly facilitated as a function of the organism's current degree of alertness and S-R associations acquired in alert states are likely also favored in retention due to their relevance to persisting dynamic orientations. The associative effect of structural isolation (see Chapter 7) is viewed, in the present analysis, not as evidence for a third learning process, but rather as an enhancement of learning (by either canalization or incorporation) due to facilitation of attention to the stimulus-response patterns to be integrated into a dynamic structure.

It is our opinion that the processes of canalization and incorporation can operate simultaneously and in parallel fashion. Learning by canalization of a need is conceived as a slower process than learning by incorporation into a cognitively elaborated motive system. One or the other mechanism may be said to be dominant to the extent that cognitive processes play a role in the elaboration of motivational states. Further, the degree of cognitive elaboration of a need may be expected to vary from moment to moment as a function of personal and situational factors. Learning by canalization will be dominant — and learning will be relatively slow — in situations involving the acquisition and retention of motor skills as well as those in which the subject has a passive attitude. On the other hand, acquisition of material of an informational nature and learning in situations in which cognitively elaborated needs are operating would be expected to proceed by the incorporation mechanism and to occur relatively rapidly. The conditions favoring the incorporation process are more likely to occur in humans with increasing age; this perhaps explains why our results in experiments with young children typically do not manifest the cognitive learning process by incorporation as clearly as do our experiments with older subjects.

It must be noted that, while the present theoretical analysis specifies the parallel operation of two learning processes — canalization and incorporation — only the latter of these has been the subject of study in the experiments reported in this volume. Our theoretical discussion of learning by need reduction (canalization) is to be viewed as a hypothesis that allows us to treat the psychological aspect of all learning in terms of integration with motivational processes — either cognitively elaborated or unelaborated.

In the next section, we shall direct ourselves to the problem of interpreting the constructive aspects of human behavior in terms of the interplay of cognitive and dynamic processes and in terms of the utilization of information and skills acquired and retained in accordance with the principles just discussed.

A THEORY OF PERFORMANCE

To understand performance requires an analysis of the processes involved in construction and evocation of behavior. It is clear from earlier remarks that our conception of performance is not simply as a process of evocation of a response by virtue of its being connected with a currently presented stimulus.

In the present conception, performance (or behavior) consists of meaningful responses to meaningful situations. Meaningful responses are not restricted to motor action, although movement will generally be an important component of behavior. I may be listening to or looking at something (an accident or a concert, for example) and may engage in movement in order to see or to hear better; in such cases, movement is a subordinate component of behavior. On the other hand, in walking home, movement is the principal component of behavior and hearing and seeing are subordinate. Similarly, experiencing an emotion is sometimes the main component of behavior (for example, when one is startled) while at other times affect plays the subordinate roles of accompanying or energizing other actions.

The extent to which the principal component of behavior is overt depends on the situation in which it is observed. In everyday situations, judgment of what a person is doing involves some degree of inference. I may see that a person is moving his arms and legs in a specific way; what I judge that he is doing is not simply a description of these movements, but an inference such as that he is going home or working. In experimental situations, behavior is more overt in the sense that the situation contains less ambiguity as to what is being done. Thus, a rat who is oscillating at a choice point may be said to be engaging in vicarious trial and error behavior; in a more naturalistic and less controlled setting, such an inference as to what the rat was "doing" (i.e., the principal component of its behavior) would be less warranted.

THE STIMULUS SITUATION IN HUMAN BEHAVIOR

"Stimulus" is one of the most ambiguous and most misused terms in psychology. It designates not only the physical energy impinging on the organism, but also the meaningful situation in which behavior occurs. Freud and others have employed stimulus to indicate the source of instigation of action while, in the phrase goal stimulus of S-R theory, reference is made to the goal or end point of behavior. All of these uses of stimulus have merit, since organisms can be described as responding to stimulation in each of the senses implied by the various usages. Nonetheless, it is difficult to proceed with a theoretical analysis of performance without more precision as to what is meant by stimulus.

The stimulus to which human behavior can be said to respond is a complex elaboration of impinging physical energy. It is possible to infer, from the behavior of various organisms, the very different ways in which different species elaborate the physical stimulus. Stimuli from solar radiation produce, in some simply structured organisms, reactions that we call phototropism; for humans, the same physical stimuli produce a variety of more complex responses, including a perceptual response of recognizing the sun as well as more complex activities such as astronomical research and composition of poetry declaiming the beauty of the sun, etc.

If a psychologist is to understand human behavior in its natural complexity, it is necessary to investigate the relationships between behavior (in the sense of what the person is doing) and the meaningful situations and objects that the person constructs from impinging physical stimulus energy. There is no reason to believe that the psychology of human behavior can successfully develop laws relating performance strictly to the physical properties of incoming stimuli. This observation in no sense is intended to diminish the importance of research into relations between physical stimulus dimensions and certain types of response, such as in investigations of judgment responses to varying physical stimuli. Our intent is rather to indicate the overriding importance of research in which the terms stimulus and response are accorded the complexity that is apparent in everyday human behavior.

In the present view, the construction of the stimulus situation is an extremely active process. The route traversed between reception of physical stimulus energy and recognition of an object (a component of the meaningful stimulus situation) is an enormous one.

Many psychologists, it may be noted, are reluctant to conceptualize stimulus in other than physical terms; they assume that discourse about the meaningful stimulus situation could not be conducted in objective terms. This restrictive assumption, however, is quite unnecessary. The basis for rigorous analysis of objects of cognition (i.e., recognized objects) is our next topic.

"COGNIZED" OBJECTS AND BEHAVIOR: THE MEANINGFUL STIMULUS AS A BEHAVIORAL CONSTRUCTION

We have already indicated our view that human behavior is more appropriately analyzed in terms of responses to meaningful situations than in terms of responses to physical stimuli. In order to establish the basis for scientific discussion of meaningful or "cognized" objects, we must first ask: What are these objects, and what is the process by which they are constructed from the physical stimulus?

To speak of cognized objects as patterns of physical stimulation is insufficient. It is possible to perceive a stimulus pattern quite clearly as a form (i.e., a figure against a ground) without that form being a meaningful (that is, recognizable) object. I may see, for example, something displayed on a shelf in a store and wonder what it is. I can see that it is metallic and has a specific shape, but I do not know what it is. When I find out that is is a nutcracker, I am able to see it fully as a meaningful object and not simply as an irregular form made of metal. The perceptual form has become a cognized (or recognized) object by virtue of my knowledge of the function it serves—that is, when I am able to place it in a behavioral context with which I am familiar.

Similar comments could be made concerning any other object—one can distinguish between the sensory pattern and the object that is cognized when one knows what to do with it. A perceived form becomes a cognized object when the percept includes representations of object-relevant responses. To state this in other words, meaningful objects are constructed by the addition of appropriate behavioral dispositions to patterns of sensory stimulation.

The process by which perceptual forms combine with behavioral dispositions may be considered in terms of a child's gradual discovery of his world. The child is predisposed to attend to motion in his environment. It follows that much of the child's early perceptual experience with the objects of his environment (for example, a spoon or a chair) will occur in the context of observing his own or others' actions (for example, eating or sitting down). The object is typically perceived, in other words, as an integral part of a configuration that includes action. When the object is later viewed in isolation, it evokes in the viewer the total object-action configuration in which it has previously been perceived, much as a rectangular form seen on a shelf in a library evokes the total perceptual configuration that is recognized as a book. This is not a matter of evocation of a memory of something previously seen or done; rather, it is the evocation of the object-action configuration that constitutes the act of recognition.

It must be noted that this analysis implies a certain degree of abstraction or generalization of the cognitively represented object-action configuration. That is, the cognitive representation does not incorporate a single specific action that has been observed or performed by the perceiver; rather, the action representation is of a more generalized schema such as eating (in relation to the object: spoon) or sitting down (in relation to the object: chair). Just as the representation of the object component of the object-action configuration is a generalized schema (our idea of a spoon is an abstraction based on a large variety of distinct perceptual experiences), so is the cognitive representation of the action component schematic, generalized, and abstract.

Once the child has developed a cognitive repertory of the basic object-action schemas of his culture, the language system of the culture takes over much of the function of further development and elaboration of cognitive representational functioning; verbal description of behavior replaces cognitively represented perception or execution of action in a large number of object-action schemas. With the aid of language, then, the generalization and abstraction of the action component of schemas increases. Thus, the action component of schemas such as vacuum cleaner, drill press, or shaving cream may be more or less abstract as a function of the relative proportion of behavioral versus verbal experience involved in the acquisition of the schema.[4]

---

[4]As an aside from our main line of discussion, it may be noted here that cognition of an object may include more than just sensory pattern plus behavioral dispositions. For example, one's cognition of the object mountain may include knowledge concerning the origin of mountains in faults in the earth's crust, the effects of natural erosion on the appearance of mountains, etc. Such knowledge is not in the form of behavioral dispositions but is, nonetheless, relevant to behavior in relation to the cognized object. It would appear that one of the required interactions between man and his environment is the acquisition of objective knowledge about the interrelationships among environmental objects and events. This need for theoretical knowledge may be found in the most primitive cultures, which have their own explanations of reality. Such theoretical knowledge allows man to have a better grasp on his environment and to achieve a necessary feeling of security. A few major unexplained natural phenomena (e.g., the origins of life and of the universe) are sources of insecurity and anxiety. Whatever

To summarize: In the present view, cognized objects are networks of behavioral dispositions integrated with patterns of physical sensory stimulation. The object as cognized is thus an active behavior potentiality that may be seen as inviting particular types of action in relation to it. What we call our perceptual or phenomenal world is not only the passive registration of incoming stimulus information; it is also an active construction including behavior potentialities derived from previous learning experiences.

The organic substrate of cognized objects may be conceptualized in terms of traces of learned responses. In fact, since meaningful objects are conceived here as repositories of learned behavior, there is obviously no difficulty in conceiving the substrate of this cognitive activity in the same terms as the substrate of more overt behavior. The retention of cognized objects is therefore readily interpreted in terms of the retention processes described earlier in regard to learned behavior in general.[5]

THE EVOCATION OF LEARNED BEHAVIOR

In this chapter, we have attempted to point out both that cognition involves an important behavioral component and that overt behavior includes an important cognitive (preparatory or pre-executive) component. The domains of mental content and overt response are thus not considered to be conceptually separate. Rather, the two are extensively interwoven and the organic structures associated with each are of the same nature.

Our present concern is to specify how learned cognitions and overt reaction patterns are activated at any given time. The central thesis of our theoretical formulation for learning was that associations are retained by virtue of their integration into a dynamic orientation. It follows from this that whenever a given dynamic state is aroused by virtue of internal or external stimulation, the learned cognitions and action patterns associated (by canalization or incorporation) with that state are also evoked.

objective knowledge man achieves about the events and objects of his environment— that is, whatever objective knowledge is included in man's cognitions of the objects in his environment—is of use in gaining mastery over the environment; thus, scientific knowledge, even though not in the form of behavioral dispositions, is not divorced from behavioral interaction with the environment.

[5]The reader may be interested in comparing Nuttin's conception of the role of behavior in cognitive processes with those of Bruner (1966), Osgood (1953), and Piaget (1954). [AGG]

In the case of canalization of a need in a specific response, the re-awakening of the need state results in the activation of the canalized action pattern—that is, the need's arousal occurs in the form of the canalized action. When the need has previously been satisfied by several different responses, the need state activates a collection of response traces that are more or less likely to occur as overt responses (i.e., they are more or less prepotent) as a function of the similarity of the current stimulus situation to situations in which the canalization originally occurred.

In the case of learning of a cognitive nature, by the incorporation process, activation of the dynamic state will similarly tend to evoke associations (cognitions or overt responses) that have been incorporated into the dynamic state.

The proposition that learned behavior is evoked by virtue of the reoccurrence of dynamic states associated with original learning transfers some of the burden of explanation of performance to the conditions that produce arousal of a dynamic condition. There are several sources of motivational arousal, including most obviously somatically originated, periodically recurring need states. It is most important to note that external stimulus conditions also can arouse dynamic states; that is, observed responses and cognized objects can arouse the dynamic states into which they have been incorporated or canalized. As we have noted earlier, however, man's motivation is frequently more than just a reactivation of an earlier dynamic state. Specifically, each time a goal is achieved the individual proceeds to a new stage of his current project or poses for himself new projects and goals rather than simply directing his actions toward already obtained goals. As a result, the situations in which man finds himself and his motivational orientations are continually undergoing much more change than is anticipated in most approaches to behavior theory or in most experiments on learning-performance processes.

For man, evocation of learned associations—following from the arousal of a motivational state—does not necessarily lead to repetition of earlier responses; rather, the evoked associations have the status of response dispositions or behavioral potentialities—performance will be a novel construction based on current motivation in conjunction with the evoked cognitions and action potentialities.

We do not intend to deny that performance can occur as an automatic repetition of learned behavior. However, as remarked earlier, such behavior occurs only in special conditions or else as the minor units from which novel behavior sequences are constructed. We are not presently concerned with the evocation and performance of these units of behavior; explanation of them is quite within the scope of our previous discussion. Our present concern is, rather, with the formulation of an explanation for the more flexible, constructive aspects of performance.

THE CONSTRUCTION OF PERFORMANCE

Much experimental data indicate that human performance is quite often a novel construction of behavioral elements, adapted to specific present conditions. This observation applies to skilled motor performances as well as to performances of a highly cognitive nature. It is not our present purpose to review relevant studies here. Rather, we shall illustrate our point with some examples representing both motor and cognitive performance.

Talking about the stroke in a skilled athletic game, Bartlett (1932) observed:

> We may fancy that we are repeating a series of movements learned a long time before from a textbook or from a teacher. But motion study shows that in fact we build the stroke afresh on a basis of the immediately preceding balance of postures and the momentary needs of the game. Every time we make it, it has its own characteristics (p. 204).

The well-known experiment of MacFarlane (1930) showed, as have many subsequently, that previous experience and practice enter readily into the coordination of present performance even when repetition of movements is made impossible by experimental conditions. Rats who had learned to run through a dry maze were quite capable, by constructing novel responses, of swimming correctly through the maze when it was filled with water.

The fact that performance is a novel construction, composed of behavioral elements selected according to the novel demands of current problem situations, is particularly well illustrated by tasks requiring cognitive work. For example, Köhler and von Restorff (1935) conducted an experiment in which subjects were given practice multiplying 19×21 by the procedure: $(20-1) \times (20+1) = 20^2 - 1^2 = 400 - 1 = 399$. Later the same subjects were given the new problem of finding the product for $28 \times (15 + 64 - 47)$. Many of the subjects solved the new problem by applying the previously practiced procedure; that is, by rephrasing the problem as $(30-2) \times (30+2)$, etc. It is apparent that, in this situation, previously learned elements of behavior were adapted to solve a new problem. In Köhler's experiment, as in MacFarlane's, what was learned was not simply a specific response to a specific stimulus. The residue of previous experience was, rather, a relatively flexible schema which was potentially usable in a variety of novel problem situations; the response to the novel situation was determined by the previously established schema in conjunction with the particular features of the new problem. The concept of generalization in S-R theory deals with modification of response to novel stimuli; however, the adaptiveness of performance in the illustrations cited here is beyond what would be expected from generalization of previous learning along dimensions of stimulus similarity. Tolman's (1932) conception of creative instability, Maier's (1931) discussion of reasoning, and the Gestaltist conception of restructuring are more closely analogous to the present view.

Earlier, we noted that reactivation of a motivational state carried with it evocation of learned material that had previously been incorporated into that state. Our present observations indicate that the form in which the learned material is re-evoked is not something so simple as a trace of previous responses. The re-evoked entity, rather than being some precise replica of an earlier response, must be of a more complex nature in order to allow for flexible application to novel situations.

The process of making adaptive and creative use of previously learned behavioral and cognitive elements must certainly occur during what we have described as the preparatory phase of cognitive activity that precedes the executive phase of overt action. Many psychologists have commented on the great flexibility of cognitive or representative processes. Krechevsky's (1932, 1933) hypothesis behavior, Hilgard's (1948, 1956) notion of provisional try, and Muenzinger's (1938) and Tolman's (1939, 1959) vicarious trial and error are conceptions that attempt to express the flexible pre-executive processes involved in the construction of performance from previously learned materials. Earlier in this chapter it was suggested that the bridge between cognition and the executive stage of behavior is a direct one, assuming that cognized objects are actually object-action schemas.

In the present conception, a state of need (or a problem situation) acts to elicit preparatory cognitive activity in which various performance possibilities are represented. By virtue of its flexibility, cognitively represented performance lends itself to tentative explorations that can become crystallized into the kinds of means-end structures we have referred to as projects or plans for action.

Although, as we have observed, overt performance is constructed with a degree of plasticity determined by the current stimulus situation and current needs, it must be emphasized that the novel construction is always derived from past learning. Performance is never constructed in entirety on the basis of current situational and motivational determinants; rather, it is constructed of pieces that have been preformed to a certain extent through prior learning. This is true not only for the behavioral skills involved in overt performance, but also for the cognitive schemas and motivational systems (i.e., plans and projects) that enter into the constructive process. This dependence on learned material provides the stability, continuity, and even rigidity that can characterize a human personality, in juxtaposition to its flexibility and creativity. Rigidity of performance is the rule, however, only in extreme cases that we designate pathological. In normal individuals, a tendency toward rigidity is perhaps favored by factors such as fatigue and situational familiarity.

The fact that man possesses at birth very few ready-made behavioral techniques for establishing the required relationships with his environment makes it possible for him to develop a highly individualized repertoire of behavior both at the overt and cognitive levels. The extent to which this individualized development takes place constitutes the degree of uniqueness of a human personality. The content of past actions, projects, and attitudes tend to be well preserved and integrated in present personality structure. To lose this personal past—as is occasionally the case in some phases of a psychotherapeutic process—creates a feeling of emptiness and rootlessness that indicates the important role played by these residues of experience in the normal personality. In terms of our conception of the human personality as an active insertion into its environment, the loss of these residues of the past means the loss of established patterns of interaction with the environment and the necessity for a new start.

In the present view, then, the human organism starts from a dynamic core of needs or required types of organism-environment relationships. The original interaction with the environment consists of canalization of this dynamic core into specific actions that fulfill the required relationships with the environment. Through the cognitive (incorporation) learning process, man acquires an increasing repertoire of potential actions so that, as an active insertion into its environment, the human organism or personality has progressively increasing adaptive flexibility. In the context of this view of the developing organism, the learning process plays a dual role. It provides the pieces with which performance is constructed, at any given time, in accordance with requirements of the current situation; and, in turn, the learning process can be directed by a current project to acquire the pieces that will be useful for construction of performance at some future time.

In closing, it must be acknowledged that the theoretical picture of the learning and performance processes that has been presented here goes substantially beyond a direct interpretation of the experimental data described in the preceding chapters. These theoretical views are intended as a general framework in which more concrete hypotheses about human behavior can and should be developed.

APPENDIX

•

FURTHER EXPERIMENTAL ANALYSIS OF
REWARD AND PUNISHMENT

INTRODUCTION

The reader is already aware that Nuttin has employed novel experimental paradigms to obtain data supporting a theoretical position divergent from currently prevalent views of reward (e.g., Postman, 1962). In the remainder of this volume, we shall present the results of a research program of more modest proportions than Nuttin's, yet concerned with the same basic problems of reward and punishment in human learning. Although this program was conducted in settings widely different from those employed by Nuttin, the results, as we shall see, provide strong confirmation for his major conclusions.

The research to be presented falls under two headings: (a) comparison of connection-strengthening effects of reward and punishment; and (b) analysis of effects of reward and punishment due to the structural properties of tasks in which they occur. Before presenting this research, we shall give brief attention to the current status of the law of effect and then consider in some detail the methodological problems involved in assessment of reward and punishment effects.

CURRENT STATUS OF THE LAW OF EFFECT

THE ACCEPTED LAW OF EFFECT — THE EMPIRICAL FORM

The "empirical law of effect" refers to a principle that is observable in all organisms that make adaptive modifications of behavior, i.e., that learn. Stated in a form designed to avoid circular definition (Meehl, 1950), the empirical law of effect combines two types of observations. First, certain events (called reinforcers) appear to have positive or negative motivational value to the organism, i.e., the organism may reliably be observed to approach or avoid them, respectively. Second, if an event of positive motivational value is made contingent on the performance of some arbitrarily selected novel response, the probability of that response will be observed to increase and, correspondingly, an arbitrary contingency between a response and an event of negative motivational value will decrease the response's probability.

In its empirical form, the law of effect is the basic law of learning. There has been some debate and there continues to be some disagreement about whether rewards and punishments are symmetrically opposed in their effects (see summaries in Hilgard & Bower, 1966; Postman, 1962; Solomon, 1964). Although some theorists have eliminated any statement about punishments from the empirical law of effect, it is not incautious to assert that, in one form or the other, the empirical law of effect is espoused by all students of learning.

THE CONTROVERSIAL LAW OF EFFECT—THE THEORETICAL FORM

Although it is the basic law of learning, the empirical form of the law of effect is unsatisfactory to many psychologists because it is merely descriptive of the effects of reinforcers and offers no insight into how these effects are accomplished in a mechanical sense. Thorndike's earliest statement of a "law of effect" (1911) did suggest the mechanics of the operation of reinforcers. His "connectionist" point of view was that rewards or "satisfiers" acted by strengthening afferent-efferent neural connections operative in near temporal proximity to the reward. Punishments or "annoyers" were originally conceived, by Thorndike, as weakening connections correspondingly. As a result of findings (referred to above) indicating asymmetry of reward and punishment effects, Thorndike subsequently (1932) emended his law of effect by removing its statement about punishment weakening S-R connections. The conception of the mechanism of satisfiers was, however, left unchanged.

The form of the law of effect that proposes a specific mechanism for the effects of reinforcers will be referred to as the "theoretical" form, to contrast it with the above-described empirical form. When stated in the theoretical form, the law of effect has been and currently remains the subject of controversy among learning theorists. In the earlier years of the law of effect, this debate concerned whether or not a mechanism such as that proposed by Thorndike was necessary to account for the phenomena described by the empirical law of effect. This is no longer the focus of debate, largely as a consequence of the theoretical efforts of Tolman (1932) and Guthrie (1935). Their cognitive and contiguity learning theories, respectively, have been influential in demonstrating the possibility of accounting for empirical reward phenomena without a theoretical law of effect. The extent of their influence may be seen in the fact that several former theoretical-law-of-effect advocates have either removed that law from their most recent theoretical statements (Miller, 1963; Mowrer, 1960) or have greatly deemphasized its importance (Hull, 1952; Spence, 1956).

The present focus of debate may be more clearly seen in recent discussions by Postman (1962, 1966), Greenwald (1966), Marx (1967), and Hilgard and Bower (1966, Chapter 2) and, also, in the experimental work of Nuttin presented in this volume. This debate concerns the interpretation of subtle types of evidence that point to an automatic action of rewards in strengthening afferent-efferent connections exercised near in time to reward. Such evidence has been obtained from demonstrations of a spread of effect (e.g., Marx & Goodson, 1956) and from experiments showing differences in the effects of rewards and punishments in incidental learning situations (e.g., Postman & Adams, 1955). The history of research on these problems in the past thirty years has consisted of cycles of demonstration and counter-demonstration in which a result indicating automatic action has been obtained and then subjected to replication attempts with added controls, most often showing that the result failed as a crucial demonstration.

IMPACT OF NUTTIN'S RESEARCH FINDINGS

In the context of the debate over the theoretical law of effect, Nuttin's findings constitute a large set of counterdemonstrations, calling into question the necessity for any reward- or punishment-specific process in accounting for experiments on effects of rewards and punishments.

The impact of Nuttin's research has recently been discussed by the present writer (Greenwald, 1966), in a presentation of the case against the theoretical law of effect that can be made from Nuttin's findings, and by Postman (1966), who discussed the bases on which it can be argued that Nuttin's data are inconclusive. It may be concluded from this recent discussion that a resolution of the debate over the theoretical law of effect must be preceded by some agreement among adherents of opposing views as to appropriate procedures for assessing possible automatic effects of rewards.

In the case of Nuttin's research, it is certainly apparent that the dependent measures of learning he used (see Chapter 5) were essential in obtaining results damaging to the theoretical law of effect.

Postman (1966) contended that these dependent measures were frequently inappropriate for testing the law of effect. In the next section, this issue will be analyzed in detail in an attempt to produce a clear specification of procedures appropriate to testing the theoretical law of effect.

DEPENDENT MEASURES AND THE LAW OF EFFECT

REPETITION MEASURES

In the experimental paradigm typically used to test the law of effect, a subject is required to respond to each of a serial list of stimuli by trial and error selection of a response from a defined set of response alternatives. The experimenter provides the reinforcing operation by remarking *right* or *wrong* (or semantic equivalents of these) after each response. This paradigm may be referred to as the serial trial and error (STAE) experiment. To simplify the paradigm, we will consider that the experiment consists of one acquisition trial, during which each response is called *right* or *wrong*, and one test trial, on which the subject responds again to each stimulus but, this time, without any rewards or punishments.

The traditionally used dependent measure of learning in the STAE paradigm is the probability of repetition of acquisition-trial responses on the test trial. This probability is calculated separately for rewarded and punished acquisition-trial responses. Following Postman (1966), we shall label this type of dependent measure as a repetition measure.

Repetition measures can be used in either of the two basic variations of the STAE paradigm—the intentional learning experiment and the incidental learning experiment. The type of learning observed is a function of the instructions given prior to the acquisition trial. In intentional learning, the subject is instructed that the list of stimuli will be presented at least one more time, at which time(s) he should give as many *right* responses as possible (i.e., he should repeat successes but not errors). In the incidental learning variation, the subject is led to believe that *right* and *wrong* have no significance for his future experimental performance. This incidental learning set is frequently accomplished (e.g., Porter, 1957) by presenting the acquisition trial disguised as an ESP (extrasensory perception) task in which the subject learns, after each response, whether or not he made a correct clairvoyant guess. An identical stimulus list is then presented, the subject being asked to give more ESP guesses (presumably, responses originally *right* are no longer necessarily correct). Repetition rate is measured on this test trial, separately for *right* and *wrong* responses, in the same fashion as for intentional learning.

CUED RECALL MEASURES

To the reader of this volume, it is obvious that repetition measures were not used in Nuttin's experiments on the law of effect. In terms of the STAE paradigm, Nuttin's subjects received the same type of acquisition trial used for the repetition measure, but a highly different kind of test trial. For the test trial, instead of being instructed to repeat successes but not errors, the subject was asked to repeat both *right* and *wrong* responses, i.e., to recall his acquisition trial responses as the series of stimuli was re-presented. The measure of learning is the probability of correct recall of acquisition-trial responses, calculated separately for rewarded and punished responses. This type of measure has been designated a cued recall procedure since each response is to be recalled upon re-presentation of the stimulus to which it was originally made. Cued recall has been most often used in tests of paired-associate learning and may be distinguished from free recall, a procedure in which acquisition responses are recalled with no representation of stimuli.

In commenting on Nuttin's dependent measures, Postman (1966) quoted the following remark of Thorndike:

> The Law of Effect would not lead us to remember experiences that were pleasant and to forget experiences that were painful, but to remember experiences that have been *pleasant to remember* and to forget experiences that have been *painful to remember*, a very different matter (1932, p. 458f).

In this brief remark about recall, Thorndike did not distinguish between the procedurally different free recall and cued recall procedures. From the content and context of the remark, however, it is clear that Thorndike meant to rule out the use of the free recall procedure for testing the law of effect, and rightly so; a free recall procedure, not involving stimuli, would have to be judged inadequate for assessing stimulus-response connection strength. Thorndike's remark does not, however, settle the question of the appropriateness of cued recall for testing the theoretical law of effect. The next section takes up a comparison of repetition and cued recall procedures in terms of their appropriateness for testing the theoretical law of effect.

REPETITION VERSUS CUED RECALL

One's conception of what is meant by stimulus-response connection strength depends on the assumptions one cares to make about the performance mechanisms underlying behavior.

The connectionist (e.g., Thorndike, Guthrie, Skinner) assumes that responses are directly under the control of stimuli to which they are connected; performance of a response requires only the presentation of stimuli to which it is connected. In the connectionist context, stimulus-response (S-R) strength is logically measured by probability of response repetition upon stimulus presentation.

The cognitivist (e.g., Lewin, Tolman, Nuttin) assumes that a decision process intervenes between stimulus input and response output. In the STAE experiment, a cognitivist might propose that the subject responds to each test-trial stimulus by redintegrating the events — response and reinforcer — that occurred following the previous presentation of that stimulus on the acquisition trial. A test-trial response is then selected on the basis of a set of motivational decision principles, such as repeating responses associated with *right*, changing responses associated with *wrong*, and making arbitrary choices when either the response or the reinforcer or both are not available for consideration by the decision mechanism. In the cognitivist context, stimulus-response strength may be taken to mean the degree of availability of the response upon presentation of the stimulus; defined this way, stimulus-response strength is most logically measured by a procedure (such as cued recall) in which the subject is equally motivated to repeat all available responses upon presentation of the stimulus. The cognitivist conception of stimulus response strength will be symbolized as "S-r strength" (the small r symbolizing an internal representation of response, as opposed to the capital R designating overt response).

It has been traditional to consider the automatic-action clause of the law of effect only in the connectionist context. However, the possibility of automatic action of reward should also be considered in the cognitivist context; in this context, the automatic action clause would be interpreted to mean greater availability of a response (given presentation of the stimulus) following the training experience of S, R, reward as opposed to S, R, punishment.[1]

---

[1]It is certainly unusual to consider automatic action of rewards in the cognitivist context. This is unusual largely because Tolman, the most prominent of the cognitive learning theorists, was a frequent and outspoken critic of the theoretical law of effect (e.g., Tolman *et al.*, 1932). As a result of the merging of the cognitivist and anti-law-of-effect viewpoints in the person of Tolman, few theorists have given serious consideration to the possibility of automatic action of rewards within a cognitivist system. This, however, is a genuine possibility, no less likely a priori than that of automatic reward action in the connectionist system.

The following discussion will consider the relative adequacy of repetition and cued recall procedures for testing automatic connection-strengthening by rewards in both the connectionist (S-R) and cognitivist (S-r) frameworks.

Assuming that there is a genuine automatic connection-strengthening effect of rewards in either of these frameworks, it matters little whether a repetition or cued recall procedure is used to test the effect. For both measures, reward superiority would be demonstrated. (It may be left to the reader to satisfy himself that this is so.)

The difference between the connectionist and cognitivist frameworks and between the two dependent measurement procedures becomes important when it is assumed that the automatic action clause of the law of effect is false. That is, we must not overlook the fact that, in testing automatic reward effects, we require a dependent measure of connection-strength capable of demonstrating no effect if, indeed, there is none; further, the measure must be able to make this demonstration assuming either connectionist or cognitivist performance principles. It may be shown that the cued recall procedure meets these requirements while the repetition procedure fails in that it has the desired property (ability to detect falsity of the automatic-action principle) only under connectionist assumptions.

An equivalent of assuming the automatic-action principle to be false is to assume that experiences of S, R, reward and S, R, punishment have identical effects on connection strength. Let us first consider this assumption in the connectionist context. It is immediately apparent that the repetition measure will yield the desired result of no difference in measured S-R strengths. It is less obvious that the cued recall measure will have the desired property because the test situation is changed from that of acquisition and, therefore, stimuli presented on the test trial are not identical to those of acquisition. However, it will be seen that the difference between stimuli stems from a general situational change (new instructions), meaning that test stimuli for rewarded and punished responses are equally different from their acquisition counterparts. Thus, the probabilities of cued recall for rewarded and punished responses will have the desired property of being equal, assuming equal connection strengths established on the acquisition trial. In summary, either cued recall or repetition may be used to demonstrate the falsity of the automatic action principle if one considers that principle in the connectionist framework. While both measures are adequate, the repetition measure must be judged somewhat superior since it does not involve change in the general stimulus situation between acquisition and test trials.

The situation is not so simple when one considers the possibility of demonstrating the falsity of the automatic-action principle in a cognitivist context. With a repetition procedure, two equally strong S-r connections, one formed by reward, the other by punishment, will not command equal response probabilities. The two responses would be equally *available* but, since the subject will be employing decision principles requiring him to repeat available rewarded responses and change available punished responses, the rewarded response will have the higher probability of occurrence. In other words, if one makes cognitivist performance assumptions, it is to be predicted that the repetition procedure will demonstrate a superiority of reward over punishment no matter whether the automatic-action principle is true or false. The difficulty in the repetition procedure is, then, that its implicit decision principles are inappropriate for comparing the strengths of rewarded and punished S-r connections. The cued recall procedure does not have this defect. Its decision rule (viz., repeat all recalled original responses) leads to equal probabilities for performance of rewarded and punished S-r connections that are equally strong (that is, available).

In conclusion, then, cued recall is to be preferred to repetition as a dependent measure of connection strength for testing automatic reinforcer effects when one is uncertain as to whether to make connectionist or cognitivist assumptions about mechanisms mediating overt performance.

INTERPRETING TEST TRIAL RESPONSE PROBABILITIES — THE NONRANDOM BASELINE PROBLEM

An entirely different methodological problem, and one that has historically haunted research on the law of effect, is the difficulty of interpreting test trial response probabilities. In order to establish the effects of rewards and punishments, whether by the repetition or cued recall procedure, it is obviously necessary to determine with some accuracy whether response probabilities are increasing, decreasing, or remaining constant from acquisition trial to test trial.

In Thorndike's experiments (e.g., 1932) on the law of effect, it was assumed that test trial response probabilities could be compared to chance probability levels in order to assess changes. If we take the digits, 0−9, as the set of response alternatives in an illustration of the STAE paradigm, the chance probability of giving any particular digit as a trial-and-error response to a given stimulus is 10% (since there are 10 digits from which one is chosen). Thus, if subjects are found, on the test trial, to have a repetition probability of 15% for responses punished on the acquisition trial, it would be inferred that a single punishment increased response probability by an average of 5 %.

It has long been recognized (Stephens, 1934) that the assumption of chance initial probabilities was incorrect, being an underestimation of actual first-trial probabilities. For example, the probabilities of "six" or "seven" as responses to the letter "S" as stimulus are likely to be above chance because of alliterative facilitation. Such above-chance responses are the ones most likely to occur as trial and error responses on the acquisition trial; they can be expected to be repeated on the test trial with their original above-chance probability even in the absence of any alterations in connection strength.

Once it was recognized that initial response probabilities differed from chance levels, procedures were instituted to attempt to compensate for these deviations. The most sophisticated procedures (e.g., Stone, 1953) involved attempts to establish the baseline of repetition that would be obtained when a response was neither rewarded nor punished (i.e., the experimenter remained silent following the response). However, results obtained with such procedures must be judged unsatisfactory in light of recent findings (Cairns, 1967; Levine, Leitenberg, & Richter, 1964) indicating that the experimenter's silence following a response is not devoid of reinforcement value. It is likely (Levine et al., 1964) that subjects most often interpret such silence as an equivalent of reward but, as Cairns (1967) concludes:

> . . . it seems reasonable to propose that the experimenter's silence, like other nonverbal events, can function as a positive, negative, or neutral signal, according to its definition within the experimental context (p. 357).

Thus, while it may be possible for the experimental context to define the experimenter's silence as a neutral signal, it will not be possible to determine the context that will accomplish this in the STAE situation until an independent solution to the problem of assessing response probability change is found. That is, since a neutral context is one in which silence will leave response probabilities unchanged from acquisition to test trial, the discovery of such a context must await a method of assessing response probability changes with some precision.

A SOLUTION TO THE BASELINE PROBLEM

The difficulty in assessing response probability changes can be stated simply: Acquisition trial-and-error responses are not generated randomly. Attempted solutions to this problem have adopted the strategy of trying to estimate the extent of nonrandomness in acquisition responding. An alternate approach to a solution is to enforce random responding on the acquisition trial! This can be accomplished simply by providing subjects with a randomizing device that functions to select (randomly) one response from the set of alternative responses. If the response set consists of the 10 digits, the device would randomly select one digit as each stimulus is presented. The subject would give his response by reading aloud the digit provided by the randomizer. If this procedure is used, it would be possible to compare test trial response probabilities with the chance baseline of 10% (in this example) and to be cofident that a change calculated from this baseline would be a genuine one. In implementing such a randomizing procedure, it probably will be important to ensure that the subject is not consigned to an entirely passive role in the response-generation process; the danger from subject passivity is that the subject may be free not to attend to his responses. An adaptation of the randomizing procedure will be seen in the experiments presented in the next section.

EXPERIMENTS ON THE LAW OF EFFECT

The experiments to be described in this section were directed at comparing the connection-strengthening effects of reward and punishment in intentional and incidental learning. Both the cued recall procedure and the random response-generation feature described in the preceding sections were employed to this end. Experiments 1−4 will be described relatively briefly, since they served mainly to highlight methodological problems that were resolved in the design of procedures for Experiments 5 and 6.

Subjects

Each experiment was conducted on a sample of 40 students from the introductory psychology course at Ohio State University. These subjects volunteered for the experiment in partial fulfillment of an experimental participation requirement of their course. Male and female subjects were assigned to procedural conditions in each experiment according to a preset random order, irrespective of subject's sex. The data were not analyzed at any time for sex differences in learning.

Apparatus and Materials

A specially constructed vertical panel served both for presentation of stimuli by the experimenter and selection of responses by the sub-

ject. The panel was 21 inches high by 12 inches wide and was supported with brackets on a table top so as to stand at an angle of 15°
from the vertical, slanting away from the subject. Three windows in
the panel were placed in a horizontal row approximately at the subject's eye level: a permanently open center window and right and left
windows that could be opened and closed by means of sliding
shutters. The panel was situated between subject and experimenter so
that the latter could control the presentation of stimuli and make necessary data records out of the subject's view. Stimulus and response
materials were printed on 5-by-8 inch index cards, decks of which
could be loaded into the apparatus from the experimenter's side. The
5-by-8 cards were prepared so that stimuli (letters or digits) would be
visible through the center (permanently open) window. Two responses (words) were printed on each card so that one was visible
through each of the right and left windows, when these were open. In
all of the following experiments, the same word was printed in the
position for the two response windows so that the subject's response
was controlled even though he was given the illusion of choosing one
of two possible responses by opening one of the two windows.

EXPERIMENT 1

Materials

The Thorndike-Lorge (1944) study of 30,000 common English
words was used as a source of 100 pairs of words with the following
characteristics: The two words in each pair (a) were matched for
length, being either three, four, or five letters long; (b) differed in
spelling only in one or both of their last two letters; and (c) were
matched approximately in frequency of usage in the language, all
words being relatively common ones in terms of absolute frequency.
Examples of three-, four-, and five-letter pairs are, respectively, FIT-
FIX, SEAM-SEED, and SNEER-SNEAK.

One word from each pair was randomly selected to be printed in
both response positions on a 5-by-8 card for use in the apparatus; the
stimulus portion of each card consisted of the one, two, or three letters
shared by the forced response word and its mate. The 5-by-8 cards
were randomly divided into five decks of 20 cards each.

Procedure

After being instructed in the use of the apparatus, the subject was
given further learning set instructions. All subjects were told that, on
the first trial, they would attempt to select arbitrarily designated *right*

words by opening one of the two response windows and reading aloud the word thus made visible. The experimenter would then inform them whether the selected word was *right* or *wrong*. All subjects were told that they would later be tested for identification of *right* words (not for opening of correct windows) upon re-presentation of stimuli, but only for a portion of the stimuli that were originally presented. Half the subjects were told that they would only be re-tested with stimuli for which their original responses were *right;* the others expected a retest only on the stimuli for which their first responses were *wrong*. The learning sets thus established were, respectively, intentional learning for *right* items and intentional learning for *wrong* items.

On the first (acquisition) trial, stimuli were presented at the rate of approximately 1 every 5 seconds, this time being used for the subject to read the stimulus letter(s) aloud, open one of the response windows, read aloud the response word, and receive feedback of *right* or *wrong* from the experimenter. Within each deck 10 responses were arbitrarily called *right* and 10 *wrong*. Between decks of 20 stimuli, there was a 1-minute rest.

In order to avoid any possible effects due to differences in the difficulty of the stimulus-response pairs on different cards, two counterbalancing procedures were employed. First, the reinforcement sequence given to one half of the subjects was reversed for the remainder; in other words, the 50 responses called *right* for half the subjects were called *wrong* for the others and vice versa. Second, the order of presentation of the five decks of 20 cards was varied by rotation so that each deck appeared equally often in the five ordinal positions.

Following the single acquisition trial, all subjects were tested (contrary to expectation) on all of the 100 stimuli that had originally been presented. As a result, data were obtained for both intentional learning and incidental learning (i.e., learning of responses to stimuli for which no retest was expected). Tests were conducted by presenting the stimuli and allowing the subjects to choose between the forced response word and its mate. For intentional learning tests, subjects were instructed to choose the *right* word from the pair; thus subjects who expected to be retested on *wrong* responses were asked to choose the word other than the one they had previously chosen. For the incidental learning tests, subjects were to select the word they had previously given as a response (no matter whether it had been called *right* or *wrong*). For these tests, stimuli were presented in the order of their original presentation and, for each stimulus, information was provided as to whether the response had originally been *right* or *wrong*.

Results

The results for Experiment 1 are given in Table A1. Data have been combined for the five decks, since block (deck) effects were slight and were not of theoretical interest here. The results can be summarized very simply. No significant differences were obtained; there was no difference between the effects of reward and punishment in either intentional or incidental learning, nor were there any differences between the levels of obtained intentional and incidental learning with either reward or punishment.

Table A1
LEVELS OF INTENTIONAL AND INCIDENTAL LEARNING
WITH REWARD AND PUNISHMENT
(EXPERIMENT 1 DATA)

| Reinforcement | Learning set | | t_{diff} |
	Intentional learning (%)	Incidental learning (%)	
Reward	80.3	76.1	1.39 (ns)
Punishment	76.1	73.2	<1
t_{diff}	1.24 (ns)	<1	

Note: Cell entries give mean percent of test stimuli for which the subject gave the requested response. The level expected in the absence of any learning was 50%. The *t* tests are for differences between independent means. Each subject contributed data to two cells (either upper left and lower right or lower left and upper right); $N = 20$ per cell.

EXPERIMENT 2

It was somewhat surprising that no significant effects were obtained in Experiment 1. The lack of any superiority in level of learning obtained with the intentional learning set as opposed to incidental learning suggested that these sets may not have been well established by the experimental procedure. Experiment 2 was a replication of Experiment 1 with a variation intended to heighten intentional-incidental learning set differences.

The change of procedure consisted of insertion of tests for intentional learning between decks on the acquisition trial. It was expected that these tests would serve to focus subjects' attention on the items for which they expected the intentional learning tests. No feedback was given for the intentional learning tests between decks; therefore these should not have functioned as additional acquisition trials. Data from these tests were not analyzed. Rather, intentional learning was assessed, as it had been in Experiment 1, by tests conducted after completion of the last acquisition deck (at which time incidental learning was also assessed).

Results

The data were analyzed in the same fashion as those of Experiment 1 and are presented in Table A2. The hypothesis of no difference between the effects of reward and punishment was rejected for intentional learning at the .01 level, but was not rejected for incidental learning. The hypothesis of no difference in magnitude of intentional and incidental learning was again not rejected, either for reward or for punishment, and it may be noted that incidental learning with punishment was better (not significant) then intentional learning.

Table A2
LEVELS OF INTENTIONAL AND INCIDENTAL LEARNING
WITH REWARD AND PUNISHMENT[a]
(EXPERIMENT 2 DATA)

| | Learning set | | |
Reinforcement	Intentional learning (%)	Incidental learning (%)	t_{diff}
Reward	80.8	75.2	1.73 $(p < .10)$
Punishment	66.6	75.1	1.65 (ns)
t_{diff}	2.79 $(p < .01)$	<1	

[a]Notes to Table A1 apply to the present data.

Discussion

The chief difference in results between Experiments 1 and 2 was the finding of a significant reward-punishment difference for intentional learning in the latter experiment. When Tables A1 and A2 are compared, the only difference between corresponding cells that exceeds 2 percentage points is that for intentional learning with punishment, for which the Experiment 2 value was 9.5% lower than that for Experiment 1 ($t = 1.83$, 38 df, $p < .10$, 2-tailed). It appears that the chief effect of strengthening the intentional learning set in Experiment 2 was to *reduce* the amount of intentional learning obtained with punishment. This was the first indication of a difficulty encountered by subjects in processing the information provided by *wrong* under the intentional learning set. Discussion of this point will be deferred until further pertinent evidence is présented.

The only evidence from Experiments 1 and 2 that might support a theoretical law of effect was superiority of reward over punishment for intentional learning in Experiment 2. This must be interpreted with much caution, for reasons discussed in our earlier section on dependent measures. That is, the intentional learning measure used in Experiments 1 and 2 was of the repetition type; differences between reward and punishment on this type of measure may be due to the operation of processes other than automatic effects of reward. A difference between reward and punishment on our incidental learning measure, which was of the cued recall variety, would have been much more decisive evidence for automatic reward effects; such a difference was not obtained in Experiments 1 and 2.

EXPERIMENTS 3 AND 4

Because of the nature of the stimulus and response materials used in the first two experiments, the failure to obtain reward-punishment differences in incidental learning should not be interpreted as damaging to the theoretical law of effect. It was possible for the subject to respond to the test materials by asking himself, for each pair of response words, which he had seen recently. When this was answered, the subject could simply repeat this response for all types of test except the intentional learning test with punishment, for which the strategy would be to select the response he could not recognize. Experiments 3 and 4 were modified from the previous experiments so as to make it decidedly more difficult for the subject to adopt such a recognition strategy on test trials.

Materials and procedure

The stimulus-response materials from the previous experiments were modified so that the stimulus display on each card consisted of the stimulus letter(s) sandwiched between the two response words that were to be used on the test trial. For example:

FIT	SEAM	SNEER
F	SE	SNE
FIX	SEED	SNEAK

The subject was obliged to view the two response alternatives for each stimulus as he read the stimulus letter(s) aloud prior to making his response. In Experiment 3, there were no tests for intentional learning between decks on the acquisition trial; between-deck tests were used in Experiment 4, however, in an attempt to enhance differences between intentional and incidental learning sets. As in the previous experiments, printed instructions were used to establish an intentional learning set for rewarded connections for half the subjects in each experiment and for punished connections for the rest.

Test trials employed the 5-by-8 cards as the means of re-presenting stimuli and response alternatives. On the final test series, each deck of 20 cards was subdivided into two sets of 10, one set of those for which the subject's responses had been *right*, the other consisting of those for which his responses had been *wrong*.

Within each deck, half the subjects were tested first on the cards for which they had been *right*, while the others were tested first on

Table A3

LEVELS OF INTENTIONAL AND INCIDENTAL LEARNING
WITH REWARD AND PUNISHMENT[a]
(EXPERIMENT 3 DATA)

	Learning set		
Reinforcement	Intentional learning (%)	Incidental learning (%)	t_{diff}
Reward	69.1	70.1	<1
Punishment	67.7	59.0	1.39 (ns)
t_{diff}	<1	2.38 ($p < .05$)	

[a]Notes to Table A1 apply to the present data.

those for which they had been *wrong*. The final test series consisted, then, of an alternation between sets of 10 cards for which the subject had been *right* and sets for which he had been *wrong*. Before each set, the subject was informed as to whether his previous responses for that set had been *right* or *wrong*. During these tests, the center-window portion of each card (see above) was presented for 3 seconds, the subject responding by giving aloud his choice of one of the two displayed alternative response words.

Table A4
LEVELS OF INTENTIONAL AND INCIDENTAL LEARNING
WITH REWARD AND PUNISHMENT[a]
(EXPERIMENT 4 DATA)

| Reinforcement | Learning set | | |
	Intentional learning (%)	Incidental learning (%)	t_{diff}
Reward	75.3	71.4	1.40 (ns)
Punishment	64.4	54.2	2.30 ($p < .05$)
t_{diff}	3.78 ($p < .01$)	3.95 ($p < .01$)	

[a]Notes to Table A1 apply to the present data.

Results

Data were analyzed as in the preceding experiments. Mean levels of performance of requested responses in each experiment are given for the four learning-set categories in Tables A3 and A4. For Experiment 3, the hypothesis of no difference between effects of reward and punishment was not rejected for intentional learning, but was rejected at the .05 level for incidental learning. As for differences between intentional and incidental learning levels, the hypothesis of no difference was not rejected for either reward or punishment. In Experiment 4, significant reward-punishment differences were obtained for both intentional and incidental learning. Further, the addition of the between-deck tests was apparently successful in establishing a difference between intentional and incidental learning sets; for punished responses, the intentional learning level was significantly higher than that for incidental learning.

Discussion

It would appear that evidence indicative of automatic action of reward was obtained in Experiments 3 and 4. We have argued that cued recall measures are appropriate for testing the automatic-action principle and, in Experiments 3 and 4, significant reward-punishment differences in incidental learning were found using the cued recall procedure. It would further appear that such evidence was not obtained in the previous two experiments only because an easy recognition strategy could be used for the test trials in those experiments. The evidence that the stimulus-display modifications used to eliminate or reduce this strategy were successful took the form of decidedly inferior learning levels in Experiments 3 and 4 (compare Tables A3 and A4 with A1 and A2), despite use of the same response materials.

Further examination of the data for individual subjects in Experiments 3 and 4, however, indicated that automatic connection-strengthening by reward was certainly not the only, and perhaps not the best, explanation of the obtained reward-punishment differences in incidental learning. It was observed that a number of subjects had performed below chance on incidental learning tests of the effects of punishment. These subjects contributed heavily to the obtained differences between reward and punishment in incidental learning; their below-chance performance, however, had no reasonable interpretation in terms of a theoretical law of effect except by invocation of the widely abandoned principle that punishment can weaken S-R connections. The below-chance performance could, however, be readily explained in cognitive terms. Bear in mind that subjects were informed, before each set of 10 cards on the test trial, of the reinforcements originally received for that set of cards (all *right* or all *wrong*). On incidental learning tests for originally *wrong* responses, a subject may frequently have recalled his response but assumed that the response he recalled was the *right* one (his previous task had been to remember only *right* responses); his test-trial strategy would then have been to guess the response other than the one he recalled. This explanation is consistent with Nuttin's finding (see pp. 42-43) that subjects tend to label accurately recalled responses as *right* irrespective of the reinforcement actually received; this principle would also account for the nonoccurrence of such interference in tests for incidental learning of *right* responses.

Due to the unique features of the random-baseline learning measures used in the present experiments, an alternative procedure for testing hypotheses about learning was available. Any deviation from 50% accurate performance of requested responses on the test trial could be considered as evidence for learning, in the broad sense of a modification of behavior due to past experience. In other words, just as learning was the only reasonable explanation for above-chance performance on the test trial, so was it the only reasonable explanation for below-chance test-trial performance. Below-chance performance would, of couse, reflect the operation of learning in the negative sense of a reduction of S-R strength or it could represent an increase in S-r strength (i.e., response availability) coupled with confusion in the cognitive processes involved in recall of responses and reinforcements.

For these reasons, the data of Experiments 3 and 4 were reanalyzed in terms of deviations from chance performance. Each subject was given a deviation-from-chance score for each of the 10 sets of 10 cards on which he had been tested; these scores were calculated by taking the absolute value of the difference between the number of requested responses actually given for each set of 10 cards and the chance value of 5. The resulting scores were then summed separately for the five sets of cards testing incidental learning and for the five sets testing intentional learning. For a given type of learning, the maximum score possible was 25, the minimum zero. In Tables A5 and A6, the reanalyzed data for Experiments 3 and 4 are presented as mean percentages of the maximum attainable score.

Table A5
EXPERIMENT 3 DATA REANALYZED IN TERMS OF
DEVIATIONS FROM CHANCE PERFORMANCE

| Reinforcement | Learning set | | t_{diff} |
	Intentional learning (%)	Incidental learning (%)	
Reward	42.2	45.8	<1
Punishment	45.4	44.0	<1
t_{diff}	<1	<1	

Note: Data are presented in terms of mean percent of maximum possible deviation from chance performance, averaged for five subtests (10 items apiece) of intentional learning and five subtests of incidental learning for each subject. Since the standard deviation of scores on 10 item subtests should be $1.58 = (n\,p\,q)^{1/2}$, with $n = 10$, $p = .50$, and $q = .50$, the baseline mean percentage in the absence of learning can be taken as 31.6%.

In Experiment 3, the reanalysis resulted in the disappearance of the difference between reward and punishment in incidental learning (compare with Table A3). For Experiment 4, the previously significant reward-punishment difference in incidental learning no longer obtained an acceptable two-tailed significance level; however, the significant superiority of reward over punishment in intentional learning was maintained (compare with Table A4).

When the data for Experiment 3 (Tables A3 and A5) are compared with corresponding data for Experiment 4 (Tables A4 and A6), it is apparent that the procedure used to heighten the difference between intentional and incidental learning sets had the effect of increasing

Table A6
EXPERIMENT 4 DATA REANALYZED IN TERMS OF
DEVIATIONS FROM CHANCE PERFORMANCE[a]

	Learning set		
Reinforcement	Intentional learning (%)	Incidental learning (%)	t_{diff}
Reward	51.4	46.4	1.02 (ns)
Punishment	36.0	38.4	<1
t_{diff}	3.00 ($p < .01$)	1.88 ($p < .10$)	

[a]See note for Table A5

intentional learning with reward and *decreasing* intentional learning with punishment. This is most noticeable with the deviation-from-chance-responding measure (Tables A5 and A6). The increase in intentional learning with reward from A5 to A6 was 9.2%, for which $t = 1.71$, $p < .10$, two-tailed. For punishment, the corresponding decrease from A5 to A6 was 9.4%, for which $t = 1.94$, $p < .10$. These near-significant findings add support to our observation made in reference to the Experiment 2 data, that strengthening the intentional learning set had detrimental effects on intentional learning with punishment.

In summary, the only reliable result of Experiments 1–4 was the superiority of reward over punishment in intentional learning when, as in Experiments 2 and 4, the difference between incidental and intentional learning sets was enhanced by means of between-decks intentional learning tests during the acquisition trial.[2] Since these findings were due primarily to reduced intentional learning of punished connections under the stronger learning set conditions, it appeared that subjects had difficulty processing the information transmitted by a punishment administered in the context of an intentional learning task. This difficulty was readily interpreted in terms of Nuttin's findings (Chapter 3) that subjects tend to recall responses more accurately than outcomes (reward or punishment) and that

[2]The reader will have noticed that, despite the use of between-decks tests to enhance intentional-incidental learning differences in Experiments 2 and 4, the levels of learning for the two sets remained nearly equal. It is possible that the tests may have been partly self-defeating. That is, subjects may have believed their intentional learning task to be completed with the test after each deck; this could have reduced subsequent retention of the intentional material (cf. Chapters 5 and 6 of this volume).

accurately recalled responses tend to be recalled as rewarded. Thus, accurately recalled *wrong* responses are likely to be remembered as *right*, interfering with correct test-trial performance; of course, the tendency to remember accurately recalled *right* responses as *right* only facilitates correct test-trial performance.

EXPERIMENTS 5 AND 6

Although significant reward-punishment differences were obtained for intentional learning in Experiments 2 and 4 and for incidental learning on the initial analyses of both Experiments 3 and 4, it seemed that these findings could be plausibly accounted for without the aid of a theoretical law of effect. Since the results were thus not conclusive as regards automatic reward effects it was desirable to seek further evidence. The results of the previous experiments suggested that our procedures would have to be modified in order to remove possible sources of reward-punishment differences other than a genuine automatic reward effect. In particular, it was most desirable to have a procedure in which the tendency to judge an accurately recalled response as having been rewarded could not interfere with tests of the automatic-action principle. Further, it was desirable to eliminate any possibility of use of simple recognition strategies (described earlier) on test trials.

The procedural modifications introduced in Experiments 5 and 6 consisted chiefly of employing a final test series composed of items for which the subject was required to choose between two responses, *both* of which he had previously given during acquisition. This change required several other alterations, as follows.

Procedure

Sixty of the cards previously used in Experiments 1 through 4 were modified by changing the stimuli (center window displays) to two-digit numbers. The 60 resulting cards were divided into five decks of 12 cards each. The cards in the first deck were stimulus-numbered 01–12; the second deck 21–32; and so on, through 81–92 for the fifth deck. Within each deck the numbers were ordered randomly, the same random order being used for all subjects.

Acquisition trials were conducted much like those in the previous experiments. The subject read the stimulus number from the center window, made a response by opening one of the two sliding windows and pronouncing the word he saw, and received reinforcement when the experimenter removed the stimulus-response card from the apparatus, leaving either the word *right* or *wrong* visible through the sliding window that had been opened by the subject. This automatic presentation of reinforcement was employed to simplify the experimenter's task and was accomplished by inserting an appropriate reinforcement card after each stimulus-response card. The reinforcement card was removed after the subject had reclosed the sliding window, exposing the next stimulus number. As in the earlier experiments, each stimulus-response-reinforcement sequence took about 5 seconds; the order of presentation of decks was rotated so that each was used equally often in the five ordinal positions; six responses were *right* and six were *wrong* per deck; cards for which responses were *right* for half the subjects were *wrong* for the remainder and vice versa; and half the subjects were instructed that they would be retested only on originally *right* cards while the rest expected to be retested only on those for which they had been *wrong*.

In both Experiments 5 and 6, subjects were tested between decks on those six items from the previous deck for which they expected a retest. The between-deck test lasted about a minute and was conducted after each of the first four decks, but not after the fifth. After the fifth deck, new instructions were given for the final test series. For this, the subject was first given a deck of twelve 3-by-5 inch cards. Each card contained one of the two-digit stimulus numbers from the fifth deck seen by the subject as well as two response words, one of which had been made originally to that stimulus, the other having been made to a different stimulus in the fifth deck. The subject was instructed to choose, for each card, the response word he had originally given for its stimulus, no matter whether that response had originally been called *right* or *wrong*. This test was conducted for all 12 stimuli from the fifth deck, in a new random order. After completion of this test, which took about 1½ minutes, the same type of test was conducted for the deck the subject had seen third, followed by one for the deck seen first.[3]

On each card in these final test decks there was a "correct" test response (the subject's original response to the test stimulus), that may have been either *right* or *wrong* originally, paired with an

---

[3]The tests for learning were conducted first on the deck seen last by the subject since it was assumed that (a) the difference between intentional and incidental sets would be most strongly established for the last deck, and (b) learning levels would be highest for the last deck, thereby providing the most powerful tests possible for reward-punishment differences. It may be seen, then, that the focus of the analyses for Experiments 5 and 6 was intended to be on the learning data for the deck that was presented last during acquisition and tested first.

"incorrect" test response that, likewise, may have been either *right* or *wrong* originally (but for a different stimulus). For each 12-card test deck, there were three correct *right* responses paired with incorrect *right* ones and three paired with incorrect *wrong* ones; similarly there were three correct *wrong* responses paired with incorrect *right* ones and three paired with incorrect *wrong* ones. In each 12-card test deck, each of the subject's six original *right* responses appeared once as a correct alternative and once as an incorrect alternative and similarly for his six original *wrong* responses. The subjects were not allowed to view more than one test card at a time, since this would have facilitated use of strategies based on the structure of the test deck (e.g., a response selected for one stimulus could be eliminated from consideration for another stimulus).

Difference between Experiments 5 and 6

The sole difference between the two experiments was that whereas only symbolic punishments were used in Experiment 5 (i.e., the word *wrong*), Experiment 6 employed aversively loud bursts of white noise (105 db for .80 seconds) delivered simultaneously with presentation of the word *wrong*. The white-noise punishment was delivered by the experimenter's pressing a foot-switch at the same moment that he presented *wrong* via the reinforcement card.

Subjects

Each experiment was conducted with a basic group of 40 subjects, and then replicated with an additional group of 40. The results will be presented combined for the 80 subjects in each experiment.

Discussion of Procedure

Because of the increased difficulty of the learning task, the quantity of materials employed in Experiments 5 and 6 was reduced from the previous experiments. The total number of items was reduced from 100 to 60 and only 36 of the 60 were included in the final test series, as compared to all 100 in the previous experiments.

The use of pairs of response words given previously by the subject as choice alternatives for the final test series had several desirable effects. First, it eliminated the possibility of any use of a recognition strategy for test response selection; while this strategy had been reduced in Experiments 3 and 4 (compared to Experiments 1 and 2), it almost certainly had still been employed to some extent. Second, since with the present procedure the subject could likely recall both responses as having been made before, the problem of a bias favoring reward due to interactions between response-recalls and outcome-recalls was eliminated. Third, the new test procedure allowed some very stringent tests of automatic reward effects. If it could be demonstrated that subjects correctly recalled *wrong* responses at an above-chance rate when they were tested against incorrect *right* ones, and if this level of correct recall is equivalent to that for *right* responses tested against incorrect *wrong* ones, we will have obtained results quite incompatible with a theoretical law of effect.

One other aspect of the procedure bears comment. It is conceivable that a theoretical law of effect may be valid for nonsymbolic reinforcements only. Experiment 6 pursued this possibility by employing an aversively loud noise as punishment. While it was inconvenient to employ a corresponding nonsymbolic positive event as a reward, there is perhaps some merit in the argument that the symbolic reward of *right* acquired enhanced positive value by virtue of contrast with the noise punishment. In fact, there may have been decided anxiety reduction associated with the word *right* in Experiment 6 because, after each response, the subject could expect the aversive noise with 50% probability.

Results

In each experiment, there were several possible tests of automatic reward effects.[4] At the simplest level, the theoretical law of effect predicted greater connection-strengthening with reward than with punishment. This was not found in either experiment. In both Experiments 5 and 6, there was no difference in the mean number of correct test choices as a function of reward versus punishment ($F < 1$ in both), nor was there any difference when the reward-punishment comparison was made examining only incidental or only intentional learning (see Tables A7 and A8).

The theoretical law of effect might also be supported if it could be demonstrated that subjects performed better on test items when the incorrect test choice was a previously punished response rather than a rewarded one. While there was a near-significant trend in this direc-

---

[4]The data from Experiments 5 an 6 were analyzed using, for each, a complex analysis of variance with one between-subjects factor (expectation of retest on *right* responses only or on *wrong* ones only) and three within-subjects factors (reinforcement of *right* versus *wrong*; incorrect choice on test item either originally *right* or *wrong*; and fifth, third, or first test deck). We shall not present these analyses in detail since much of them is not pertinent to tests of the theoretical law of effect. However, all significance tests presented are based on these analyses.

tion in Experiment 5 ($F_{1,78} = 2.93$, $p < .10$), the trend in Experiment 6 was in the reverse direction ($F < 1$). Again, the theoretical law of effect was unsupported.

It is apparent from Tables A7 and A8 that, in both experiments, intentional learning was far superior to incidental learning. We may also observe that there was apparently no incidental learning whatsoever in Experiment 6. Let us examine this result in more detail by looking at data for only the last acquisition deck in each experiment (i.e., the first deck on which subjects were tested). These data are given in Fig. A1. It may be seen that there was, in fact, above-chance performance on tests for incidental learning for the first test deck in Experiment 6; this learning reached a one-tailed .05 significance

Table A7

EXPERIMENT 5 DATA

| | Learning set | | |
| | Intentional | Incidental | |
Reinforcement	learning (%)	learning (%)	t_{diff}
Reward	65.3	53.5	4.37 ($p < .001$)
Punishment	65.2	53.5	4.32 ($p < .001$)
t_{diff}	<1	<1	

Note: Cell entries indicate mean percentages of associations accurately reproduced, combined over the complete final test series (36 responses per subject). As in Experiments 1–4, each subject contributed half of his data to each of two cells of the table (either upper left and lower right or lower left and upper right); $N = 40$ per cell. The expected level of reproduction is 50.0%, in the absence of learning.

Table A8

EXPERIMENT 6 DATA[a]

| | Learning set | | |
| | Intentional | Incidental | |
Reinforcement	learning (%)	learning (%)	t_{diff}
Reward	61.9	50.1	4.33 ($p < .001$)
Punishment	61.1	49.0	4.43 ($p < .001$)
t_{diff}	<1	<1	

[a]See note to Table A7.

level ($t = 1.85$, 156 df) when averaged over reward and punishment and both types of test item. However, the fact that evidence for learning was confined to types of test in which the test alternative was a response that had been intentionally learned (to a different stimulus) suggests that the above-chance performance on incidental learning tests was only a by-product of intentional learning; that is, subjects might have recognized the incorrect alternative as one that had been (intentionally) learned to a different stimulus, therefore rejecting it and selecting the correct test alternative.

In the case of Experiment 5, however, there was significant evidence for incidental learning on choices involving an incorrect alternative that received the same reinforcement as the correct one. This indicates genuine incidental learning in Experiment 5. Although

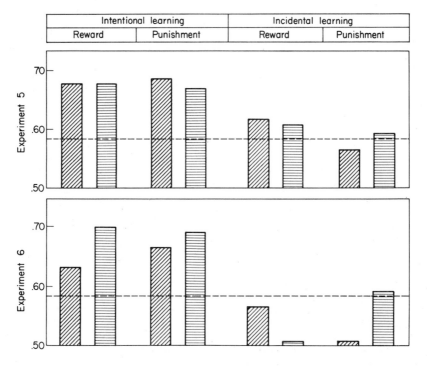

FIG. A1. Probability of reproduction of associations from last acquisition deck (first test deck) as a function of reinforcement (reward or punishment) and learning set (intentional or incidental). (Diagonally striped bars give data from test items for which the incorrect alternative was an originally punished response; for horizontally striped bars, the incorrect test alternatives had originally been rewarded. Bars exceeding the horizontal line at .579 indicate performance exceeding the chance (.50) level at the one-tailed .05 level.)

the incidental learning level for punished responses when tested against incorrect *wrong* alternatives was not in itself significant in Experiment 5, neither was it significantly inferior to the comparable level for rewarded responses tested against incorrect *right* alternatives ($t = 0.63$, ns).

The intentional learning data in Fig. A1 also provide no evidence for any enhanced position of rewarded connections in memory. Rewarded and punished connections were equally well intentionally learned and it made no difference whether the incorrect test alternative had previously been rewarded or punished. The overall intentional learning levels for the first test decks in Experiments 5 and 6 were nearly identical. This indicates that the reduction in intentional learning in Experiment 6 (compare Tables A7 and A8) was confined to the decks tested later.

In summary of the results of Experiments 5 and 6, there was no evidence for any differences between reward and punishment, either in intentional or in incidental learning. In comparing the two experiments, the only apparent result of supplementing symbolic punishment with aversively loud noise was a reduction in levels of learning. It is interesting to note that the reduction in learning levels due to white noise was equally distributed over rewarded and punished connections for both intentional and incidental learning; the effect of white noise was not at all specific to the connections for which it was received.[5]

CONCLUSIONS

The results of the first four experiments presented in this section were equivocal as regards automatic effects of reward. They served, nonetheless, to highlight some methodological problems as well as to provide some interesting data on the difficulty encountered by subjects in processing the information contained in punishments. This difficulty appeared to stem from a tendency to label an accurately recalled response as rewarded, whether or not it had been. When the experimental procedures were adjusted to strengthen the intentional learning set, data were obtained indicating that intentional learning

---

[5] Berlyne, Borsa, Hamacher, and Koenig (1966) found no decrease in paired associate learning when 6 seconds of white noise at 75 db followed response terms of each pair. The present experimental conditions were sufficiently different from those of Berlyne *et al.* to warrant much caution in assuming relevance; however, the present findings do suggest that louder noise levels might have had negative effects in their situation.

for punished connections was thereby reduced. Reanalysis of the data from Experiments 3 and 4 demonstrated that these findings were due more to a breakdown of storage-retrieval processes for information acquired in conjunction with punishment than to reductions in quantities of stored information. It is difficult to estimate the significance of these findings for the interpretation of previous studies of reward and punishment, since previous studies cannot be reanalyzed by the methods we have used here. Nonetheless, it is quite conceivable that previous findings indicating superior learning with reward than with punishment may actually have been the product of faulty processing of information stored in conjunction with punishment.[6]

The problems encountered in the first four experiments were used as the basis for modifying procedures to provide fair and stringent tests of automatic reward effects in Experiments 5 and 6. The procedural features incorporated in Experiments 5 and 6 included (a) use of cued recall in testing for both intentional and incidental learning; (b) use of the random acquisition-response-generation procedure to guarantee chance baselines against which to test learning; and (c) use of previously given responses as incorrect alternatives on test trials in order to remove biases due to influence of response-recall on test-trial guessing strategies. Experiments 5 and 6 indicated no difference in the connection-strengthening effectiveness of reward and punishment for both intentional and incidental learning procedures.

The evidence was particularly strong for this conclusion in the case of intentional learning, since the learning levels for both reward and punishment were well above the chance baselines and were virtually identical to each other. Since the procedure for intentional learning of punished connections was one that required subjects to recall the punished connection in order to perform successfully at the intentional learning task, it might be objected that the present results should not be regarded as pertinent to reward-punishment comparison. That is, the conditions were designed to "reward" memory for punished connections. This observation, in fact, is not quite accurate. Subjects were not rewarded for memory of punished connections; rather they were *motivated* to remember them. The point of our

[6]The present findings of difficulty in processing punishment information almost certainly bear also on findings indicating difficulty in processing the information contained in negative instances in concept learning (Hovland & Weiss, 1953; Weber & Woodward, 1966). That is, in both cases the subject faces the problem of trying to learn something about the members of one set (instances of the concept or correct responses) from information about members of another set (noninstances of the concept or incorrect responses).

criticism of earlier literature, and of Nuttin's earlier criticism (stated in Chapter 5) is that typical learning experiments have motivated the learner to retain only rewarded connections, thus unfairly biasing retention in the direction of reward superiority. In the procedures of Experiments 5 and 6, manipulated learning sets served to control levels of motivation to retain rewarded and punished connections; it was intended that the only difference between intentionally-learned rewarded and punished connections would be the fact of success or failure for the acquisition-trial performance. We can assert now, with confidence, that there is no difference in connection-strengthening effectiveness of reward and punishment in intentional learning when the learner is not differentially motivated to retain rewarded and punished connections. This conclusion is, of course, in precise sympathy with Nuttin's conclusion that it is the motivational orientation of the learner at the time of reward and punishment that is important to connection strengthening, rather than an automatic effect of reward or punishment per se.

The incidental learning data from Experiments 5 and 6 equally showed no reward-punishment differences. However, the conclusion drawn from these findings must be a bit reserved since incidental learning was weak in Experiment 5, and virtually absent in Experiment 6. That is, not enough learning may have been obtained to allow observation of possible reward-punishment differences. It would thus be desirable to repeat our experiments, modifying the procedures of Experiments 5 and 6 so as to increase the levels of incidental learning.

While the present findings support the conclusion of no automatic connection-strengthening effects of rewards, we are obliged to state this conclusion in somewhat less-than-intrepid fashion. The present research constitutes a counterdemonstration, i.e., a demonstration failing to find evidence for automatic action of rewards and suggesting that previous demonstrations of such may well have been spurious. While we have faith in the methods used to produce this counterdemonstration (and have attempted to justify that faith in the preceding section), it would be brash to suppose that we have reached the ultimate in methodology for testing the theoretical law of effect. The present data do, however, place the burden of proof once again on the shoulders of adherents of the theoretical form of the law of effect.[7]

[7]A few colleagues who have been kind enough to comment on the present experiments (particularly Experiments 5 and 6) have suggested that the interference conditions of the STAE learning situations employed here probably warrant a qualified conclusion—that of no difference between connection-strengthening by reward and punishment under associative interference-producing conditions. It is certainly true that

One final observation on the present findings: As a result of demonstrating no difference between reward and punishment in intentional learning, we must disagree with Nuttin's assertion (Chapter 5) that reward is more effective than punishment in strengthening connections in open tasks (i.e., when the subject has intent to learn). It will be recalled that Nuttin's data on structural determinants of learning (Chapter 7) provided a basis for reservations about his earlier assertion. (He found that the ratio of rewards to punishments in a learning task was important in determining their relative connection-strengthening effectiveness.) The present experiments (particularly Experiments 5 and 6) indicated that when reward and punishment were equally likely their connection-strengthening effects were equally strong. In the following section, we shall consider further evidence on the role of task reward-punishment structure in learning.

LEARNING AS A FUNCTION OF TASK REWARD-PUNISHMENT STRUCTURE

Nuttin's experiments, particularly those reported in Chapter 7 of this volume, have clearly demonstrated that the effectiveness of reward and punishment in connection-strengthening varies with task structure in the sense of reward-punishment ratio. His results can be summarized by the generalization that the connection-strengthening effectiveness of an outcome, whether it be reward or punishment, is inversely proportional to the outcome's probability of occurrence. In the present section, we shall explore variations on this theme in learning tasks quite different from those employed by Nuttin in Chapter 7. The results will demonstrate the generality of Nuttin's conclusion as well as providing the basis for some further speculations

---

associative interference was generated in Experiments 5 and 6. Nonetheless, in light of the procedures used by other investigators in arriving at conclusions supporting automatic reward effects, it seems inappropriate to attenuate the present conclusion. That is, serial trial-and-error procedures have been the rule in tests of the law of effect. Postman (1962, p. 394) pointed out the extreme interference properties of the Wallach and Henle experiments (1941, 1942) in which the list of stimuli was presented 20 times in the course of a task with ESP instructions. He suggested that automatic reward effects might be submerged in such extreme interference conditions; Postman's suggested remedy was to use only a single acquisition trial for the list of stimuli (e.g., Postman & Adams, 1954). Thus, the present procedures, while not devoid of interference properties, were in keeping with Postman's suggestion for procedures necessary for keeping interference within tolerable bounds for testing the law of effect. Further, the body of evidence supporting the law of effect comes entirely from STAE experiments with associative interference-generating procedures. In the absence of firm evidence indicating automatic reward effects in low interference tasks, it seems inappropriate to limit the conclusiveness of the present findings.

about the role of task reward-punishment structure in learning.

The three experiments to be described in this section were conducted at Educational Testing Service (Princeton, New Jersey). Since a student population was not readily available for research at that location, available personnel of the Research Division at ETS participated as subjects. The subject samples consisted, then, of adults between the ages of 20 and 35, almost all of whom were employed as secretarial-clerical assistants.

EXPERIMENT 7

This experiment combined procedural features of both paired-associate and serial-trial-and-error learning. The task structure involved the use of three equally probable outcomes, two neutral in value to the subject, the third a punishment. It also employed the random-response-generation procedure described and used previously, as well as a test for learning in which subjects were motivated equally to perform neutral and punished associations. Eighteen subjects participated in the experiment.

Apparatus

A rectangular array of 30 holes (10 rows by three columns), drilled through a 4-by-12 inch piece of plywood, served as a response matrix. A metal stylus when inserted in any of 10 of the 30 holes resulted in the ringing of a bell; responses in another 10 holes sounded a buzzer; and responses in the remaining 10 holes produced no sound. The three outcomes (Bell, Buzzer, and Silent) were randomly distributed through the response matrix with the one restriction that each of the 10 rows of the matrix contained one Bell, one Buzzer, and one Silent hole. The rows of the matrix were plainly labeled 1 through 10 and the columns were marked A, B, and C. The response matrix was made of two layers of plywood, with metal contacts at the bottom of the lower layer. A paper roll that could be pulled between the two layers served to record responses, since the stylus had to pierce the paper in order to reach the metal contact. The apparatus was powered by a 1.5-volt dry cell; a switch in the circuit allowed the experimenter to disconnect the bell and buzzer, as required in the second part of the experiment.

Procedure

Subjects were run individually. Prior to their arrival, they were told only that they were to participate in an experiment. There was no mention of learning or punishment or any other indication of the experiment's purpose. Upon the subject's arrival, the experimenter demonstrated the three outcomes (Bell, Buzzer, and Silent) by inserting the stylus in three holes outside the 3×10 array and informed the subject that one of each of the three outcomes was located in each of the 10 rows of the matrix.

Acquisition

The first part of the experiment was presented as a game of chance. The subject was told that he would draw slips (designating the coordinates of specific holes in the response matrix) from a bowl and that, for each slip, he would insert the stylus in the designated hole and observe the outcome. Payoffs for this game of chance worked as follows. The subject was given 90¢ — in 30 white chips worth 3¢ each — at the start of the game and was told that whenever one of the outcomes occurred (the Bell, say), he would lose a chip (punishment); whenever either of the other two outcomes occurred, he would not have to give up a chip (neutral outcomes). The subject was told that, with these rules, he could expect to break even at the completion of the game which was to last 90 trials. (This information was accurate; the container had 240 slips, 8 marked with the coordinates of each of the 30 holes in the response matrix.) Each subject also received several red chips (each representing 3¢ of negative earnings) to be used in case all the white chips were lost before 90 trials were completed, and he was told: "There will be ways for you to earn money in a second part of the experiment so that, even if you end up losing a little in the first part, you should still be ahead by the time the whole experiment is done." In order to ensure that the subject would attend to the outcome and payoff on each of the 90 trials, he was placed in charge of the payoffs; that is, he gave the experimenter one chip each time the punished outcome was encountered.

The acquisition trials were conducted rather rapidly. Subjects were encouraged to play the game quickly and were told to increase speed if they hesitated during or between trials. As a result, the mean trial duration (including intertrial interval) was approximately 6 to 7 seconds.

Retention Testing

Immediately upon completion of the 90 acquisition trials, the apparatus was disconnected so that the bell and buzzer would no longer sound. The subject was then asked to take the stylus and locate all

10 instances of one of the outcomes (the Buzzer, say) by making one and only one response in each of the 10 rows. A 2¢ reward was offered for each correct location and there was a 1¢ penalty for each incorrect location. This retention testing procedure was then repeated for the other two outcomes. Prior to testing retention on each outcome, a fresh piece of paper was pulled through the response matrix so that the subject's 10 responses were recorded automatically. Payment for accuracy in locating the outcomes and knowledge of accuracy were delayed until all retention testing was completed.

Assignment of payoffs to the three outcomes during acquisition (three methods) and order of retention testing on the outcomes (six orders) were completely counterbalanced over the 18 subjects.

Since the lottery procedure guaranteed randomly selected responses during acquisition, we may state with confidence that the baseline probability of locating a particular outcome (Bell, Buzzer, or Silent) in a particular row was exactly ⅓ – the chance probability value – in the absence of learning. The game-of-chance procedure also had the useful side effects of keeping the subjects actively involved in the acquisition procedure while distracting them from the fact that they were in a learning experiment and assuring approximately equal exposures to the three outcomes.

Results

Table A9 presents the retention data, showing subjects' performance in relation to chance (or 33.3%) success at locating punished and neutral responses. Subjects performed significantly above chance ($p \cong .01$) at locating punished responses, but not significantly above chance at locating neutral responses. Performance in locating punished responses bordered on being significantly superior ($p < .10$) to performance in locating neutral responses.

It is worth noting how little incidental learning took place as a result of the 90 acquisition trials. If one made the meager assumption that subjects learned, on the average, only the locations of 2.00 punished responses, one could predict all of the retention data of the present experiment virtually without error. That is, knowledge of the locations of two punished responses would lead to the obtained average of 46.7% correct locations of punished responses (when chance success is additionally taken into account), and the avoidance of guessing those two locations when attempting to locate neutral responses would inflate chance success at locating neutral responses to 36.7%, just short of the observed figure of 37.2%.

Table A9

RECALL OF PUNISHED AND NEUTRAL RESPONSES[a]

(EXPERIMENT 7 DATA)

	Type of response	
	Neutral	Punished
Mean percent correctly recalled[b]	37.2	46.7
Standard deviation[c]	10.6	19.7
Difference from chance value (%)	+3.9	+13.3
t	1.56	2.87
p	ns	<.02

[a]$N = 18$.

[b]For the difference between recall of punished and neutral responses: $t = 1.76$, $p < .10$, two-tailed. This t-test is based on the difference, for each subject, between the number of correct locations of the punished outcome and the mean number of correct locations of the two neutral outcomes.

[c]The data in the neutral and punished columns are based on two observations per subject and one observation per subject, respectively. Error terms for the two t-tests in the fourth row of the table were computed separately.

Discussion

In this experiment, associations between locations in the response matrix and outcomes (Bell, Buzzer, or Silent) were better learned when punishment was associated with the outcome than when it was not. The learning obtained was incidental in that subjects were not instructed to expect a learning test. This finding supports results of Nuttin's experiments (IR_{1-5}, Chapter 7) that showed superior connection-strengthening by punishment when it was an infrequent outcome in a closed-task (i.e., incidental learning) situation. The present result extends the phenomenon to a situation in which the associative materials were not verbal (although the subjects certainly were free to code them verbally). The interpretation offered by Nuttin, that isolation by virtue of an infrequent outcome serves to enhance learning, seems entirely appropriate to the present data; however, let us briefly consider some alternative interpretations.

Stone (e.g., 1953) reported a series of experiments in which it was consistently found that punished responses (in a verbal serial-trial-and-error task) were repeated more frequently than responses that had been neither rewarded nor punished, despite the fact that the subjects were under explicit instructions not to repeat punished responses. Stone attributed these results to a response "fixation" by punishment, a process by which subjects would tend to perseverate on punished responses. If subjects in the present experiment were fixating on punished responses, we should expect that they would have selected the punished responses at an above-chance rate not only when under instructions to locate them, but also when under instructions to locate neutral responses. In fact, however, subjects in Experiment 7 selected punished responses at the below-chance rate of 27.2% when they were attempting to locate neutral ones. We can therefore reject the fixation explanation for the present results.

Additionally, it is possible that the experimenter or the procedures unintentionally cued the subjects to attend to and learn the punished response locations during the lottery (acquisition) procedure. While possible, this seems unlikely for the following reasons: There was no mention of a learning task in connection with the experiment; acquisition trials were conducted with sufficient rapidity that the subjects were really not free to reflect on what the experiment might be about; the use of two different outcomes on neutral trials acted to draw special attention away from the punished responses; and, finally, the generally poor retention performance of the subjects indicated that few, if any, could have approached the experiment as a learning task; in fact, several of the subjects voluntarily apologized for their poor retention by saying that they had not expected to be tested for learning.

Experiment 7 adds to the body of results reported in this volume that are inconsistent with a theoretical law of effect. Since the neutral outcomes in this experiment were (in relative terms) actually worth 3¢ apiece and, therefore, might be construed as rewards, the law of effect should predict superior learning of their locations – the opposite of the obtained results.

With this experiment, we conclude our presentation of research pertinent to the theoretical law of effect and turn to further experiments concerning task reward-punishment structure. In the following experiments, we shall be considering aspects of reward and punishment that have received relatively little empirical attention, perhaps because of their irrelevance to the law-of-effect related problems with which many reward-punishment experiments have been preoccupied.

EXPERIMENT 8

In *The fundamentals of learning* (1932), Thorndike reported a number of tests of the law of effect in which subjects who were blindfolded drew straight lines of specified lengths and were rewarded (told *right*) or punished (told *wrong*) as a function of their accuracy. Not surprisingly, he found that accuracy of line drawing improved with practice in this situation. Thorndike attributed this improvement to automatic reinforcing effects of the rewards received. Experiment 8 was based on the assumption that information other than reward and punishment could serve to improve accuracy at blindfolded line drawing. Our initial aim was to compare the line-drawing performance of subjects who received reward and punishment with that of subjects who received information in a different form. Since the reward-punishment procedure consisted of making one of the two words, *right* and *wrong*, contingent on the subject's performance for each attempt, we employed a comparison condition which also made one of two words contingent on performance. We chose the words *long* and *short*, expecting that these would be successful in producing improvement in line-drawing accuracy when appropriately used. Twenty subjects participated in the experiment with 10 each in the right-wrong and long-short conditions.

Procedure

The subject was first instructed that his task would be to draw a series of lines while blindfolded, each as close as possible to 7½ inches long. He was told that, after each try, information about accuracy would be provided and that this should enable improvement of performance as the task proceeded. The subject was then blindfolded and placed (standing) next to a desk. He was instructed to draw his lines on a sheet of paper placed on this desk. The experimenter placed the subject's pencil back at the starting point after each trial and provided a straightedge against which to draw the lines.

The experimenter moved the sheet of paper on which the subject was drawing a short distance after each response so that a sequential record of performance was generated. The sheet had been prepared with markings at every quarter inch, allowing the experimenter to announce feedback information immediately upon the subject's termination of his pencil movement.

In the right-wrong condition, the subject was told that he would be informed *right* after each trial for which his line was within 1 inch of 7½ inches, i.e., between 6½ and 8½ inches; if it was outside this margin, he would be told *wrong*. It was emphasized that the task was to draw lines exactly 7½ inches long, not just to draw lines between 6½ and 8½ inches.

In the long-short condition, the subject was told that he would be informed *long* if his line was longer than 7½ inches and *short* if his line was shorter than 7½ inches; further he was told that lines exactly 7½ inches long would be called either *long* or *short* on a random basis.

Fifty trials were conducted in the manner described for subjects in each condition, followed by an additional 20 trials for which subjects received no verbal feedback following performance. The trials were conducted at an average rate of one every 5 seconds. There was a short break prior to the last 20 trials, while the subject was informed that he would no longer receive information about his performance but was, nonetheless, to try to draw 7½ inch lines.

Results

A fair means for comparing the two conditions in terms of overall accuracy of performance is to use the accuracy criterion of the right-wrong condition – number of responses within 1 inch of 7½ inches. (Subsequently, responses within this margin will be referred to, for both conditions, as *hits*, and responses outside this margin will be called *misses*.) In these terms, the long-short condition was significantly superior to the right-wrong condition (see Table A10) during the 50 information trials. The long-short condition remained superior during the following 20 no-information trials, but not significantly so.

Comparison in terms of total hits and misses yielded only a very gross characterization of the differential effects of the two conditions on performance. A finer grain comparison was obtained by examining improvements in accuracy on the trial immediately following a hit or

Table A10

RESPONSE ACCURACY IN LONG-SHORT AND RIGHT-WRONG CONDITIONS[a]

(EXPERIMENT 8 DATA)

	Percentage of obtained hits[b]						
	Reinforced trials					Extinction	
Condition	1 – 10	11 – 20	21 – 30	31 – 40	41 – 50	51 – 60	61 – 70
Long-short	52	84	85	90	90	80	68
Right-wrong	36	51	60	66	76	69	59

[a]$N = 10$ per condition.

[b]Hits are defined as responses between 6½ and 8½ inches in length. This was the criterion for a *right* response in the right-wrong condition. For trials 1–50, there were significantly more hits in the long-short condition ($t = 2.39$, 18 df, $p < .05$). For trials 51–70, the conditions were not significantly different ($t < 1$).

Table A11
PROBABILITY (IN PERCENTAGES) OF IMPROVEMENT[a]
ON THE TRIAL IMMEDIATELY FOLLOWING A HIT OR
MISS UNDER TWO FEEDBACK CONDITIONS
(EXPERIMENT 8 DATA)

Condition	Probability of improvement following	
	Hits (%)	Misses (%)
Long-short	51.86	87.88
Right-wrong	43.33	71.23
CR_{diff}	2.14	3.23
p	<.05	<.001

[a]Improvement is defined as a gain in accuracy over the preceding trial. Improvement was not scored following direct hits (responses that could not be improved upon).

Table A12
PROBABILITY (IN PERCENTAGES) OF IMPROVEMENT[a]
ON THE TRIAL IMMEDIATELY FOLLOWING A MISS
BEFORE AND AFTER THE FIRST HIT
(EXPERIMENT 8 DATA)

Condition	Probability of improvement (%)		CR_{diff}	p
	Before first hit[b]	After first hit		
Long-short	78.13	92.53	—[c]	.09
Right-wrong	62.69	85.90	3.60	<.001

[a]See footnote [a] of Table A11.

[b]It took a mean of 4.2 trials to obtain the first hit in the long-short condition as opposed to a mean of 14.4 trials in the right-wrong condition.

[c]Due to extremity of the probability of improvement following a miss in the long-short condition, the significance of this difference was determined by the Fisher exact test.

a miss. Table A11 summarizes these results. (Although hit and miss are not particularly meaningful in terms of the long-short condition, still it is reasonable to compare improvement in the two conditions when the position of the previous response is controlled for by the device of separating responses into hits and misses.)

It may be noted that the probability of improvement following a hit was significantly greater in the long-short condition. Further, the long-short condition was also significantly superior to the right-wrong condition in terms of the probability of improvement after a miss.

Internal analysis of the right-wrong condition showed a remarkable change in the probability of improvement following misses from before to after the first rewarded response (i.e., the first hit). These data are shown, together with comparable data from the long-short condition, in Table A12. It may be seen that improvement following misses in the right-wrong condition increased substantially after the first hit had been made.

Discussion

We have already noted that Thorndike interpreted improvement in blindfolded line drawing accuracy in his own experiments as a function of automatic effects of rewards. He referred briefly to interpretations in terms of "higher" cognitive processes as follows:

> There is the possibility that the beneficial action of the reward in these experiments consisted, in whole or in part, in the temporary retention in memory by the subjects of some methods or ideas or guiding sensations, and the deliberate effort to make such movements as were in harmony with these. The possibility is slight since the existence and helpfulness of such methods, ideas, or sensations are very problematic. . . .
> Conceivably the subject may, as learning progresses, revive memories of how he behaved in making past shoves [i.e., line-drawing movements] plus memories of their respective success or failure. . . . I do not think this occurs, save very rarely, in experiments of only 750 or 1050 shoves. . . . The right responses in this experiment do not easily become available for ideational representation; and guiding sensations have little chance to act in the course of so simple and rapid a movement (Thorndike, 1932, pp. 189-195).

The following aspects of the data of Experiment 8 suggested that higher processes of the type dismissed by Thorndike did play an important part in line-drawing improvement, even though only 50 "shoves" were involved: (a) the relatively good performance in the long-short condition (see Table A10); (b) the high probability of improvement on the trial following a *wrong* (see Table A11); (c) the fact that the probability of improvement following *wrong* increased sharply after the first reward (see Table A12); and (d) the fact that performance more often deteriorated than improved following *right* (see Table A11).

In combination, these findings suggested that useful information was provided by punishment as well as by reward in the right-wrong condition and that the information received after a given response was used as the basis for a deliberate attempt to correct the just-made error (if any) while performing the immediately following response. The information provided by *wrong* became useful only after the first *right* response, presumably because the subject was able to infer the direction (long or short) of his error reliably only after he had first stored in memory the approximate feel of a *right* response.[8]

It appeared that feedback information in the line-drawing task (even in the right-wrong condition) was not serving primarily to increase the strength of the response of drawing lines of the specified length. Rather, subjects seemed to be handling the task as a slow-motion tracking task in which feedback played more of an error-correcting role than a habit-strengthening role. Alternatively, this conclusion might be stated in terms of subjects using the feedback information to acquire complex habits of responding to the proprioceptive and verbal feedback received on one trial by producing a more accurate response on the next trial. The fact that performance noticeably deteriorated when feedback was discontinued (see Table A10) supports this interpretation.

The conclusions to be drawn from Experiment 8 must be limited for two reasons. First, in comparing the right-wrong and long-short conditions, it would be inappropriate to assume that reward-punishment features were absent from the latter; in particular, it might have been rewarding for a subject to receive feedback of *long* after having just made a *short* response (and vice versa) and receipt of the same feedback on two successive trials may have had some properties of punishment. In the second place, the size of the reward margin used in the right-wrong condition may have been an important determinant of the obtained results; it should be noted that in Thorndike's experiments the typical reward criterion allowed a deviation of no more than ¼ inch from the target length, compared to 1 inch in the present experiment. That is, part of the relatively poor performance in the right-wrong condition must be attributed simply to the fact that relatively inaccurate responses were called *right* (cf., Trowbridge & Cason, 1932). These limitations suggested further research in which feedback was limited to *right* and *wrong* for all subjects, but with different reward criteria for different conditions.

[8]This particular finding bears on Skinner's analysis (e.g., 1953) of punishment. Skinner deplores the use of punishment in education because, he claims, it does not serve to reduce the probability of incorrect responses or to increase the probability of correct responses. Our results support this assertion as regards the learner's situation prior to making the first correct response, but suggest that punishment is highly useful in decreasing incorrect responses and facilitating correct ones after a correct response has once been made.

EXPERIMENT 9

Procedure

The procedure in Experiment 9 was similar to that for the right-wrong condition of Experiment 8. The target length was set at $5\frac{1}{2}$ inches and subjects were divided into two conditions ($N = 15$ in each) with different reward criteria. In the wide margin (WM) condition, responses within 1 inch of the target length were called *right* and those outside this margin were called *wrong*. In the narrow margin (NM) condition, the rewarded zone was reduced to within ½ inch of the 5½ inch length. In neither condition were the subjects informed of the reward criteria. All subjects knew only that they would be told *right* if they were within a "small margin" on either side of the 5½ inch target length.

One important change from Experiment 8 was that each subject was guided through one correct response prior to his experimental trials. For the guided trial, the subject was asked to draw a line slowly and to stop when instructed by the experimenter (this was done when the subject's pencil was in the middle of the target zone). The purpose of the guided trial was to avoid problems associated with the change in effectiveness of *wrong* from before to after the first correct response (see Experiment 8). The experiment was completed after 50 trials, all of which were followed by feedback of *right* or *wrong* as appropriate for each condition.

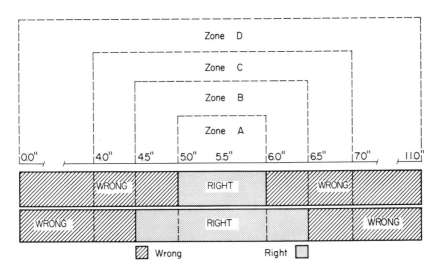

FIG. **A2.** Schematic representation of narrow-margin (upper bar) and wide-margin (lower bar) feedback conditions.

Results

Figure A2 schematically depicts the feedback arrangements for the NM and WM conditions. Our analyses of performance in the two conditions will focus on the effects of the feedback received on a given trial on accuracy of performance for the next trial. In order to control for position of previous response in this analysis, we shall employ the device of classifying responses in terms of the zones depicted in Fig. A2. Table A13 summarizes various characteristics of performance on trials following responses in zones A, B, and C for the NM and WM conditions. (Zone D has been omitted because relatively few responses occurred outside A, B, and C.)

Table A13
MEAN IMPROVEMENT AND VARIANCE OF BEHAVIOR ON TRIALS IMMEDIATELY
FOLLOWING RESPONSES IN ZONES A, B, AND C[a,b]
(EXPERIMENT 9 DATA)

Condition	Zone A	Zone B	Zone C
Frequency of response (%), by zones			
Narrow margin condition	57.95	26.92	8.33
Wide margin condition	46.54	34.23	13.08
Improvement on next response (inches)[c]			
Narrow margin condition	+.008	+.205	+.288
Wide margin condition	+.001	+.056	+.392
t	0.24	3.05[d]	1.03
Variance of improvement[e]			
Narrow margin condition	.155	.419	.465
Wide margin condition	.215	.170	.366
F	1.38[d]	2.47[f]	1.27

[a] $N = 15$ per condition.
[b] Zones A, B, and C are described in Fig. A2.
[c] Following responses shorter than 5½ inches, positive improvement scores were given to all responses of increased length; following responses longer than 5½ inches, positive scores were given to all responses of decreased length. This scoring is not too meaningful for zone A, since such improvement might well lead to less rather than greater accuracy when the starting point is close to 5½ inches.
[d] $p < .01$, two-tailed.
[e] These are within-subject variance estimates, pooled for the 15 subjects in each condition.
[f] $p < .001$, two-tailed.

In zone A, subjects in both conditions were rewarded, but reward was relatively a less frequent event for the NM subjects than for the WM subjects, who were rewarded also for responses in zone B. Since overall accuracy was superior for NM subjects (see frequency of response data) and since performance following a zone A reward was more reliable for NM than WM (see variance of improvement data), it appears that *right* was more effective when it was less frequent.

In zone C, subjects in both conditions were punished, but punishment was relatively more frequent for the NM subjects, who were punished also in zone B. The data indicate more improvement after punishment in zone C for WM than NM, i.e., greater effectiveness of punishment when it was less frequent. The statistical nonsignificance of this difference may be due to the relatively small number of zone C responses for the two conditions.

Zone B provided very interesting data because the two conditions received different feedback for responses in that zone. In particular, it was found that there was significantly more improvement on the response following a zone B response for subjects who had been punished (NM) than for subjects who had been rewarded (WM). That is, punishment provided more useful information than reward for zone B responses. Consulting Table A13, we find that punishment for the NM subjects was, on the average, a less frequent outcome (42 % of trials) than was reward for the WM subjects (81 % of trials). Therefore, the findings for zone B are also consistent with the generalization that outcome effectiveness is inversely proportional to outcome probability.

The generalization just stated was earlier stated by Nuttin, in Chapter 7 of this volume, in connection with experiments in which reward-punishment probability was manipulated in a fashion quite remote from that presently used. Before accepting the generalization as applicable to the line-drawing situation, let us look at some relatively fragmentary data obtained from the line-drawing situation with a more stringent criterion for reward than that used in the present NM condition.

Five additional subjects performed 50 trials at the blindfolded line-drawing task of Experiment 9 with responses within ¼ inch of the 5½ inch target called *right* and all others called *wrong*. Data for these very narrow margin condition (VNM) subjects are presented in Table A14. Several aspects of the VNM condition data may be compared with corresponding data for the NM condition given in Table A13. First, overall accuracy of performance during the 50 trials in VNM was inferior to that for NM. Second, improvement of performance following punishment in zones B and C for VNM was inferior to that in NM and variance of this improvement in VNM was greater than in NM. Finally, variance of improvement following rewarded responses in zone A was greater for VNM than in NM.

Table A14
MEAN IMPROVEMENT AND VARIANCE OF BEHAVIOR ON
TRIALS IMMEDIATELY FOLLOWING RESPONSES IN
ZONES A, B, AND C FOR VNM CONDITION[a,b]
(DATA SUPPLEMENTARY TO EXPERIMENT 9)

Condition	Zone A (right)	Zone A (wrong)	Zone B	Zone C
Frequency of response (%)	18.80	20.00	28.00	16.00
Improvement on next response (inches)[c]	−.016	−.030	+.082	+.250
Variance of improvement[d]	.226	.710	.621	.725

[a]$N = 5$.
[b,c]See corresponding footnotes for Table A13.
[d]See footnote [e] for Table A13.

The data indicated, then, that reducing the reward criterion beyond ½ inch (the NM condition) did not have a beneficial effect on performance accuracy during the 50 trials of the line-drawing task. In addition, the fact that punishment was less effective in the VNM condition than in the NM condition was consistent with the generalization that an outcome's effectiveness is inversely proportional to its probability. However, the fact that reward was less effective in VNM than in NM was not consistent with this generalization, since reward was less probable in VNM than in NM.

Discussion

Before attempting to interpret these data, let us note the possibility that the results might have been different had we extended the task substantially beyond 50 trials. Part of the difficulty experienced by the VNM subjects may have been due to their relative inexperience with reward over the 50 trials of the task; the mean number of rewarded responses was only 9.4 in VNM as compared to 29.0 for the NM condition.

We have noted the rough approximation of the line-drawing data to the generalization that an outcome is effective (in producing accurate performance) in inverse proportion to its probability. Further, we have noted that a similar generalization was made by Nuttin in regard to the connection-strengthening effects of reward and punishment in serial-trial-and-error verbal learning tasks; also, the generalization was consistent with our own results in Experiment 7. In the cases of Nuttin's experiments in Chapter 7 of this volume and Experiment 7 of the present series, it seemed most reasonable to assume that the enhanced effects of infrequent outcomes could be attributed to selective attention focused on the connections to which they were attached, this selective attention being a direct concomitant of the outcome's novelty or infrequency. While it was possible that outcome infrequency in the line-drawing tasks did have effects on attention, the results obtained were consistent with an interpretation that does not rely primarily on such attention effects.

This alternative interpretation is based on our earlier observation, from Experiment 8, that subjects employed feedback information of *right* or *wrong*, in conjunction with proprioceptive or kinesthetic information, to infer the direction of their error after each response; only if the feedback information conveyed this information successfully were the subjects able to improve their performance reliably on the subsequent trial. Reward and punishment thus served (at least) two functions in the line-drawing experiment: (a) providing error information that cued the subject as to the direction in which he would have to alter his next performance (longer or shorter); and (b) providing information concerning the success of the alteration made on the next trial, i.e., information as to which responses would subsequently be useful and which would not.

It must be obvious that *wrong*, by itself, could not be sufficient to provide direction-of-error information. The subject had to infer from additional sensory information (primarily proprioceptive) whether a *wrong* response was too long or too short. This, of course, was easy to do when the reward margin was a wide one (e.g., the WM condition), since the proprioceptive information associated with a too-long *wrong* had little in common with that for a too-short *wrong*. When the reward margin was very narrow (e.g., the VNM condition), the proprioceptive information associated with a just-too-long *wrong* was probably nearly indistinguishable from that accompanying a just-too-short *wrong*. Thus, the extent of the reward margin was an important determinant of the subject's successfully obtaining error information from feedback of *wrong*; it was coincidental that the probability of *wrong* also varied inversely with the size of the reward margin.

A similar case can be made to demonstrate that *right* was relatively unsuccessful in informing the subject of the extent of his error (or, more properly, the extent of his accuracy) when the reward margin was wide; again, it was only coincidental that the probability of *right* varied as a function of the size of the reward margin.

The second function of feedback of *right* or *wrong* in the present interpretation — informing the performer as to which responses he should try to repeat and which not — was more directly a reward and punishment function, in the customary sense of those terms. In regard to this function, it is quite possible that outcome frequency may have had effects on attention that mediated differences in learning. Our feeling, however, is that over the relatively short course of the 50-trial line-drawing experiments, the error information-providing function of *right* and *wrong* may have been more important to accurate performance than was their reward-punishment function. This perhaps explains why performance was relatively poor for the subjects in the VNM condition; they were required to deal very frequently with feedback of *wrong* that conveyed little error information.

In summary, then, we suggest that the effects of *right* and *wrong* in the line-drawing situation should be construed in terms of a dimension of reward-punishment effects that was not relevant to the serial-trial-and-error tasks discussed previously in this volume. This added dimension is one of the adequacy of feedback in providing error information that contributes to the stimulus situation for the immediately following response.

While we shall not proceed further with this area of experimentation in this volume, we may note that the line-drawing task is an instance of a general category of positioning tasks (the kinesthesiometer task employed by Nuttin in Chapter 6 is another instance). Positioning tasks, in turn, can be seen as slow motion versions of tracking tasks. In tracking tasks, the subject's assignment is to respond continuously to a continuously moving target by matching the movements of the target; in positioning tasks, the target is stationary and the subject makes repeated separated attempts, as in the line-drawing task, to hit the target. Both positioning and tracking tasks are basic to the study of perceptual-motor skills.

The findings of the present experiments should be considered in the context of previous studies of target size and variations of information feedback in positioning tasks (E. A. Bilodeau, 1956; I. Bilodeau, 1966). The studies by the Bilodeaus suggest that overall positioning accuracy is not particularly sensitive to variations in manner of presenting information feedback. However, our Experiments 8 and 9 show substantial sensitivity of positioning performance to information feedback variations during the first 50 trials of positioning performance. The observed variations in performance were particularly noticeable in analyses of trial-to-trial dependencies in performance — that is, when the effects of different types of feedback were compared in terms of performance on trial $n + 1$ as a function of amount of error and feedback received on trial n. It is not unreasonable to assume that continuation of the line-drawing tasks well beyond 50 trials (say, to 500 trials) would have reduced or eliminated between-group differences in line-drawing skill. Nonetheless, our trial-to-trial analyses indicate that the process by which the asymptote is achieved would vary significantly as a function of variations in presenting feedback.

CONCLUSION: THE ROLE OF REWARD AND PUNISHMENT IN HUMAN LEARNING

If there has been a consistent theme running through the present series of experiments and through this volume as a whole, it is that rewards do not have any inherent property of enhancing stimulus-response connection strength or in otherwise facilitating learning in laboratory learning tasks. This, however, is only a negative manner of stating the conclusions that may be based on the research presented in this volume.

In a more positive fashion, we may assert that there are a variety of effects associated with the task context of rewards and punishments and that influence performance in learning tasks, but which are not to be identified with a theoretical law of effect. Specifically:

1. If task instructions indicate that retention of either rewarded or punished responses will be of greater use in regard to future task performance, the designated outcome will control more learning in the task situation.

2. When either reward or punishment occurs relatively infrequently in the course of trial-and-error performance, selective attention to responses receiving the more infrequent outcome will be responsible for increased learning.

3. Due to a process that Nuttin attributes to "transfer of affect" (Chapter 3), correctly recalled responses tend more often to be recalled as having been rewarded than as having been punished. This represents a defect of information processing in the serial-trial-and-error learning situation; the evidence suggests that this defect does not occur at the level of stimulus-response association formation, but rather in the process of retrieving learned information.

4. In positioning tasks, and perhaps also in other skilled perfor-

mances such as continuous tracking tasks, reward and punishment take on a function of providing error information. This error information serves not only the customary reward-punishment function of indicating which responses will subsequently be useful and which not, but also contributes to the stimulus situation for the immediately subsequent response. We have found that an important variable in the positioning task situation is the range of responses that is considered as on target. The extent of this range plays an important role in determining the extent to which *right* and *wrong* can be utilized in terms of the just-described stimulus function. In general, it appears that as the target range is narrowed, the value of stimulus information provided by reward increases relative to that provided by punishment.

The first three of the conclusions just listed may be used to explain why much experimental evidence in the reward-punishment literature, particularly the major segment contributed by Thorndike (e.g., 1932), appears to indicate superior learning with reward than with punishment. That is, the experimental tasks used to demonstrate reward superiority have frequently (a) employed instructions indicating that rewarded responses would be subsequently more useful than punished ones, or (b) used reward as a relatively infrequent outcome, or (c) allowed the transfer of affect process to bias results in the direction of indicating more learning with reward. An additional source of bias that may tend to produce results indicating reward superiority, we have had occasion to argue, may be found in the procedures most frequently used to assess connection strength in serial-trial-and-error learning tasks (Appendix, pp. 148ff).

In regard to our fourth conclusion, one interesting implication is that varying the target range in a positioning task will have the effect of increasing the error-information effectiveness of one outcome at the expense of the other. (We assume a task in which outcome information is limited to *right* and *wrong* or their equivalents.) Our data indicate that there may be an optimal value of the target range for a given task (note the variations in overall performance accuracy for the three target-range conditions of Experiment 9). Specifying the principles that may be used to determine the optimal target zone is a potentially interesting problem for future research. As a speculation, we may venture that optimization will involve narrowing the target zone as performance accuracy increases through practice at the tracking or positioning task.

In the process of providing evidence against automatic effects of reward, we have obtained evidence supporting the four above conclusions and, in addition, have arrived at an overall theoretical interpretation of reward and punishment quite far removed from that of the theoretical law of effect. We have found that rewarded and punished connections are generally equally available for performance after learning experiences involving equivalent exposures to reward and punishment. The fact that human learners are, nonetheless, selectively able to perform successful responses and to avoid performance of punished ones must, then, be taken as evidence supporting what we have described as cognitivist performance principles (Appendix, pp. 150ff) in which available responses are performed or not performed as a function of whether or not, respectively, they are recalled as having been rewarded. Although the work reported in this volume has been much stimulated by the extensive research and theoretical efforts of Thorndike, it would be difficult to arrive at a conclusion that is much more in contradiction of his law of effect.

REFERENCES

Aall, A. Die Bedeutung der Zeitperspektive bei der Einprägung für die Dauer der Gedächtnisbilder. *Bericht über den Kongress für experimentelle Psychologie*, 1912, **5**, 237-241.

Aall, A. Ein neues Gedächtnisgesetz? Experimentelle Untersuchung uber die Bedeutung der Reproduktionsperspektive. *Zeitschrift für Psychologie*, 1913, **66**, 1-50.

Allport, G. W. *Personality: A psychological interpretation.* New York: Holt, 1937.

Alper, T. G. The interrupted task method in studies of selective recall: a reevaluation of some recent experiments. *Psychological Review*, 1952, **59**, 71-88.

Bartlett, F. C. *Remembering. A study in experimental and social psychology.* Cambridge: Cambridge Univ. Press, 1932.

Berlyne, D. E., Borsa, D. M., Hamacher, J. H., & Koenig, I. D. V. Paired-associate learning and the timing of arousal. *Journal of Experimental Psychology*, 1966, **72**, 1-6.

Bilodeau, E. A. Studies of target size and the control of psychomotor behavior through systematic transmission of knowledge of results. *National Academy of Sciences — National Research Council, Publication*, 1956, **445**, 17-24.

Bilodeau, I. Mc.D. Information feedback. In E. A. Bilodeau (Ed.), *Acquisition of skill.* New York: Academic Press, 1966. Pp. 255-296.

Bruner, J. S. On cognitive growth. In J. S. Bruner *et al.* (Eds.), *Studies in cognitive growth.* New York: Wiley, 1966. Pp. 1-67.

Cairns, R. B. Informational properties of verbal and nonverbal events. *Journal of Personality and Social Psychology*, 1967, **5**, 353-357.

Cartwright, D. The effect of interruption, completion, and failure upon the attractiveness of activities. *Journal of Experimental Psychology*, 1942, **31**, 1-16.

Courts, F. A., & Waggoner, D. The effect of "something happening" after a response. *Journal of Experimental Psychology*, 1938, **22**, 383-387.

Dembo, T. Der Aeger als dynamisches Problem. *Psychologische Forschung*, 1931, **15**, 1-144.

Donceel, J. Le rôle du souvenir dans l'interprétation de la loi de l'effet. Unpublished thesis, University of Louvain, Belgium, 1934.

Feigenbaum, E. A., & Feldman, J. *Computers and thought.* New York: McGraw-Hill, 1963.

Greenwald, A. G. Nuttin's neglected critique of the law of effect. *Psychological Bulletin*, 1966, **65**, 199-205.

Guthrie, E. R. *The psychology of learning*. New York: Harper, 1935.

Harlow, H. F. Learning and satiation of response in intrinsically motivated complex puzzle performance by monkeys. *Journal of Comparative and Physiological Psychology*, 1950, **43**, 289-294.

Heider, F. The gestalt theory of motivation. In M. R. Jones (Ed.), *Nebraska Symposium on Motivation*. Univ. of Nebraska Press, 1960. Pp. 145–171.

Hilgard, E. R. *Theories of learning*. New York: Appleton, 1948.

Hilgard, E. R. *Theories of learning*. Second edition. New York: Appleton, 1956.

Hilgard, E. R., & Bower, G. H. *Theories of learning*. (3rd ed.) New York: Appleton, 1966.

Hilgard, E. R., & Sait, E. M. Estimates of past and future performances as measures of aspiration. *American Journal of Psychology*, 1941, **54**, 102-108.

Hoppe, F. Erfolg und Misserfolg. *Psychologische Forschung*, 1930, **14**, 1-62.

Hovland, C. I., & Weiss, W. Transmission of information concerning concepts through positive and negative instances. *Journal of Experimental Psychology*, 1953, **45**, 175-182.

Hull, C. L. *Principles of behavior*. New York: Appleton, 1943.

Hull, C. L. *A behavior system*. New Haven: Yale University Press, 1952.

James, W. *Principles of psychology*. New York: Holt, 1890. 2 vols.

Jones, E. *The life and work of Sigmund Freud*. Vol. 1. New York: Basic Books, 1953.

Köhler, W. *The place of value in a world of facts*. New York: Liveright, 1938.

Köhler, W., & von Restorff, H. Ueber die Wirkung von Bereichsbildung im Spurenfeld. *Psychologische Forschung*, 1933, **18**, 299-342.

Köhler, W., & von Restorff, H. Ueber die Wirkung von Bereichsbildung im Spurenfeld. II. Zur Theorie der Reproduktion. *Psychologische Forschung*, 1935, **21**, 56-112.

Krechevsky, I. 'Hypotheses' in rats. *Psychological Review*, 1932, **39**, 516-532.

Krechevsky, I. The docile nature of 'hypotheses.' *Journal of Comparative Psychology*, 1933, **15**, 429-443.

Leeper, R. W. What contributions might cognitive learning theory make to our understanding of personality? *Journal of Personality*, 1953, **22**, 32-40.

Levine, M., Leitenberg, H., & Richter, M. The blank trials law: The equivalence of positive reinforcement and nonreinforcement. *Psychological Review*, 1964, **71**, 94-103.

Lewin, K.   Das Problem der Willensmessung und das Grundgesetz der Assoziation. *Psychologische Forschung*, 1922, **1**, 191-302; **2**, 65-140.

MacCorquodale, K., & Meehl, P. E.   Edward C. Tolman. In W. K. Estes *et al.*, *Modern learning theory*. New York: Appleton, 1954. Pp. 177-266.

MacFarlane, D. A.   The role of kinesthesis in maze learning. *University of California (Berkeley) Publications in Psychology*, 1930, **4**, 277-305.

Maier, N. R. F.   Reasoning in white rats. *Comparative Psychology Monographs, 1929*, **6**, No. 3.

Maier, N. R. F.   Reasoning and learning. *Psychological Review*, 1931, **38**, 332-346.

Marks, R. W.   The effect of probability, desirability, and "privilege" on the stated expectations of children. *Journal of Personality*, 1951, **19**, 332-351.

Marx, M. H.   Spread of effect: A critical review. *Genetic Psychology Monographs*, 1956, **53**, 119-186.

Marx, M. H.   Analysis of the spread of effect: A comparison of Thorndike and Nuttin. *Psychological Bulletin*, 1967, **67**, 413-415.

Marx, M. H., & Goodson, F. E.   Further gradients of error reinforcement following repeated reinforced responses. *Journal of Experimental Psychology*, 1956, **51**, 421-428.

Meehl, P. E.   On the circularity of the law of effect. *Psychological Bulletin*, 1950, **47**, 52-75.

Miller, N. E.   Some reflections on the law of effect produce a new alternative to drive reduction. In M. R. Jones (Ed.), *Nebraska Symposium on Motivation*. Lincoln, Neb.: University of Nebraska Press, 1963. Pp. 65-112.

Mowrer, O. H.   *Learning theory and behavior*. New York: Wiley, 1960.

Muenzinger, K. F.   Vicarious trial and error at a point of choice. I. A general survey of its relation to learning efficiency. *Journal of Genetic Psychology*, 1938, **53**, 75-86.

Muenzinger, K. F.   Motivation in learning. II. The Function of electric shock for right and wrong responses in human subjects. *Journal of Experimental Psychology*, 1934, **17**, 439-448.

Nuttin, J.   Respective effectiveness of success and task-tension in learning. *British Journal of Psychology*, 1947, **38**, 49-55. (a)

Nuttin, J. La loi d'effet et la finalité du comportement. *Miscellanea psychologica Albert Michotte*. Louvain, Belgium: Publications Universitaires, 1947. Pp. 611-633. (b)

Nuttin, J. "Spread" in recalling failure and success. *Journal of Experimental Psychology*, 1949, **39**, 690-699.

Nuttin, J. *Tâche, réussite, et échec*. Louvain, Belgium: Publications Universitaires, 1953.

Nuttin, J. The future time perspective in human motivation and learning. *Acta Psychologica*, 1964, **23**, 60-82.

Nuttin, J. *La structure de la personnalité*. Paris: Presses universitaires de France, 1965.

Nuttin, J. Adaptation et motivation humaine. In F. Bresson, J. Nuttin, J. Piaget *et al.*, *Les processus d'adaptation*. Paris: Presses universitaires de France, 1967.

Osgood, C. E. *Method and theory in experimental psychology*. London and New York: Oxford University Press, 1953.

Ovsiankina, M. Die Wiederaufnahme unterbrochener Handlungen. *Psychologische Forschung*, 1928, **11**, 302-379.

Piaget, J. *The construction of reality in the child*. New York: Basic Books, 1954.

Porter, L. W. The effect of "right" in a modified Thorndikian situation. *American Journal of Psychology*, 1957, **70**, 219-226.

Postman, L. The history and present status of the Law of Effect. *Psychological Bulletin*, 1947, **44**, 489-563.

Postman, L. Rewards and punishments in human learning. In L. Postman (Ed.), *Psychology in the making*. New York: Knopf, 1962. Pp. 331-401.

Postman, L. Reply to Greenwald. *Psychological Bulletin*, 1966, **65**, 383-388.

Postman, L., & Adams, P. A. Performance variables in the experimental analysis of the law of effect. *American Journal of Psychology*, 1954, **67**, 612-631.

Postman, L., & Adams, P. A. "Isolation" and the law of effect. *American Journal of Psychology*, 1955, **68**, 96-105.

Rapaport, D. *Emotions and memory*. Baltimore: Williams & Wilkins, 1942.

Rosenzweig, S., & Mason, G. An experimental study of memory in relation to the theory of repression. *British Journal of Psychology*, 1934, **24**, 247-265.

Skinner, B. F. *Science and human behavior*. New York: Macmillan, 1953.

Solomon, R. L. Punishment. *American Psychologist*, 1964, **19**, 239-253.

Spence, K. W. *Behavior theory and conditioning.* New Haven: Yale University Press, 1956.

Stephens, J. M. A change in the interpretation of the law of effect. *British Journal of Psychology*, 1934, **24**, 266-275.

Stone, G. R. The effect of negative incentives in serial learning: VII. Theory of punishment. *Journal of General Psychology*, 1953, **48**, 133-161.

Thistlethwaite, D. A critical review of latent learning and related experiments. *Psychological Bulletin*, 1951, **48**, 97-129.

Thorndike, E. L. Animal intelligence: An experimental study of the associative processes in animals. *Psychological Review Monograph Supplement*, 1898, **2**, No. 8.

Thorndike, E. L. *Animal intelligence.* New York: Macmillan, 1911.

Thorndike, E. L. *The fundamentals of learning.* New York: Teachers College, 1932.

Thorndike, E. L. An experimental study of rewards. *Teachers College Contributions to Education*, 1933, No. 580.

Thorndike, E. L. *The psychology of wants, interests, and attitudes.* New York: Appleton, 1935.

Thorndike, E. L. *Man and his works.* Cambridge, Mass.: Harvard University Press, 1943.

Thorndike, E. L., & Lorge, I. *The teacher's wordbook of 30,000 words.* New York: Teachers College, Columbia University, 1944.

Tolman, E. C. *Purposive behavior in animals and men.* New York: Century, 1932.

Tolman, E. C. The determiners of behavior at a choice-point. *Psychological Review*, 1938, **45**, 1-41.

Tolman, E. C. Prediction of vicarious trial and error by means of the schematic sowbug. *Psychological Review*, 1939, **46**, 318-336.

Tolman, E. C. Principles of purposive behavior. In S. Koch (Ed.), *Psychology: A study of a science.* Vol. 2. New York: McGraw-Hill, 1959. Pp. 92-157.

Tolman, E. C., Hall, C. S., & Bretnall, E. P. A disproof of the law of effect and a substitution of the laws of emphasis, motivation and disruption. *Journal of Experimental Psychology*, 1932, **15**, 601-614.

Trowbridge, M. H., & Cason, H. An experimental study of Thorndike's theory of learning. *Journal of General Psychology*, 1932, **7**, 245-258.

Wallace, W. P.   Review of the historical, empirical, and theoretical status of the von Restorff phenomenon. *Psychological Bulletin,* 1965, **63**, 410-424.

Wallach, H., & Henle, M.   An experimental analysis of the law of effect. *Journal of Experimental Psychology,* 1941, **28**, 340-349.

Wallach, H., & Henle, M.   A further study of the functions of reward. *Journal of Experimental Psychology,* 1942, **30**, 147-160.

Watson, J. B.   *Behaviorism.* Chicago: Univ. of Chicago Press, 1930.

Weber, R., & Woodward, A., Jr.   Transformations of positive and negative information in a modified learning-set task. *Journal of Experimental Psychology,* 1966, **72**, 492-496.

Weiner, B.   Effects of motivation on the availability and retrieval of memory traces. *Psychological Bulletin,* 1966, **65**, 24-37.

Woodworth, R. S.   *Dynamic psychology.* New York: Columbia University Press, 1918.

Zeigarnik, B.   Ueber das Behalten von erledigten und unerledigten Handlungen. *Psychologische Forschung,* 1927, **9**, 1-85.

Zirkle, G. A.   Success and failure in serial learning. II. Isolation and the Thorndike effect. *Journal of Experimental Psychology,* 1946, **36**, 302-315.

AUTHOR INDEX

SUBJECT INDEX

The letter *n* indicates footnoted material.